"In *How to Cook a Crocodile* Bonnie Lee Black has not only channeled the spirit of M.F.K. Fisher with style and wit, she has provided an entertaining account of the trials and tribulations of her service in Gabon and a collection of inventive recipes. She has also succeeded in writing a guide to living with grace and gusto, wherever you are, and whatever you happen to be doing."
— Thurston Clarke, author, *The Last Campaign: Robert F. Kennedy and 82 Days that Inspired America*

"We enter Black's world with the initial thrill of discovery and then fall in love, as she did, with the world she describes. What truly seduces us is experiencing it through her fine prose and expert storytelling."
— Cherie Burns, author, *Searching for Beauty: The Life of Millicent Rogers, the American Heiress Who Taught the World About Style*

"There's a sensuous gravitational tug to Bonnie Lee Black's memoir-with-recipes *How to Cook a Crocodile*. Her vivid prose draws you into a world that is rife with humidity and sweat, sharp aromas, the lively voices of children, exotic birds, swarming insects, trash and flowers and diesel exhaust. ... To readers who engage it fully, the book brings this tiny slice of Africa into both mind and body. The masterfully wrought narrative stimulates the intellect as much as the palate..."
— Kevin Cassell, blogger, *Rapid Pulse*

"*How to Cook a Crocodile* ... succeeds due to Black's honesty, humor, and astonishingly creative resiliency. If given the chance, I'd travel — and eat a crocodile — with Bonnie Lee Black just about anywhere."
— Becca Lachman, book reviewer, *Alimentum*

"*How to Cook a Crocodile* reminded me of *Eat, Pray, Love,* another story I loved. Both books are about self-discovery, about love of humanity and laughter and certainly love of good food ... but Ms. Black's book offers something more to her readers — or at least this one: the sense from page one that we have all we need to cope with any challenge. ... Ms. Black, without preaching, by way of her wonderfully humorous stories, also teaches us that the simple act of trying to make even the tiniest bit of our world a better place is remarkably powerful..."
— Paul Griffin, author, *Burning Blue*

"This is a profile in courage and good taste, the story of a woman's singular journey into the unknown, where she discovers not only the culture, people and food of Gabon, but also uncovers new dimensions of her own being. This is a book of physical energy and movement, of emotional love and loss, acceptance and surrender. And, too, it is a metaphysical lesson of how to embrace change — at any age — with grace, poise and a lively sense of humor. ..."
— Davida Singer, poet and author, *Port of Call*

"Armchair adventurers, take note: Bonnie Lee Black is a wonderful writer and this is a wonderful book that should not be missed by any connoisseur of world culture, travel, or cuisine."
— Sean Murphy, author, *The Time of New Weather*

"*How to Cook a Crocodile* is a lovely book. It was a pleasure to read and a privilege to have Bonnie Lee Black as a guide. With humor, grace, and uncommon intelligence, she takes the reader into kitchens in Gabon and New York and shares stories that are intimate and fascinating..."
— Jane Bernstein, author, *Rachel in the World*

"Black's stirring and inspiring story is jazzed with a nice dollop of actual recipes, thus providing the reader with a filling combo for both the literary and taste palette. Put this book on your 'must-read' list."
— David Perez, author, *Wow!*

"Black takes readers on a journey to a land they may never encounter … Pick up this book and join Bonnie Lee Black in the kitchen and across the world."
— Catherine Meyer, book reviewer, *Izilwane*

"*How to Cook a Crocodile* … relates not only the author's dogged, inspiring, and, ultimately, successful efforts to bring a modicum of improvement to the lives of women and children in Lastoursville, Gabon; it does so with insightful wisdom, intelligence, sensitivity, and humor…"
— Jeffrey Newman, contributor, *The New York Times*

"For the wanderlust in us all, get this book for someone who needs to pick him- or herself up and bootstrap somewhere else."
— Carol Durst-Wertheim, contributor, *Oxford Encyclopedia of Food and Drink in America,* 2nd ed.

"*How to Cook a Crocodile* is destined to shatter negative stereotypes about Africa and illuminate the richness and complexity of that continent."
— Teresa Dovalpage, author, *Habanera: A Portrait of a Cuban Family*

NIGHTHAWK PRESS
TAOS, NEW MEXICO
www.nighthawkpress.com

ISBN: 978-0615773391
Library of Congress Control Number: 2013933803

Also by Bonnie Lee Black:

How to Cook a Crocodile: A Memoir with Recipes
(Peace Corps Writers, 2010)

Somewhere Child
(Viking Press, 1981)

Front and back cover photos:
"The Quilt," by Bonnie Lee Black, 2001 (www.bonnieleeblack.com)
Cover design: Kathleen S. Munroe, Starr Design, Littleton, Colorado (www.starrdesign.biz)
Interior page design: Barbara L. Scott, Final Eyes, Taos, New Mexico (www.finaleyes.net)

Type is set in Adobe Garamond and Calligraphic 421.

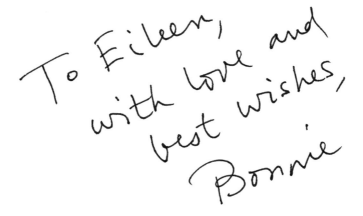

To Eileen,
with love and
best wishes,
Bonnie

To African women,
who are the hope

ALSO BY BONNIE LEE BLACK

How to Cook a Crocodile: A Memoir with Recipes

Somewhere Child

How to Make an African Quilt

The Story of the Patchwork Project of Ségou, Mali

by Bonnie Lee Black

Africa

Gabon

Mali

Niger

Ségou

"Patchwork is the beginning of a new life for me...
Truly, I love patchwork with all my heart. This Patchwork Project
creates a liaison between our country and other, cold, countries,
where [quilts are] appreciated. What I have learned in patchwork
I will use to perfection — if it pleases the Good Lord."

— ASSITAN TOGORA, Patchwork Project graduate
(translated from the French)

Contents

Prologue

ONE FRIDAY AFTERNOON IN MAY 1999, when the core group of women from Centre Benkady, a local women's center, was at my home in Ségou, Mali, for a lesson on how to make mango jam, a few of the women stopped in my living room to admire a child-size bed quilt I'd hung on the wall. It was a quilt I had made the year before while serving in the Peace Corps in Gabon, Central Africa; it was my first, amateurish, patchwork-quilted effort, colorful, yet valuable only to me.

"What is this called?" Ami, a tall, regal Malian woman, head seamstress of the women's center, asked me in French, pointing to the wall quilt, then circling her strong brown hand over the pinwheel block design made of wild African fabrics. "This technique?"

"Patchwork," I told her.

"Le Patch-work?" She mulled the foreign term over slowly and then announced to me firmly, "We want to learn how to do it. We must learn this."

"D'accord," I said, taking up the challenge. *"Je vais essayer."* I agreed to try.

By some fluke, I'd brought with me to Mali some months before a hardback primer on patchwork quilting that had sat on my bookshelf in New York for nearly twenty years but I had never had occasion to open. This fluke proved to be fortuitous because, once settled in Ségou, I found I needed to teach Malian women — as well as myself — how to quilt. "We must learn this" became the imperative, my *raison d'être*, my reason for being, and staying, in Mali.

1

*"The Patchwork Project is a project that I have loved a lot
because I think it is a good thing for us.
I will never throw fabric scraps away in the future;
I will make good things from them."*

— MARIAM DOLO, Patchwork Project graduate
(translated from the French)

Centre Benkady

It is 4:30 a.m. by my watch, and I'm writing by the dim light of the smudgy kerosene lamp beside me on the floor as I wait for a small pot of water to boil to make some instant Nescafe. I'm sitting cross-legged on a straw mat on the earthen floor of an otherwise empty spare room in Youssef's family's compound. From the ten-inch-square window set high in the adobe wall to my right, I can see a patch of black sky speckled with countless tiny stars, more stars per square inch than seem even possible.

Soon the call to prayer from a nearby mosque will wake the faithful, women will begin their morning chores, donkeys will bray, roosters will crow, and tethered goats will complain. But for now all is still, in the relatively cool, early morning air, and I am alone with my thoughts while everyone else still sleeps.

Youssef is back asleep in our makeshift bed, a thin foam mattress spread out on the earth floor of the adjoining spare room. His long, slim body, curved like a parenthesis on his side of our bed, is still. He is a quiet man, asleep and awake.

I'd woken Youssef in the cool, pitch-darkness a few minutes ago to help me light the charcoal in this tiny brazier so I could make myself some coffee while I write. In the year we've been together, he has always respected my need to rise early, to claim time alone in the predawn hours. He understands my need to preserve my thoughts and observations in words on paper, the way he must preserve in photographs every remarkable thing he sees. In many significant, unseen ways we are alike.

Without grumbling, he quietly set about making a fire for me. He carefully poured a few drops of kerosene from the lamp onto the broken pieces of charcoal in the brazier. He tried several times to light the charcoal with a match before we saw a flame. He fanned the fragile red embers vigorously with a hand-woven reed fan until the charcoal took. Then, without a word, he went back to bed, leaving me to blow on the embers to keep them alive as I write and wait for my coffee-water to boil in the small metal teapot resting atop the brazier.

There's a lesson in this for me, isn't there. It takes some effort to keep the embers alive. This is precisely why I want to stay in Africa. The challenges here fan the embers for me. And Mali is a whole new world: exotic, like the Islamic Middle East; familiar, like the American Southwest; earthy and real, like the Africa I've always loved and where, mysteriously, I've felt at home. My heart tells me I must try to stay in Mali for as long as the fire inside me is still alive.

- - - - - - - - - - - -

Ten days ago, Youssef and I arrived in Ségou after a three-hour bus trip from Mali's capital, Bamako, where we'd flown in from Libreville, the capital of Gabon. From Ségou's bus depot in *centreville*, we traveled to his family's compound by donkey cart, which must have been a rare sight for the locals. From what I've observed so far, there are few white people to be seen here in Ségou, and those that are here, or are passing through, speed by in air-conditioned four-wheel-drive SUVs with the windows up.

Children as well as adults gawked and laughed and pointed when they saw me, a thin, middle-aged white woman with short blond hair dressed in jeans and a T-shirt, sitting beside Youssef, a younger African man in a T-shirt and khakis, along with our baggage, on the back of a donkey cart clomping along the dusty side roads at glacial speed. The younger children called out to me, giggling, *"Toubob! Toubobbooooooo!"*

"What are they saying?" I asked Youssef.

"White person," he said.

"Oh."

I smiled and waved back at the gawkers, secretly enjoying the idea of shattering stereotypes. "You might as well get used to it," I wanted to tell them but didn't, "we may be here for a while."

- - - - - - - - - - - - -

In Lastoursville, Gabon, where Youssef and I had met in the course of his vast African travels, I had taught health, nutrition, cooking and crafts for two years to women and children as a Peace Corps volunteer. Youssef, a tall, slender, dignified Malian in his thirties, a self-described "adventurer" and freelance photographer, often attended my classes and took photos of me and my work. He helped me prepare my lessons in French; he helped me carry the health posters, hand puppets, recipe ingredients, crafts supplies, or whatever I needed for whichever women's group or elementary school class I was teaching.

Youssef and I, both *étrangers* (foreigners) in this remote Gabonese town nestled in the rain-forested interior of this equatorial African country, became friends and allies, and — after he saved my life when I had a serious burn accident and he came to live with me to help me convalesce — lovers.

In the evenings after supper, when we sat together in the study of my house on the hill in Lastoursville, sipping a nightcap of cheap Spanish wine, Youssef would tell me about his homeland. He spoke softly in French, the only language we had in common, a second language for both of us, about how tolerant the people of Mali are, how creative, resourceful, resilient, and proud. "You would *love* Mali," he said to me as we studied the large map of Africa on one wall of my study, wondering where in the world we could go next. "And the people of Mali would love you and your creative ideas."

One thing had become clear to me in the course of our first year together: I could not leave this man and return to my previous life in Manhattan. I could not live alone again in a tiny studio apartment, struggling to survive in that gray, cold, soulless city. I could not reestablish my catering business, which I'd closed to join the Peace Corps at the age of fifty. I felt I could not start over elsewhere in the States, either, as a single, self-supporting woman now in her early fifties, feeling sidelined by America's youth culture. I could not envision living through days that didn't begin with Youssef's gentle embrace and his sweet words, *"Je t'aime beaucoup, cherie."*

Sometimes he even added, sincerely, *"Il faut que nous restons toujours ensemble"* (we must stay together always), and I dreamed that might be possible.

So, in Gabon, we weighed our options. Neither the United States nor anywhere in Europe we could think of would work for us, we felt, because the industrialized, so-called "first world" was notoriously racist, sexist, and ageist; and we both were too thin-skinned to withstand the inevitable discrimination we would face as a couple that seemingly broke their unwritten rules. We narrowed our choices to the continent of Africa, where Youssef would more likely be accepted anywhere and where, somewhere, I might feel adopted.

In numerous letters to my best friend and neighbor Martha Cooper, a documentary photographer in New York, who was managing the sublet of my Upper West Side studio apartment, I tried to share my reasoning and solicit her always cool and rational thoughts. "I would like to live where my low-tech talents can be best put to good use," I wrote to her some months before my scheduled close of service from the Peace Corps. "That just about narrows the globe to the Third World. And of all the places in the Third World, Africa interests me the most. ... The world is big, and I don't want to be confined to one room in it anymore."

For many months before leaving Gabon I'd written letters to non-governmental organizations worldwide that focused their efforts on food and nutrition, inquiring about the prospects of my finding a job in Africa along the lines of the community health and nutrition work I'd been doing in Gabon. Most of these letters went unacknowledged. One of the few to respond to me was the World Health Organization in Geneva. They informed me that the minimum requirements for the type of position I was seeking were a master's degree, at least three-to-five years' experience in the field, computer savvy, and foreign-language fluency.

In addition, they made it clear that even for those who met these minimum requirements, the competition was stiff. "Very often," their letter stated, "there may be hundreds of applicants for a single vacancy notice." With no master's degree, only two years' experience as a community health volunteer, no computer skills, and still far-from-fluent French, I knew I would have to find my own way.

When I left New York for the Peace Corps in 1996, my friend Martha had given me an enormous map of Africa, which I'd hung in my study in Lastoursville. On those evenings, Youssef and I would sit in front of that map as if watching a movie screen, waiting for the sound track to reveal some clues, as we discussed the possibilities.

South Africa? Perhaps. But Youssef didn't speak English and wasn't especially keen to learn.

Zimbabwe? No. I'd been there for a visit the Christmas before I met Youssef and found the whites to be as racist as ever. Privately, I'd heard some refer to Africans as "ants."

Nigeria? No. Youssef had told me most Nigerians despise whites. He said it wouldn't be at all safe for me there.

East Africa? No; too Anglophone.

Togo? Youssef had been there once, briefly, and said he liked what he saw; but he had heard rumors recently of political instability in the face of their upcoming elections.

Burkina Faso? A possibility. We'd have to look at it more closely.

Morocco? I'd been there on a food writers' junket a few years before and loved it — especially the food, art, textiles, music, and culture. As a Muslim, French-speaking country, Morocco might be a good choice for Youssef, we felt; but as a mixed couple, we probably would have trouble fitting in.

We needed to find a racially tolerant country, ideally Francophone and preferably hospitable to Muslims. Over time, after weighing the pros and cons, by a process of elimination, we found that country, Youssef's homeland, Mali. Tolerance, Youssef said, was an integral part of Mali's national ethos. The nomadic desert people of the north, the Tuaregs and Moors, were fairer skinned than those of the southern ethnic groups, such as Youssef's tribe, the Malinke. "In Mali people of all colors and all religions live together in peace," Youssef told me. "And older people are revered. Age means wisdom. Age is a plus."

- - - - - - - - - - - - -

So here we are now in the ancient city of Ségou, Mali's second-largest city after the capital, Bamako, staying temporarily with Youssef's older cousins and their wives and many children. His family has welcomed Youssef, the family's long-lost travel-adventurer, and me, his American *copine*, warmly. Youssef was right; I do love Mali already. He, on the other hand, has seemed less than happy and more quiet than usual since our arrival. Sometimes I notice him walking, head down, back and forth, in the courtyard of his family's compound, like a bird with clipped wings pacing in a cage.

As Youssef paces, I sit at a comfortable distance and note the new world around me.

This compound, like most others in *centreville*, I've observed, is built of thick mud bricks. It consists of a large, walled-in square with an arched entryway from the street. Inside, there is a series of small contiguous rooms around the perimeter. Each room has a wooden door that opens onto the central communal courtyard, where most of the family life takes place.

Even in the short while Youssef and I have been here, I've noticed a clear pattern to the family's daily routine. The mothers, Nene and Fatimata, Youssef's older cousins' wives, rise just before dawn to draw water from the central well to fill buckets for their family members' baths and to start the outdoor fire to prepare the family's breakfast. This breakfast is always the same — millet porridge, which tastes to me like soupy, citrusy tapioca pudding. As the sun rises, people begin to stir and go through their morning regimen, quietly, privately, like sleep-walkers crossing paths in the courtyard. By eight, the men, brothers Moussa and Makan, Youssef's cousins and heads of this household, along with their older children, have left for work and school, respectively, while the mothers and younger children remain at home.

The six preschoolers, wearing nothing but white cotton under-pants, race around the courtyard, laughing, squealing, sometimes whining and crying, while Nene and Fatimata busy themselves with other things, such as sewing, pounding millet in a wooden mortar for the next day's breakfast, hand-picking rice-size pebbles out of kilos of raw white rice, washing laundry in large metal buckets stationed near the well, and watching the stew pots gurgle on the open fire.

At noon, the men and schoolchildren return home for lunch, which is always boiled rice plus some kind of tasty, saucy stew contain-ing small chunks of meat or fish and various vegetables. People gather in clusters here and there around the dusty courtyard, sitting on low stools, sharing round platters of food they eat with their right hands. By 3 p.m., after everyone has had a midday nap, the men and older children are off again to work and school, and the women continue their chores at home while the little ones romp.

Dinner, too, is always the same — a cooked, congealed, thick millet *gateau*, or savory cake, served with a dipping sauce, such as gumbo, as flavorful as the gumbos found in New Orleans. After nightfall, a good-size color TV is hauled out to the courtyard close to Fatimata and Makan's rooms — the only section of the compound that has genera-tor-powered electricity. Small aluminum folding chairs and straw mats are spread out on the ground, and everyone, including neighbors who don't own a TV, gathers around this modern, noisy hearth for the rest of the evening to watch whatever programs are being broadcast on Mali's one-and-only television channel.

The TV blares until almost midnight every night, but Youssef and I excuse ourselves at nine and go to bed, wearing earplugs. The family knows I wake early, at 4:30.

One of the children, Makan and Fatimata's impish four-year-old, Mohammed, and I have fallen in love. He follows me everywhere I go, sometimes peeking through a crack in the wooden door to my room when I'm dressing. He seems fascinated by my pale skin and light, straight hair, so different from his own. When we sit side by side, he strokes my hair with his right hand. This is after he's emptied his hand of his treasure for the day, his *objet d'art du jour*, which he's been clutching, waiting for the right moment for our game to begin:

"Qu'est-ce que c'est?" I ask him, tapping the chubby clenched hand he holds out to me. He speaks only Bambara, but he knows by my tone and facial expressions what I'm asking. Slowly, he unfolds his stubby fingers one by one to reveal the small found item that had captured his curiosity that day — a dented bottle cap, perhaps, or a six-sided metal bolt, or a silver bobby pin. I overdramatize my astonishment when I spy the surprise lying in his palm, and he laughs at my clownish behavior. "What does it *do?*" I ask him in French, which Youssef translates

into Bambara for me, at which point Mohammed takes pains to demonstrate the object's function. He inserted the bobby pin, for example, with great care into the front of my hair.

Lately, little Mohammed has taken to sauntering around the courtyard wearing a pair of oversize plastic sunglasses, presumably because I always wear prescription sunglasses to protect my light-blue eyes from the sunlight's fierce glare. Already, at age four, he knows he's a charmer, he knows that imitation is flattering, and he knows he has me in the palm of his hand.

I told his father, Makan, the only person in the family other than Youssef who speaks French and therefore the only other person I've been able to converse with, that his youngest son Mohammed is surely destined to be a mechanical engineer one day. Of his three sons, Mohammed is the most like him, in his broad facial features, strong, stocky build, and keen interest in how things work. Makan has his own business in Ségou repairing motorcycles and *motos* (mopeds). I'm convinced Mohammed could take this talent even further. "If Mohammed does well in school," I tell his father, "I know he'll be a great success in life. He'll support you in your old age. You'll see." Makan seemed pleased to hear my impromptu prophesy.

Besides Makan, his brother Moussa, a tailor, their wives, and all of their children, two other members of the family live in the compound. Zou, a single man about Youssef's age and also a cousin, is partially paralyzed from an accident he suffered as a younger man. He walks with enormous difficulty, as though one leg refuses his commands, and he only has the use of one arm. Nevertheless, he manages to earn a small income as a *charrette* (donkey cart) driver. The family provides for all his basic needs — his own room, three meals a day, clean laundry, community.

And in a room at the far end, a skeletally frail, elderly aunt is treated by everyone in the family with immense deference and care. Every morning, after his ablutions and prayers, I notice, but before he does anything else, Makan spends time with the old woman, whom he calls *"La Vieille"* (the old woman) and pays her his respects. "We honor our elders," he tells me in French on his way back from visiting her room. "We must never let them suffer in any way."

- - - - - - - - - - - -

To celebrate Youssef's birthday in late October, I tried to make him a cake. I decided to turn the effort into a *plein air* cooking lesson, similar to the ones I used to give in Gabon, for Nene and Fatimata and their women friends from the neighborhood. I taped a poster-size recipe I'd made for Youssef's favorite chocolate cake, illustrating the measurements, ingredients, and procedures in pictures rather than language, onto a mud-brick wall not far from the tethered goat being fattened for the family's next *fête*. I had no table to work on, so I used the ground; no oven to bake in, so I used a large *marmite* (cookpot) with a tight-fitting lid, set over an open fire; no cake pans, so I used an aluminum bowl. There was dirt and dust flying everywhere, due to the dozens of fidgety little children who'd arrived from all over the neighborhood to be in my audience.

But by some miracle, a fully baked, dome-shaped chocolate cake emerged when I upended the bowl onto a round platter. I drizzled the top with melted chocolate as icing and I decorated it with flowers. The women were amazed. The children were clamorous. I cut the cake into thirty-six tiny pieces, hoping each child might get at least a taste. In an instant, the cake was gone. There was nothing left for Youssef.

"The problem with Africa," Youssef said to me later in our room, "is that there are too many hands reaching out for the same small cake. Africa has too many children." He said he was thankful that he and I would never add to their numbers. He was glad I was too old to get pregnant.

- - - - - - - - - - - -

In the afternoons, after lunch and a *sieste*, Youssef and I explored Ségou on foot in the dry Arizona-like heat. There was so much to see in this historic, exotic, yet strangely familiar city, I knew it would take years for me to take it all in.

Youssef, who never went anywhere without his cherished camera, took photos of everything that interested him. I borrowed his camera once to take a picture of him standing outside a photographer's studio: smiling his sweet, broad smile, his wide-brimmed straw hat tilted jauntily to one side, sunglasses hanging from the neck of his hand-woven, white cotton traditional Malian shirt. His narrow, pale-blue jeans look clean and pressed; his beige shoes, despite the red mud in the streets, are spotless. In the photo, he looks happy and hopeful, as though a photography studio like this one could be his own one day.

I paint small watercolors of the sights that most captivate me: the vast, smooth, serene expanse of the Niger River; a gigantic baobab tree at the water's edge, almost as wide as a house at its base, which must have been alive when Ségou was the capital of the Bambara Kingdom in the 19th century; the haunting red-mud Muslim mosques; the former-French colonial administrative buildings built in the neo-Sudanese style, flanked by towering palms; the men in their hand-built, outdoor looms weaving long, thin strips of colorful cotton cloth, the way it's no doubt been done for centuries; the textile merchants in the *marché* with their mountain ranges of lively African-print cotton fabric manufactured right here in Ségou.

- - - - - - - - - - - -

One afternoon not long after our arrival in Ségou, Youssef and I went for a *pirogue* (canoe) ride across the Niger to a village on the other side, a distance of about two kilometers each way. It was a beautiful, tranquil little voyage across the great, mirror-smooth river. Besides Youssef and me, there were two young men, one at either end of the long boat, poling and paddling — depending on the river's depth — and a young boy in the middle, behind me, bailing out excess water with a tin can.

The river was high due to good rains, which I was told was a blessing, but part of this small fishing village of round mud huts with thatched straw roofs had been flooded. The marketplace on the former riverbank was now half under water.

Inside the village, Youssef noticed a family that read signs in cowry shells. One family member read our future this way: by tossing a handful of shells onto a blanket, then interpreting their significance based on their relative positions. The old fortuneteller said Youssef and I would remain together, and I would stay in Ségou. He said I would have great *bonheur* (happiness) in Ségou, and I would do good things.

Perhaps the man is just a mind reader, I thought, *and he is reading my wish list*. But by that evening I knew I'd seen enough to know I had to stay. I asked Zou to take Youssef and me on his donkey cart to outlying areas to look at available rental property. I felt sure that if this was meant to be, we'd find a place to call our own.

- - - - - - - - - - - -

AMINATA WAS THE FIRST PERSON I MET BY NAME the day Youssef and I moved in to our rental house in the Pelangana *quartier* of Ségou. She was the unofficial chairperson of the little welcoming committee of neighborhood children who came to greet me. As she approached, she held out a small, square, bamboo stool; then she placed it in the shade of the neem tree just outside the front gate of my house and indicated I should sit down. Youssef had gone in search of the man with the keys to our front gate, and, as the children well knew, it could be a long wait.

She patted her boney breastbone with a weatherworn hand that looked older than her years. "Aminata," she said.

"Bonnie," I said, holding out my large, white, right hand to shake her small brown one. The cluster of dusty, little, half-clothed children giggled shyly and huddled together behind Aminata. To them my name sounded familiar — Bani, the name of the sister river to the Niger. "Bani!" they sang in a happy chorus. "Bani, Bani, Bani!"

Aminata, I guessed, was only eight or nine years old, but she had the time-tested bearing of a person who had lived a much longer life. Her body was thin as a whippet's, and her hair was cropped close, like a boy's. Her quarter-moon smile was warm but tentative, her large, bright eyes, seeking. She was, I could see, a pretty girl who was destined to be a beauty.

"Maison," she said, patting her chest again, and then pointing to the one-room, tumbledown, traditional adobe house in the bare-earth courtyard next door. She seemed proud, especially in front of the other children, to claim me, the only white woman to live in this *quartier*, as her own, her new next-door neighbor.

"Papa?" I asked her, motioning toward the large, middle-aged man sitting outside Aminata's mud-brick house in the shade of the thatched overhang, hunched over his work, hammering metal with a steady ferocity.

Her smile slipped away, and she shook her head. *"Non,"* she said. "Camara."

- - - - - - - - - - - - -

In the weeks that followed, as Youssef and I busied ourselves settling in to our new, nontraditional, cement-brick house — cleaning, painting, and furnishing it to make it as livable as our home in Lastoursville, Gabon, had been — Youssef made neighborly conversation in Bambara with Camara next door and then relayed to me what he had learned. Camara, who was in his early fifties, made a subsistence living as a *forgeron*, turning scrap metal into saleable recycled objects, such as wok-like pans for cooking over an open fire. His much-younger wife, Sarah, a diminutive woman with short limbs, a large head, and a bad temper, could not have children. "She was pregnant once," Youssef told me, "but the baby was born dead." So her sister, who had more children than she could handle, gave Sarah one of her own: Aminata.

Aminata, then, became their unpaid servant-girl. She was assigned all of the tasks neither Camara, due to his advanced age and fatigue, nor Sarah, due to her physical limitations and innate inertia, could do: Drawing buckets of water from their well. Washing the dishes, pots, pans, and laundry outdoors by hand. Tending to their scrawny chickens and raggedy plants. Pounding the millet for porridge in a large, wooden *mortier* every morning. Shopping at the local *plein air marché* (open-air market) every afternoon.

Aminata even helped supplement the family's income by going door to door throughout *quartier* Pelangana selling fingers of fresh ginger root from a large, round metal tray balanced on her head.

Camara told Youssef that Aminata was too busy to attend school; her purpose was to help Sarah, whose sole responsibility was to sit on a low stool all day, in front of their outdoor cook-fire, stirring sooty pots of porridge, sauce, or rice, preparing the three-person-family's meals. From this low perch, Sarah shouted orders at Aminata in a steady, grating stream.

From her tone alone I could surmise her angry words in Bambara: "Get this!" "Do that!" "Move faster!" "You must listen!" "You must do as I say!" Her scolding, rancorous voice, along with Camara's incessant hammering on metal, became the discordant daytime background music of my new neighborhood in Ségou.

Because neither Camara nor Sarah spoke French, my communication with them was limited to the few words of greeting I learned in Bambara — *"A'ni so go ma"* (good morning) and *"A'ni wu la"* (good evening) — sent with a half-hearted wave at the appropriate times of day across the chest-high cement-block wall that separated our courtyards. Aminata and I, however, found creative ways to communicate with each other, through a patchwork of elemental French, which she picked up from her girlfriends in the *quartier* who did attend school, plus pantomime, and telepathy. Her searching eyes seemed to read my mind. Or heart. Or both.

On the rare occasions when Camara took Sarah into *centreville* and Aminata was left alone at home, I could hear her from my kitchen as I kneaded bread or prepared lunch, singing to herself as she worked outside. She sang light, happy, repetitive little tunes; and, no doubt thinking no one could see her (though I could, from my kitchen window), she danced alone to her own, made-up music, twirling her arms, clapping her hands, bending at the waist, tapping her bare feet on the dusty earth. At such moments, remembering doing a similar solo dance whenever I was alone as a little girl, I felt that this tiny brown waif and I were soul sisters, both more spirited than our early circumstances would allow.

Sarah complained to Youssef, he told me over lunch one day, that Aminata was "stupid" and "stubborn." *"Pas du tout!"* I insisted. *"Aminata est très intelligente! Elle a l'esprit. Sarah est jalouse d'elle."* Youssef concurred that Sarah's unstoppable rage could only stem from deep-seated jealousy of the young girl's spiritedness and latent beauty.

- - - - - - - - - - - - -

One afternoon, while I was in my kitchen making tea for Youssef and me, I heard Aminata begin to scream as though in great fear and pain. When I opened the kitchen shutters, I saw, to my horror, Camara pulling Aminata by one of her twig-thin arms, as though she were a recalcitrant animal. He was pulling her across their courtyard with one hand and whipping her repeatedly with a long switch held in the other.

I stood at my kitchen window, frozen, though the day was scorchingly hot, waiting for him to stop; but he didn't. He whipped her with the force of his hammer blows on scrap metal. She screamed and writhed and tried to pull away from his grasp. Yet this man, who was normally a quiet, hard-working, God-fearing Muslim — a man at least five times larger than this little girl — would not stop lashing her.

I ran to my front door, opened and slammed it loudly behind me, then stood on my terrace, plainly visible, clearly horrified. I said nothing. What could I say? I didn't speak his language. I didn't practice his religion. I didn't know the reasons for his out-of-control behavior. I couldn't know his mind. Although I stood less than one hundred feet away from him and we were next-door neighbors, we lived in different worlds. I knew it was not for me, nor even Youssef, to tell him what to do. Yet when Camara looked up and saw me standing there, rigidly staring at him from my front porch, he stopped whipping, dropped the stick, and opened his grasp of Aminata's arm. Aminata ran off, hugging herself and whimpering.

For the next several days, wanting somehow to convey my indignation, I ignored him. When he greeted me, sheepishly, in Bambara, I turned away, saying nothing. It was a good thing, I thought then, that I couldn't speak his language because if I could I would tell him exactly what I thought. I would tell him his cruelty toward Aminata was inexcusable. I would tell him I'd lost all respect for him. I might even go so far as to say that Allah would punish him for what he'd done.

In the ensuing days, Camara tried to make amends. As I was leaving my house to bike into town one day, I saw him outside my front gate, crouched down to the ground on his hands and knees, pulling weeds as if groveling in the dirt in an act of contrition.

"Pardons, Bonnie," he said in French, the only French I'd ever heard him use. *"Pardons."*

I leaned my bike against the nearest neem tree and picked up a long stick from the side of the road. Then, like an actor in a silent movie, I acted out my sentiments with dramatic gestures: "You are too strong to use a stick on a little girl," I told him wordlessly. "You made me cry too."

"Pardons," he repeated, still on all fours.

I gestured toward heaven. "Ask Allah for pardon," I added. Then I pointed to myself and shook my head, "Not me."

- - - - - - - - - - - -

After this incident, Aminata visited me more frequently, as though my home were her refuge. I noticed she timed these visits to coincide with her Aunt Sarah's frequent naps and Camara's forays into town to search for more scrap metal or to sell his wares. At first she sat quietly beside me, her weatherworn hands folded tightly in her lap, watching with keen interest whatever I was doing. Then I could see she wanted to play a more active role.

So when I wove a floor mat with strips of scrap fabric on a nail-studded wooden loom, I gave her a small, square loom like it on which to weave a potholder. When she helped me plant impatiens around the base of a mango tree in my front courtyard, I gave her several impatiens plants to take home and plant at her house. When I kneaded bread dough in my kitchen, I gave her a turn at kneading. When I read a book in the shade of my front terrace, I pointed out the letters and gave her a pencil and paper on which to practice the alphabet. The first whole word she learned to write was "Aminata."

And when I learned from a local Peace Corps volunteer how to crochet using recycled plastic bags as yarn, I gave Aminata a crochet hook of her own and taught her how to do it too. More than anything else, she loved this. When we were not sitting side by side on my porch crocheting with plastic, she was crocheting at home after dinner in front of their outdoor cook-fire. Even Sarah approved of this pastime, as long as Aminata's other daily chores were done.

One day Aminata appeared with a friend about her age whom she introduced to me as Bintou. Bintou, who spoke some French, asked me whether I would also teach her how to crochet with plastic bags. She, like Aminata, was quick to learn the technique of folding and cutting the whisper-thin, pastel-colored bags into fine strips, then using this as yarn to make small items, such as change purses and pencil cases, for possible sale in the weekly open-air Pelangana *marché*.

Acting as Aminata's translator, Bintou boldly approached me with a proposal: Could we invite other neighborhood girls to come to my house and do the same? Could we call it a "club," just for girls? Would I teach them all, maybe one afternoon every week, how to crochet using plastic bags as yarn? Please, please, please, please, *please?*

"Quelle bonne idée" (what a good idea), I told the two smiling little girls, as we swatted away a swarm of attacking black flies.

- - - - - - - - - - - -

I HAD BROUGHT MY BELOVED BIKE, a black, ten-speed Specialized Hybrid, to Mali from New York so that biking could be my primary means of transportation in Ségou. I couldn't afford a car, or even a moped, which was the way most middle-class Ségouvians got around. The average Malian couldn't afford a car any more than I could; even second-hand cars cost more than most of them earned in ten years.

Halfway decent automobiles, usually older-model Mercedes Benz, were for *grands types* (big shots), such as well-connected politicians and highly successful businessmen, and there were relatively few of them in Ségou. The poorest people traveled by donkey cart. The not-quite-so-poor, such as Peace Corps volunteers and now me, got around on push-pedal bikes.

My house in *quartier* Pelangana was about 6 kilometers (roughly 4 miles) from *centreville* Ségou, so biking to town and back was at least a 12 km trip, generally in over 100-degree (F.) heat. Fortunately, Ségou's main road, which came up from Bamako and led to the popular tourist destination of Mopti, was flat and paved, and the forward motion of biking provided a pleasant breeze. Unfortunately, it was a narrow road and a busy route, crowded with heedless pedestrians and all types of bikers, plus impatient cars, dilapidated taxis, and barreling trucks.

As I wrote in a letter to my friend Martha in late December, soon after settling in to Pelangana, "Biking to the post office is a 40-minute harrowing experience — dodging potholes, sand pits, donkey carts, huge trucks, hordes of sleepwalkers and other bikers. But what a great workout!"

I biked to and from *centreville* several times a week, returning from town with heavy, bulging plastic grocery bags dangling precariously from both sides of my handlebars. Most days I felt physically fit — like a teenager, in fact — even though I was in my early fifties. When locals would remark, "A Malian woman of your age could never bike back and forth to town the way you do!" I felt strong and proud.

- - - - - - - - - - - - -

The one day I could never miss biking into town was Monday. Ségou's Monday *marché,* when all of *centreville* becomes an open-air marketplace, was one of the highlights of my week, as I suspected it had been for countless others for centuries. Both *commerçants* and customers flock to town by road and river from far outside the city to buy and sell and reconnect as though this weekly extravaganza were a family-of-man reunion.

Early every Monday morning farmers and craftspeople from outlying areas make the journey into town on slow-moving donkey carts bearing their fresh-picked produce and handcrafted wares. Then, in designated areas, they set up their makeshift stands, offering glistening pyramids of Italian plum tomatoes, fluffy mounds of pale-green lettuces, cumulous clouds of raw cotton, hand-woven baskets and prayer mats, handmade traditional furniture fashioned of wooden slats tied with cowhide, and myriad other goods.

Long, low-lying boats arrive on Ségou's riverbank overloaded with more items for sale. Villagers from Kalabougou across the Niger carry their sturdy, functional pottery to display along the shore. Fishermen unload their fresh catches in large baskets to sell from rickety wooden tables by the water's edge to eager women buyers.

As a center of Mali's textile industry, Ségou's *marché* also proudly displays stacks of pre-cut *pagne*-lengths (about 5 feet) of colorful African-print cotton fabric, bolts of hand-woven strip cloth, and countless examples of *bogolan* mud cloth art.

On most Monday mornings I headed from home on my bike directly to Nene and Fatimata's stand at the *marché*, where I visited with them before making my rounds. Youssef's cousins' wives sold small sachets of a sweet-smelling potpourri concoction I liked to buy as gifts. Then I chained my bike under their watchful eyes, and I set out into the crowded *marché* alone on foot.

Despite the crush of people filling the narrow labyrinthine streets, the mood, I found, was always friendly and festive. There was never any pushing or shoving or sales pressure, no hawking or haggling. No one was in a hurry, it seemed. Everyone was too busy enjoying the colorful human spectacle.

This is theater, I thought: The timeless drama of the bazaar, where people come to offer up the fruits of their labors and others come to get the goods they need. It's a give and take as old as hunger. It's also a meeting place for people for whom social ties are beyond price. This is where the people reinforced their bonds. This is where they learned their news — not from newspapers or television but from face-to-face communication.

I walked among these regal, resourceful Malians for hours, taking it all in — the sights and smells, the colors and cacophony of voices in Bambara — greeting some vendors I'd come to know who spoke some French, buying the items I needed for the upcoming days' meals. And then I'd head home by bike, both exhilarated and already exhausted by the sensory overload.

- - - - - - - - - - - -

One Monday at noontime, while I was slowly pedaling home from the *marché*, with a strong wind coming toward me like an invisible, almost-impenetrable obstacle I had to push through, feeling hungry, thirsty, hot, sweaty, dirty, and most of all tired, a young motorcyclist came up behind me at top speed, sideswiped me, and sent me and my bike flying onto the graveled shoulder of the road. If I hadn't been wearing sturdy blue jeans and a long-sleeved shirt, I might have been badly scraped. My bike's handlebars were bent with the impact of the fall and my grocery bags were sent flying, but I was thankful that neither my bike nor I had broken anything. I was only slightly bruised and badly shaken.

As I picked the bike and myself up and stood, dazed, by the side of the road, a crowd of dusty, aimless little children gathered around me to gawk. The teenage motorcyclist looked terrified, as if he fully expected to be hauled off to jail. *"Pardons,"* he said to me penitently. *"Pardons."*

Sure enough, out of nowhere a policeman arrived on the scene, offering to take me to the hospital to be checked and then to the police station where I could file a complaint against the reckless young motorcyclist who'd hit me. But the prospect of standing in a long line in the blazing midday heat at the hospital, and the thought of the red tape at the police station, made me refuse the policeman's offer. I was beginning to feel nauseated and dizzy, in addition to thirsty and hungry. All I wanted was to get home, have some lunch, and take a nap.

"Ce n'est pas grave" (it's not serious), I told the solicitous policeman. I'm okay, I insisted. *PLEASE let me go home*, I thought.

The young motorcyclist appeared relieved that I wasn't about to press charges.

"Merci," he said, bowing.

"Ce n'est pas grave," I repeated to him, still in a daze. The gawking children helped me gather up my groceries, and then I walked my bike as though it were a wounded horse the rest of the way home, reassuring myself I was fine.

In fact, I was sore for days afterward. At fifty-something, I realized, the body takes longer to bounce back from such blows. Suddenly, I felt old and frail. But that didn't stop me from riding my bike, sometimes just for the pure, childlike pleasure of it.

Every once in a while, in the late afternoon, I would ride alone for nearly an hour in the opposite direction from Ségou's *centreville*, toward Mopti. This ride was thrilling to me: the flat expanse of Mali's heartland, its scrubby trees and occasional massive baobab dotting the landscape, the descending slanting African sunlight, the smell of dried hay in the sun-scorched fields. I felt embraced by Nature, which restored my soul. I felt like the carefree child I had never been — or a large, wild, low-swooping African bird. Free.

- - - - - - - - - - - -

OUR SIX-ROOM, ONE-STORY, cement-block house in Pelangana, which I rented for the equivalent of only $100 a month, sat toward the back of a cement-walled courtyard, which, except for a few established mango trees in the front, was a blank canvas of flat, baked earth, begging to be transformed. The house, which belonged to a Malian businessman, a *grand type* who lived in Bamako, was nine years old and had never been lived in or loved. Like the other relatively modern houses in our *quartier*, this house had been built during an optimistic time, but those times had obviously changed for Ségou. Many of these new houses dotting Pelangana's wide, tree-lined dirt roads remained empty, while the longstanding residents in their traditional adobe homes continued their timeless lives, traveling by donkey cart to and from town along back roads, raising goats and chickens — and countless children — within their walled-in, mud-brick family compounds.

One afternoon soon after Youssef and I moved into our house in Pelangana, we went for a long walk along the dusty streets of our new neighborhood and happened upon an intriguing enterprise. At the far end of the *quartier*, before it became open, uninhabited fields, we found a man with a nursery business, a *pepinieriste*, by the name of

Abdoulaye Mariko, a member of Mali's Malinke tribe, like Youssef. Mariko was a tall, broad-shouldered, middle-age man with a wide smile framed by a close-cropped white beard. When I told him we were new to Pelangana and anxious to transform our barren courtyard into beautiful gardens, he invited us into his compound for tea and for a tour of his vast nursery.

This was a second career for him, he told us in perfectly accented French over small glasses of sweet black tea in the shade of a rustic arbor set up amidst hundreds of seedlings and saplings. He had been a teacher in the interior of Mali for many years and then the principal of a public school. He was retired now, he said, and trying to support his large family doing what he loved best — working with plants.

"C'est un defi" (it's a challenge), he told me with a brave smile. *"Mais, si plait a Deu, ça va reussir"* (but if it pleases God, it will succeed).

Yes, his new enterprise was surely challenging, and he could only hope it would somehow succeed. But there was more to his story, I could see. Mariko did not look well to me. He walked haltingly, as though every step pained him. His eyes, though kind, were worry-lined and deep-set. His dark-brown skin was tinged with gray.

With energetic words and dramatic gestures I outlined for him my plans for our courtyard: I'd like a thick hedge lining our front gate, I told him with outstretched arms; I see glorious bougainvillea tumbling over the front wall, a tiered rock garden filled with potted succulents along the length of one side of the house, a vegetable garden lining the other side, multicolored flower beds encircling the mango trees, more flowers and greenery hugging the house....

Mariko's face brightened as if he too could see what I was envisioning. I could tell my ambitious gardening plans pleased him, not just because he'd found a new customer, but because he'd found a new soulmate. We spoke the same language. We were both irredeemably in love with living, breathing, beautiful, and edible plants.

That day I paid for twenty-three tiny prickly hedge plants, plus a large bag of *terre noir* (topsoil) to be delivered to my house the next day by one of Mariko's sons on their *charrette*. Mariko assured me that hungry roaming goats or other animals would not eat these prickly plants, even though I planned to plant them along the outside walls, on either side of our front metal gate. "Goats don't like the taste of this hedge," he informed me, "nor do they like the needles that stick in their throats."

Then, with a courtly bow, he presented me with a small, pink-flowered impatiens plant to carry home. *"Cadeau de Noël,"* he said, smiling broadly. It was Christmastime 1998, and although he himself was Muslim, he wanted to give me a Christmas gift.

- - - - - - - - - - - -

Within days, dozens of dirty little hands had volunteered to help me plant the hedge in front of my house. Little helpers held the bag of topsoil open for me so I could scoop. They followed me like ducklings into neighboring fields to help me gather a bucket full of sun-dried goat manure to use as fertilizer in the beds. They watched as I dug a deep trough, then they pitched in as I followed the process Mariko had taught me: manure, sand, hay, topsoil, water — layer after layer — until, finally, the plants, equally spaced. Then I watered it well once again. *Soon these bushes will put down roots, grow up, fill out, belong,* I thought, as I yearned for the same for myself. I patted the woolly heads of all of my little barefooted helpers to thank them.

In the weeks that followed, Mariko's nursery supplied the stuff of my gardening dreams. I planted bougainvillea in fiery shades of red and orange along the inside front wall; I collected large, porous red rocks and arranged them in tiers, then planted my rock garden between them; I double-dug and ameliorated the clayey soil for a good-size vegetable garden, then planted rows of tomatoes, eggplants, and basil, dreaming of pasta sauce to come. My heart sang. My muscles ached.

Keeping the garden watered — in a climate that receives scant rainfall each year — became the biggest physical challenge. Pulling up bucket after bucket of water from our well to water our burgeoning garden became a twice-a-day, strenuous task, which Youssef and I shared. At first, though, having a well of my own was a novel experience for me, not without its charms.

All my life, I reflected, whenever I'd wanted water, I simply turned on the nearest tap. Wells for me always existed primarily in the abstract — in other places (far away), in other times (my grandmother's time), in storybook rhymes ("Ding, dong, dell…"). Now that I had a working well in my own life, in the front courtyard of my house in Ségou, I could appreciate its virtues, sing its praises, and respect its dangers.

First, it was always there, and the water was free for the taking. Second, pulling up buckets full of water (in a rubber pail made from a recycled inner tube) was terrific exercise. I used arm, shoulder, and back muscles that had never been challenged quite this way. Water, I soon learned, is *heavy*. Each bucket held enough to fill a standard-size watering tin; and I needed at least a dozen watering tins' worth to water all my newly sown plants.

Each time I lowered the black rubber bucket into the deep, cylindrical well — letting it drop the distance of its cord (roughly 50 feet) and land with a thud on the surface of the water below — I would think: How easy it would be to lose one's balance and fall, head-first, in. How tragic it would be if my prescription sunglasses fell off my face and disappeared into the deep; I could no longer see! How many Malian children — toddlers, roaming around unsupervised in the courtyards of their families' compounds — have tripped, fallen, and drowned in their well?

Well water, I also learned, is warm, abundant and soft. But the well itself was constructed of cold cement and its dangers were hard and real. *Maybe one of these days,* I told myself, *Youssef and I will buy a pulley that will make it easier for me to draw the water I need every morning for watering our growing garden.* Until then, I realized, I would have to do it the ancient way, bending over the abyss, peering into the watery depths, taking with thanks this free gift from Mother Earth, while not ignoring the well's dangers.

- - - - - - - - - - - - -

As I watched my nascent garden grow and thrive, I watched my relationship with Youssef slowly dissolve. The quiet peace and harmony we'd known in Gabon became rarer in Mali.

In our new life in Ségou, Youssef became dispirited, irritable, short-tempered, and unkind. He blamed his erratic behavior on Mali's hot-dry climate, on his sudden allergy to dust and other nameless ailments, on his frustrations with establishing himself as a professional photographer there.

In Gabon, I'd witnessed the emergence of Youssef's photographic career; in Ségou, as I saw his discouragement deepen, vivid memories of that hope-filled time flooded back to me:

Youssef's lifelong dream, he had told me in Gabon, was to one day become a professional photographer — not unlike Seydou Keita, the world-renowned Malian portrait photographer. But Youssef was realistic enough to realize the fulfillment of that dream was a long way off. His first step was to buy a decent, second-hand, single lens reflex camera, for which he needed to save a considerable amount of money. To that end, he went to work for a relatively well-paying logging company in Gabon, *Societe de Bois de Lastoursville,* known as SBL, where he became part of a small expatriate Malian community.

Sometimes in the evening, in my study in Gabon, when we sat and talked together quietly before going to bed, Youssef would share with me in tragic, lyrical terms how the earth and trees suffered at the hands of these foreign-owned logging companies.

As Youssef explained it, even carefully selected trees — which he described as several stories tall, oil-drum thick, and centuries old — take down many, many more trees with them. To get the big Okoume trees, first a path, then a clearing is cut, killing scores of other trees; then, when the sought-after tree is chain-sawed and falls, "screaming like a human being," Youssef said, to the ground, it wounds and ultimately kills all the trees it touches. The prize tree is then sliced into truck-length portions, hauled out of the rainforest in chains, loaded onto the waiting *grumiers,* and whisked off to the greedy, thoughtless world.

The problems, Youssef added, are many and complicated. One is that all these slaughtered trees and plundered forests are not being replaced. Forests that took hundreds and hundreds of years to come into being can be — and are in the process of being — destroyed in the space of decades.

Another problem, he told me, is that the damaged and dying trees are left, like garbage, to rot in place. This, plus the roads and clearings made by and for all the heavy machinery, cause, Youssef said, *"inundations"* (floods) during the heavy rains, which cause more trees to die.

"The foresters only care about *l'argent*" (money), Youssef said. "Okoume makes the best plywood in the world, and there is a great demand for plywood, especially in Asia. These French businessmen don't see the African workers who lose fingers and arms to the sawing machinery. They don't hear the trees weep."

Youssef worked at the *chantier* just long enough to save 500,000 CFA, then worth about $1,000 in Gabon, to buy his first profession-al-quality camera. He entrusted the money to his Malian friend, Kofi, who lived with his wife and children in Lastoursville and who was traveling on business to Togo, where he was more likely to find a good, second-hand camera for Youssef at a far better price than in costly Gabon. When Youssef told me this story the day we met, he was still waiting for his friend's return, and I had my doubts. But I was proven wrong: Kofi eventually returned to Lastoursville, some months later, with the camera of Youssef's dreams.

When Youssef brought his new camera, a used Canon A-E1, to my home to show me, he was overjoyed. He cradled it in his arms the way he must have seen his mother hold his newborn siblings. He turned it slowly in his large hands, inspecting it as if to see whether it had all its fingers and toes. He didn't know yet how to use it — aperture? depth of field? what did all those numbers signify? — but an instruction booklet came with it, written in French, English, German, and Japanese. He would soon learn, we both knew.

Youssef's first photo assignment was to take portraits of Kofi's fam-ily in Lastoursville for them to send back to relatives in Mali. He did this as a thank-you gesture, to show his appreciation, right away. I made a camera carrying case for him from a sturdy, canvas shoulder bag I had, which I stuffed with mattress foam hollowed to fit his camera and lens. I also gave him a khaki vest my friend Martha (Marty) had given me when I left for the Peace Corps, with all sorts of zippered pockets in the front for holding film and other small items. I tucked into one of the zippered pockets a small notebook and pen so Youssef could record his clients' names, and the dates and settings for all the photos he took.

Youssef was set. He removed the lens with a slow turn, capped it, and nestled it into the shoulder bag. He capped the camera's body and tucked it too into the bag's foam bedding. He put the vest, which matched his clean, creased khaki pants, over his bright, white T-shirt and slipped the shoulder bag's wide strap over his head. He patted the bag protectively as it hung at his side. Already tall and dignified, he stood even taller and more regally now. In his new role, he looked the part. *"Oh, vraiment, je suis professionnel maintenant. Je suis photographe!"* (Truly, I'm a professional now. I'm a photographer), he announced to me, smiling broadly.

Not long after Youssef's new camera arrived, Marty sent, through a volunteer named Chris who'd been back in the States visiting his family in New York, a surprise package for Youssef. Among the items she included were a flash attachment for his camera, a dozen good-quality batteries for it, several rolls of film, and a large, coffee-table-size book of Seydou Keita's photography. Youssef was overjoyed with these gifts and so awed by the book he lifted it up to his face and kissed it. This was the first such book he had ever owned, he told me, and it became, along with his new photo equipment, one of his most cherished treasures.

Together, we studied Keita's photographs — the way he posed his subjects in his studio space, and the way these subjects chose to include their possessions in their portraits to prove their modern identity, social status, or profession. There was one portrait of a middle-aged man in a light suit and tie sitting on his shiny, new motor scooter; another of a younger man in a dark blazer leaning possessively over a console radio with an alarm clock on top of it; two young mothers wearing identical, wildly printed traditional dresses, lavish jewelry and dramatic head wraps, each with a chubby baby on her lap; and a pensive-looking Peul woman with darkened lips and tufted hair sitting behind her hand-cranked Singer sewing machine. In these and thousands of other portraits, Keita captured the self-identity of his countrymen-and-women during a period of enormous social change in Mali.

Like my friend Marty, whose own photographic career could be traced to the Kodak Brownie camera her father, who owned a camera shop in Baltimore, gave her when she was in nursery school, Seydou Keita's career began in Bamako, Mali, in the 1930's when as a boy he received a Brownie camera as a gift from his uncle. By 1948 Keita had set up a commercial studio in downtown Bamako, not far from the train station, and proceeded to teach himself the craft. At first, he used his own lacy bedspread as a backdrop, and he photographed outdoors using available light. In time, his photographic portraiture received worldwide acclaim. Keita's success stemmed from his sensitivity to his subjects' needs, his eye for composition and detail, and his unflagging determination to learn and improve. Youssef seemed to possess these same qualities. Although he had no one to teach him the technicalities of photography in Lastoursville, Youssef chose to follow Seydou Keita from afar, as if navigating his own small sailboat at night by the North Star.

In fact, the profession of itinerant photographer perfectly suited Youssef's nature. Like me, he was independent and self-motivated, and he preferred to be his own boss. He enjoyed the freedom to choose his own hours, follow his own pace, find his own clientele, make and keep his own appointments, hold himself to his own high standards, and methodically build a reputation for reliability — in a place where reliability was rare.

By his nature, too, Youssef was sensitive to his surroundings, vigilant, and observant.

"Did you see that?" he would ask me on one of our early evening walks together by the Ogooué River which ran through Lastoursville.

"What?" I'd missed whatever it was he was pointing to.

"That bird, over there, up in the trees. It's so big! And it's plumage so beautiful, so colorful. Oh, it's flown off now."

I'd always considered myself to be an observant person. "A writer," I once noted, "is one on whom nothing is lost." But Youssef consistently eclipsed me in this regard. He seemed to see everything.

And, like his unsuspecting mentor, Seydou Keita, Youssef had a gift for posing his subjects in front of the most flattering backdrops, tilting their heads just so, saying the right word to the fussy baby to capture that curious expression, pressing the shutter at the perfect instant to preserve the ephemeral, forever. His eye for color and composition was unerring. His pride in his work was palpable.

Inspired by his emerging talents, I wrote a short poem for him in French called *"Photographe"* (photographer), which he kept folded in his wallet, like a love letter:

Quelle magie il fait	[What magic he makes
Avec un toucher il arête le temps	With one touch he stops time
Il saisit le moment pour toujours	He seizes the moment forever
Les jeunes ne vieillissent pas	The young don't age
Les vieux ne meurrent pas	The old don't die
Et tout le monde sourie	And everyone smiles
pour l'éternité	for eternity
Quel pouvoir!	What power!
Quel métier magiques.	What a magical craft.]

But his early freelance photography work in Gabon was not without its frustrations. Sometimes a whole roll of film came out overexposed, his subjects looking like ghosts standing in front of a bleached-out background. Youssef knew his clients would not accept these inferior photos, and not only would they not pay the balance due, they would demand their deposit back. In these instances, he knew that all of the time, effort, and travel expense he had incurred was for nothing.

I tried my best to cheer him by making up stories that may have been half true. I told him Marty sometimes forgot to put film in her camera when she went on a shoot; once she misplaced a whole roll of exposed film after an event she'd covered, and she never did find it. "Marty's forgetful like that," I told him. "These things happen. I'm sure Seydou Keita had lots of horror stories too." I would turn to the Introduction to the Seydou Keita book Marty had sent him and translate again for him the sections where Keita speaks about the tough time he had at the beginning of his career. *"C'est normal,"* I assured him.

To take his mind off these setbacks when he was home, I played his favorites among the cassettes I'd brought with me to Gabon — Willy Nelson, Paul Simon, and Tracy Chapman. He especially liked listening to Tracy Chapman, even though he didn't know the words she sang in English. He said he could tell just from the depths of the sound of her voice that her ancestors came from his homeland, Mali.

- - - - - - - - - - - -

But now that we were in Mali, Youssef's frustrations only seemed to deepen. He spent more and more time away from home trying to establish a clientele, only to learn that Ségou had more than enough freelance photographers already. When he arrived home, tired and coughing from the dust, he was disheartened and angry.

Although after each angry outburst, he would always apologize to me sincerely, it became clear that he was no longer content with our domestic arrangement. He appeared restless and anxious to leave, to try his luck elsewhere. The day we first met in Gabon, he'd described himself to me as an *"aventurier."* Now, in Ségou, he seemed ready for another adventure.

So my visits to Mariko's nursery became more frequent and more personal. I sought not only his advice on gardening in Mali but also his wise counsel on how to deal with Youssef. Mariko himself had been married to the same woman for more than thirty years. They had weathered many storms. *Did he think this was a storm I should patiently ride out,* I wondered aloud, *or should I encourage Youssef to leave?*

Mariko's large and sturdy wife, the mother of his nine children, now mostly grown, always welcomed me warmly into their compound when I pulled up on my bike. She seemed not to be the least bit jealous of my quiet visits with her husband in his secluded arbor, away from his bustling family of boisterous children and grandchildren, perhaps because she knew our friendship could never be more than platonic. As he stretched his long body in a handmade hammock crafted of rough, black rope, and I sat nearby him in an aluminum-and-plastic folding chair beneath the arbor's thatch, we talked of many things, and he told me more about himself.

His health was deteriorating due to chronic diabetes, he confided. The circulation in his hands and feet was *"très mal,"* he said, so bad he could barely walk anymore. His biggest fear was that his feet might have to be amputated — *What would he do then?* He had lost a lot of weight, due to illness and worry.

"When I was young, I was big and strong," he told me nostalgically. "I was *aflame,"* he added with a wink.

"I'm sure you were," I said, knowing exactly what he meant and what his illness had taken from him.

- - - - - - - - - - - -

Needing a space to call my own, I converted the small front bedroom of our home in Pelangana into a private study, making a desk of a rectangular wooden table abutting the window overlooking the courtyard. There, every morning before the sun crept around the house and forced its fiery rays into this tiny room, thereby converting it to an oven — while the predawn sky was still royal blue and the only outdoor sounds were birds singing, roosters crowing, and donkeys braying — I would sit at this desk and read and write and think and pray and marvel at my growing garden.

Straight ahead, I could see the smallest, most scraggly of the three mango trees, whose tiny, unripe fruit kept dropping to the ground discouragingly. To the left was my fledgling vegetable garden — basil plants, corn, gumbo (okra), green beans, amaranth, and tomatoes — looking like a miniature forest. Beyond the front mango trees, I could see the bougainvillea I'd planted as scrawny naked sticks now climbing up the front, whitewashed wall. And to the right was the little avocado tree I'd planted from a pit I'd saved from the day Youssef and I first arrived in Mali. This nearly knee-high avocado tree, with its fat, deep-green leaves and strong, straight trunk, seemed to be thriving — unlike my love for Youssef.

I'd brought with me to Mali a tattered copy of the Penguin Classic paperback of the Koran translated by N.J. Dawood, which I'd long had in my library in New York but had never read. There in my small, quiet study, I began reading portions of the Koran every morning, at first merely out of intellectual curiosity about Islam, Mali's predominant religion. But I soon grew to appreciate the beauty of its lyrical language, the lilting cadences, so much like David's Psalms in the King James Old Testament. I found comfort in its words and inspiration from its many references to promised gardens.

For "the people of the desert" to whom the Koran is addressed, lush gardens in the next life are offered as the reward for good behavior in this life. Believers are repeatedly reassured: "Those that have faith and do good works shall be rewarded with gardens watered by running streams. That is the supreme triumph."

"This is where my heart is now," I wrote one morning after reading the Koran, "in the earth, the soil, the garden. This is what thrills me, makes me happy to be still alive on planet earth, happy to be here in Mali: planting this garden, watching things grow."

- - - - - - - - - - - - -

THE WHOLE SOLAR SYSTEM seemed closer to me in Mali than anywhere else I'd been on earth, and its elements held greater sway in people's lives than I had ever seen.

The sun, in a yearlong loop of endless summer, sizzled everything within its grasp, paralyzing living things with its inhumane heat. The wind, especially during the season of *l'harmattan*, the first quarter of the year, picked up handfuls of sand from the nearby Sahara and sent them swirling, blindingly, like beige snow, in all directions. Angry gale-force winds threw dust and dirt into eyes, nose and teeth, enveloping the skin, encrusting the hair. One soon grew used to sand beneath eyelids, sand in the mouth, sand glued to a sweaty scalp. Open windows and doors invited sand inside the house, where a broom could gather piles of sand, several inches high, every afternoon.

During the day, both men and women wore traditional, long, loose-fitting, tent-like clothing they called *boubous* and turban-like head wraps to protect themselves from the sun's fierce rays and the wind's stinging swipes. Then at night, while the sun went elsewhere and the wind shriveled to an occasional limp breeze, most Malians slept outdoors on straw mats dotting their wall-enclosed compounds, under the moon and the star-studded sky.

At least one night every month, however, when the moon was fullest, the people wouldn't go to bed at all. Instead, they celebrated life throughout the bright, moonlit night, playing traditional Malian bluesy music, singing their repetitive call-and-response songs, and dancing to thudding drums until dawn. *"Au clair de lune, Afrique danse,"* a Malian friend told me. Yes: *In the full-moonlight, Africa dances.*

Following the windy season, *l'harmattan*, comes the hottest-driest season, *la saison chaude*, from April through June, when daytime temperatures hold steady at 45 degrees Celsius (115 F). Then comes the "rainy" season, when the hope of rain to cool the hot-humid days remains mostly a tease, because from July through September rain might fall heavily during only about five or six days.

When the rains do come, however, they turn the hard, red-clay, baked-earth roads into mini lakes in which clusters of barely clothed children splash gleefully, while little boys try valiantly to float their handmade toy boats. The children know that cars will not disturb their street play. The roads, at least until the thirsty sun sucks up these lakes as if through a short straw, become impassible to vehicles, due to the deep water and underlying mud.

What Malians called their "winter" — October through December — I came to call the "tourist season" because temperatures drop at last to a more-tolerable-for-foreigners daytime temperature of 85 to 90 degrees Fahrenheit. For the people of Ségou, who bundle themselves up in ski jackets, woolen caps and scarves, this so-called winter weather is cold. To me, it was lifesaving.

In fact, during Mali's *saison chaude*, I had never known such heat. I perspired constantly, day and night. In rebellion, my thin white skin became at first blotchy and itchy — I wanted to unzip it like a wet suit and remove it all together — then it erupted in ugly, painful boils, on my chin, inner thighs, back, arms, shins. About a dozen in all.

Unlike Mali's ancient adobe-style homes, my house was made of "modern" cement blocks, which made it ill suited for the country's intense subtropical climate. The cement absorbed the sun's pounding heat all day and then disgorged it inside every room throughout the night. The house had no air-conditioning, but I did have a few electric fans, which worked sporadically. During the hottest months, when the Niger River was at its lowest, the hydroelectric power plants shut down for long stretches of time. This meant no electricity — which meant no somewhat-cooling fans, no cold drinking water from the fridge, no reading light, no audio-tapes, no Voice of America on the radio, no frosty beer.

Every morning of *la saison chaude*, I complained privately to my journal about my personal discomfort with the heat and mused upon its broader deleterious effects. "I'm convinced," I wrote one day, "that climate is a major reason for Mali's underdevelopment. The heat is simply *paralyzing!*" And another day: "It's pointless to complain about the weather. What good does it do? People here are so strong. The hardships they withstand, such as this amazing HEAT, are more than most Westerners could imagine. I admire the locals' awesome strength."

Youssef slept Malian-style on a woven grass mat on our front terrace, while I remained in our furnace-like master bedroom, sweating all night in our mosquito-netted double bed. Rivulets of perspiration ran down my body like crawling insects, waking me. My nightclothes and sheets became soaking wet.

Youssef complained about the weather, too, but just to me. He regretted our having come to Mali. He told me often that his father had moved his family from western Mali to the coast of Côte d'Ivoire in the early '60s for this very reason: He couldn't bear Mali's climate either. *Why had I brought us here?* Youssef demanded. *Why couldn't we have stayed in Gabon, where the temperature was only 38 degrees C. (100 F.), not 45 C., as in Mali?* he wanted to know. He claimed to be allergic to *la poussiere* (dust). He blamed his unhappiness on me. He blamed the weather for the fact that we no longer slept together.

I didn't blame him. Fate had brought us to the country of his heritage, but once there he chafed at Mali's — or anyone's — claim on him. He had grown up in Abidjan, the capital of Côte d'Ivoire, where his aging parents still lived; he talked often of returning there to care for them. I, on the other hand, felt, despite the physical discomforts of its climate, more at home in Mali, the country of Youssef's origin, than I ever had in my own. For reasons even I didn't fully understand, I felt I must stay.

- - - - - - - - - - - -

A few months after making Ségou our home, Youssef bought himself a second-hand, one-speed bike, freshly painted white, in fairly good condition. So on our good days we were able to more fully explore our *quartier* by biking together, side by side. As we rode along the wide, dusty, dirt roads, passing low, adobe houses surrounded by courtyards framed by five-foot-high mud-brick walls, exuberant little children ran up to us in the street shouting *"Toubob! Toubob! Touboboooooooooo!"* and pointing at me. I waved to the kids and greeted them in Bambara. As the only white person in our neighborhood, I was reluctantly becoming accustomed to these innocent, astonished receptions, which had the sudden, stinging effect of making me feel self-conscious of and uncomfortable in my skin.

One day, on such an excursion, Youssef and I found at the extreme eastern end of our new *quartier*, about a mile from our house, a women's sewing center. The sign in front of the center read:

CENTRE DE FORMATION FEMININ

BENKADY PELENGANA

COUPE COUTURE

It was, I could make out, a place where women from the local area could take cutting and sewing (dressmaking) lessons. But I had to ask Youssef to translate for me the Bambara word "Benkady."

"It means 'good success,'" he said.

I took the name as an omen.

Centre Benkady had a small *boutique* (small, humble shop) close to the main road into town, where the women members sold their handiwork. The sign out front was meant to attract tourists who might be inclined to stop their tour-guided vehicles and briefly shop for hand-sewn souvenirs before speeding east, on their way to Mopti and Djenne, then on to the cliff dwellers' Dogon region of Mali.

When Youssef and I stopped in the *boutique* to introduce ourselves, we met the center's head *formatrice* (instructor), Ami Sylla, a tall, commanding woman who appeared to be in her mid-forties. She wore a billowing blue and white *boubou*, liberally edged at the square neckline and wide sleeves with white cotton hand-crocheted trimming, which contrasted markedly with her rich dark-brown skin. Her regal head-wrap was made of indigo tie-dyed fabric. Her unlined face was softly rounded, her smile warm and self-assured.

Standing proudly behind the *boutique's* counter, Ami showed us the center's wares on the open shelves and in the glass-doored cabinets. There were small plastic dolls with straight blonde hair dressed in frilly, wool, hand-crocheted dresses; handmade, stuffed African animals (giraffes and elephants — not normally found in Mali) made of hand-woven and hand-dyed *bogolan* (mud cloth); tablecloths with matching napkins of *bogolan*; and large *bogolan* wall hangings of African scenes, such as thatched, round huts beneath swaying palm trees.

When I asked Ami about *bogolan*, she answered in confident French: "It is an ancient tradition, specific to this region of Mali, of using natural substances, especially mud from the Niger River, to hand-dye hand-woven cotton textiles. In Bambara, the word *bogo* signifies mud; the word *bogolan* literally means 'the result of putting mud on' the fabric."

Ami may have assumed that I was a tourist and Youssef, who had greeted her in Bambara, was my tour guide, so I explained that we were in fact new residents of *quartier* Pelangana; we were her neighbors. I told her we had recently arrived in Mali from Lastoursville, Gabon, where Youssef and I had met, and where I had spent two years teaching nutrition, cooking and crafts as a Peace Corps volunteer. I'd come to Mali, I explained, to continue doing similarly gratifying work with women, but this time on my own volition; I was no longer a Peace Corps volunteer.

"Voulez-vous," I ventured, "Would you like me to give cooking and crafts classes here at Centre Benkady– on a voluntary basis — from time to time?"

Ami's broad face lit up the dimly lit *boutique*.

"Oui, bien sur! Avec plaisir," she said. *"Immediatement!"*

- - - - - - - - - - - -

In the weeks that followed this first meeting, I threw myself into planning classes for Centre Benkady and making samples of things I might teach the women how to make. I made sure to consult with Ami as to what she felt the women would most like to learn. She, a master seamstress with a tailor shop of her own adjoining her home in Pelangana not far from the women's center, taught dressmaking. This was her territory, her area of expertise, where I would not and could not encroach or compete. But I could, I offered, propose small, hand-sewn items that might appeal more to tourists than kitschy plastic dolls in frou-frou crocheted dresses. More tourist sales would bring "good success" to the center, I pointed out. Ami, clearly a born businesswoman, needed no further convincing.

Ami and I decided, since I did not yet speak Mali's native language, Bambara, and most of the dressmaking students at Centre Benkady were young, unschooled local girls who spoke little or no French, Mali's official language, that I would teach my lessons in French to the center's core group of sewing instructors. These were women mostly in their forties who had had some schooling and spoke and read French as imperfectly as I. These instructors would then in turn teach the younger women in Bambara the crafts I'd taught them in French. My classes then, held once a week on Friday afternoons, either in the center's treadle-sewing-machine-filled classroom or at my home a mile away, became teacher-training sessions.

My main criteria for choosing the crafts Ami and I decided I would teach were that they should be simple for beginner students to make and that they should be made of affordable — or, better yet, free — materials. They should also be useful, practical, durable, portable and unbreakable (in tourists' luggage). They should be charmingly African and appealing to "rich" foreigners passing through, who were, in fact, the only people who could afford to buy such items. Malians didn't need and wouldn't buy souvenirs; they spent what little money they had on the basics — food, shelter, and clothing — for survival.

Malians didn't need, for example, decorative cloths for their dinner tables and matching cloth napkins for their laps; they ate their meals with their fingers from round, communal platters, sitting in small groups outside on the ground under a shady tree in their courtyards.

As I wrote to my sister in Denver, "I couldn't be happier. I've started to teach once a week at a local women's center, where I feel appreciated and valuable. The women are terrific — so strong, intelligent, and enthusiastic." I continued:

> My first class on Friday was on weaving. ... I've been experimenting here at my house, making doormats and floor mats from all sorts of things — scraps of fabric, plastic bags, rope, nylon cord, and so on — plus potholders, and, soon, placemats. I had a local carpenter make me three different size frames (potholder size, placemat size, and doormat size), and I used the smallest one to teach the teachers the basic How-To's of it. They <u>loved</u> it. The beauty of this project is that the frames cost next to nothing, and Ségou, being the fabric capital of Mali, doesn't lack for material, especially scraps thrown away by local tailors.

- - - - - - - - - - - - -

For my second class, I brought an item I'd created in my workshop/ study at home and felt particularly proud of: a mineral-water-bottle holder made from two thick layers of traditional Malian hand-woven- and-dyed fabric with foam padding in between the layers to keep the mineral water relatively cool in Mali's blistering heat. A sturdy, wide strap wrapped around the length of the bottle-size sack would allow tourists — who were the only ones who bought bottled water, out of justifiable fear of the possible water-borne diseases found in the local well water that Malians were used to drinking — to carry the bottle holder on their shoulders. The women at Centre Benkady were ecstatic to begin this project.

My third lesson, held on a Friday in mid-May at my house because Centre Benkady had no kitchen, was on *"Confiture de Mangue"* (mango jam).

I'd asked the core group of five teachers at the center to arrive at 4 o'clock and each bring a small empty jar and a small bag of mangoes, which are inexpensive and abundant in Mali. I agreed to supply the rest: lemons, sugar, photocopies of the recipe, labels for the jars, kitchen equipment, and gas stove. To my surprise, about a dozen women, all beautifully dressed in flowing *boubous* and matching turbans, drove up to my house at four-ish on their motorbikes, carrying enormous bowls and buckets filled with fat, perfectly ripe mangoes.

With an overabundance of fruit and more eager students than I'd bargained for, yet only two stovetop burners and two decent-size pots in my kitchen, we had to make do. Using one pot filled with boiling water to sterilize some jars and the other for cooking the peeled-pitted-and-cut-up mangoes, I gave the women a basic lesson. Then, with a view to their one day selling this jam in their *boutique,* I showed them how to label and decorate the filled jars with a round of colorful African fabric and a bowtie of colored yarn.

This was the day that Ami planted the seed for my teaching patchwork quilting.

- - - - - - - - - - - -

The next morning at the center, using big pots set over wood fires outdoors, the women made mango jam from the remaining bowls of fruit they'd cut up while at my house. They filled their jars so that each one of them had a jar of jam to take home. There was no need to label and decorate the jars, the women told me later, because their large families ate all of the jam soon after it reached home.

By late May, the women had at least eight water bottle holders (which they called *"porte d'eau")* for sale in their *boutique,* each slightly different, each one wonderful, I thought. Plus, they had a woven floor mat in the making, still on the frame, which I saw as a work of art. I was thrilled to see the results of their follow-through, their initiative, energy, and creativity. The president of Benkady, Ramata N'Djaye, said she didn't know how to thank me enough for helping them. I, in turn, told her I didn't know how to express the joy that working with the women there brought me. I felt joyously free — free to do exactly what I wanted to do, and what I wanted to do was to share my creative crafts ideas with interested African women.

In subsequent weeks, with the aid of my friend and neighbor Abdoulaye Mariko, the *pepinieriste*, I gave a lesson at Benkady on potting flowering plants, to help decorate the exterior of the center. I showed the women how to make teddy bears out of *bogolan*, from a Simplicity pattern my sister Heather sent, to add to the African animal toys they sold in their *boutique*. I invited my new friend Vivica, a local Peace Corps small-enterprise volunteer, to give a talk to the women in Bambara on marketing their products. I gave a lesson on how to make puppet heads out of papier-mâché and how to crochet with recycled plastic bags. I gave more cooking lessons out of my home for simple items, such as yeast bread, vegetable soup, and pasta with tomato sauce.

In between, when I made informal visits to the center, I learned new things from the women there. In mid-July, for example, I learned how to make *bogolan* mud cloth:

- First, take dried leaves and crush them in a *mortier*; then put the crushed leaves in a large basin with four liters of water. Add your fabric (raw, hand-woven cotton) to the water and leave it there until it takes on a rusty color. Wring the water out, lay the fabric flat (right side up) to dry in the sun, and repeat this process (returning the fabric to the dye bath) two more times to fix the background color.
- Then, take the special, black, *bogolan* mud, which is scooped from the Niger River bed, and use it like paint to make designs on the right side of the dyed fabric. Let these mud designs dry completely in the sun. Wash the fabric, and *voilà, bogolan!*

The women at Benkady made their traditional, geometric, "secret" *bogolan* designs using stencils cut with razor blades from thin, pliable plastic that looked like discarded X-rays. For paintbrushes they used old toothbrushes. We sat outside on the ground, outstretched legs anchoring the fabric we were painting, talking and laughing like little girls playing with mud pies.

For my first effort I made a big banner: I drew a large tree with the thick, black mud and hand-lettered the words *"Aimez la Terre: Plantez des Arbres!"* (Love the Earth: Plant Some Trees) beneath it. The next day, Ami Sylla proudly showed me an exact replica of my banner that she had subsequently made. *"Tu es une machine de photocopie,"* I teased her. She beamed.

At night at home in my study, I experimented with new sewing projects, like an obsessed scientist driven to find some cure. In my case, I wanted to create items for the Benkady women to make that would sell in their gift shop and earn them some much-needed income. I wanted to do what I could to help "cure" their economic poverty. These ideas — for artisinal projects to share with the women — seemed to come to me out of the blue, as though someone was guiding my hands, as though I were a puppet on strings.

In late July, Centre Benkady held a *cérémonie de remise de certificats* (graduation ceremony), to which I was invited and treated like an honored guest, or even a sister. The event was filmed and televised later that evening on Mali's one nightly news program. I saw myself on their national news. The following week the Benkady women held a party at the center for the recent graduates. Once again, I was treated like a VIP, included in the women's traditional dancing, and fussed over.

I felt as though I were in my element: an artisan among artisans, a mature woman among other mature women who still needed to dance to life's drumbeat. "If there's any hope at all for this poor, poor continent," I wrote in my journal, "it's in *the women*. I love working with them, feeling one with them, in our individual and collective struggles to make something worthwhile."

- - - - - - - - - - - - -

My new Malian women friends at Centre Benkady told me in all sincerity that they believed I was African in a former life. When I tried to press them to elaborate, all they would say to me was, "You have an African soul." This compliment made me feel close to them, as though we truly were sisters under the skin. But knowing the history of my country as I did, I also felt far removed.

In Mali, griots, storytellers, still sing the people's history at nearly every social gathering. But in the United States, history is found, by those who still seek it and read it, primarily in the written word. Unfortunately, Mali and its history have been as unknown to most Americans as has Timbuktu, Mali's most fabled, ancient city. Also, because Mali was a colony of France from 1898 until 1960 and its official national language remains French, there has been a language barrier impeding Americans' knowledge and understanding of this significant West African country. Countless African-Americans, however, perhaps without realizing it, have deep ancestral ties to this region, ties that were also once inextricably bound to cotton.

From the mid-seventeenth to the late-eighteenth century, in order to satisfy the labor needs of the growing economies in the New World, the practice of slavery grew. A prime area for obtaining slaves was on Africa's west coast. Slavers knew that the peoples of West Africa were noted for their skills. The Africans of Ghana, for example, were well known for smelting iron ore. The people of southern Mali were famous for their cultivation of cotton.

After Eli Whitney's invention of the cotton gin (patented in 1794), designed to mechanically remove the sticky green seeds from the short-staple, "upland" cotton that grew well in the interior regions of the American South, the yield of raw cotton doubled each decade after 1800. Although the cotton gin did reduce the labor involved in removing seeds, it did not reduce the need for slaves to grow and pick the cotton. In fact, the opposite occurred. Cotton growing became so profitable for the planters that their demand for both land and slave labor greatly increased. In 1790 there were six slaves states; in 1860 there were 15.

By mid-nineteenth century, at the height of the plantation system in the South, when cotton had become the country's dominant cash crop, 1.8 million of the 2.5 million slaves in the United States were involved in the production of cotton.

As David Brion Davis points out in *Inhuman Bondage*, his excellent study of slavery in the New World:

> A nation conceived in liberty and dedicated to the proposition "that all men are created equal" happened also to be

the nation, by the mid-nineteenth century, with the largest number of slaves in the Western Hemisphere — a nation whose most valuable exports, particularly cotton, were produced by slaves.

Throughout the antebellum period, Davis points out, "cotton accounted for over half the value of all American exports, and thus it paid for the major share of the nation's imports and investment capital. A stimulant to Northern industry, cotton also contributed to the growth of New York City as a distributing and exporting center. ..." Cotton was America's "number-one commodity."

In 1858, three years before the start of the Civil War, South Carolina Senator James Henry Hammond protested: "What would happen if no cotton was furnished for three years? England would topple headlong and carry the whole civilized world with her. No, you dare not make war on cotton! No power on earth dares make war upon it. Cotton is King."

That "king" of the American South was deposed forever when the last of the slave laborers who made his reign possible was finally freed on June 19 (later referred to as "Juneteenth"), 1865. Today, to keep this commodity alive and to give it a competitive edge on the world market, the U. S. Government underwrites much of the costs of America's cotton farmers with checks that can total billions of dollars a year.

In Mali, however, cotton remains king. It is called *Mali nafolo* in Bambara, *l'or blanc* in French, or in English "white gold." Mali is the second largest producer of cotton in Africa, after Egypt. For Mali, cotton is generally the number one export product, with actual gold a close second.

Malian cotton, which grows along the banks of the Niger River between Bamako and Mopti and farther south to the borders of neighboring countries, is of the highest quality, with superb long staple lint (fibers over two inches in length) and black, fuzz-free seeds. In Mali cotton is still picked by hand rather than machine, so each individual cotton boll, or seedpod, can be harvested at the optimal time, as pickers make successive passes over the field. Mali's climate and soil are said to present "near-perfect agronomic conditions" for growing cotton. Early summer rainfall helps establish the cotton plants in the soil, and the grilling sun does the rest.

Just as cotton — and the African slaves who planted, tended and harvested it — helped develop the economy of nineteenth century America, cotton today in Mali, which is ranked among the world's ten poorest nations, is considered "the motor" of economic development. Sadly, however, the billions of dollars in federal subsidies paid to American cotton growers put Malian cotton growers at an economic disadvantage in international markets.

- - - - - - - - - - - - -

If my Malian women friends at Centre Benkady were right and by some unknowable chance I had been an African seamstress-slave from Mali in a past life, then my working with African women in this life, in a sewing center in Ségou, the textile capital of Mali, was like a homecoming for me.

When I mentioned the story of slavery in the American South, my friends at Centre Benkady appeared unaware of this history. This aspect of their past — the fact that so many African ancestors had been torn from their motherland and sold into slavery on cotton plantations so far away — seemed to be hidden from them. Their griots, it seemed, never sang of it. Their formal educations were scant; they obviously hadn't learned about this dark past during their brief years in elementary school. They looked at me incredulously, as if asking, "How could such a thing be?"

They were, of course, aware of France's exploitation of their country when Mali was a French colony. But America too? They seemed unable, or unwilling, to believe it. It was easier for them to believe that I was African in a previous life than it was to believe my country, *les états-unis*, the great United States of America, could once have been so evil.

I searched the "African" part of my soul, allowing my imagination full rein, to give my purported former-African self a name, a face, and a voice. I tried to imagine her into being, rescue her from oblivion, and reclaim her life, at least in words on paper.

A South Carolina Plantation, late 1822

*The griots of her village, Jeneba remembered from her childhood, told sto-
ries in song. The griots' stories were true stories, stories of Mali's glorious past
and greatest people, such as Sundiata, a brave Mandinka prince, later
known as the Lion King, who founded the Kingdom of Mali, created a
central government, and established peace and prosperity throughout this
vast west-African region. That was at a time when Europeans were still
living through the dark night of their Dark Ages and their rulers were
barbarians.*

    *The village children sat on the hardened earth and listened obediently
to the griots, the keepers of history and memories, as they sang and danced
their stories in the firelight under the star-filled sky. This was the children's
schooling, their bedtime stories.*

    *Jeneba's village was beside the Niger River, which fed the earth so the
people could plant their crops knowing they would thrive despite the fierce
sun and fickle rains. The children used hollowed calabashes to scoop water
from the river and carry it to their family's fields to give them drink. The
river was generous; the carefully cultivated fields were bounteous.*

    *The villagers grew many good things, such as okra, rice, beans, and
pumpkins, so that their large families would eat well; and they grew cotton,
as they had for centuries, so they would have homespun clothing to wear.*

    *Jeneba learned early how to cultivate cotton: the right time to plant it,
how to tend it, and exactly when the bolls were ripe and the cotton tufts
ready to be plucked from their sharp protective shells. She helped her mother
clean the soft cotton fiber of its hard, black seeds. She watched her mother
comb the cloudlike mounds and spin it all by hand onto sticks to await
weaving. As her mother worked, she entertained her children by telling stories about a cruel king who tried to force his subjects to spin cotton into gold.*

    *Jeneba's father was a weaver who made his own loom from long,
smoothed tree branches tied together with cord. He, like the other weavers
in the region, sat on a rock inside this wooden structure — as though his
body were its engine — passing the shuttle back and forth from one waiting
hand to the other, pulling with his feet the strings that shifted the loom's
shed. From the freshly spun cotton, he wove long, narrow strips of fabric
which was then sewn together to make cloth. Jeneba's mother then painted*

the cloth with black mud from the Niger River, following ancient, mean-ingful designs.

- - - - - - - - - - - -

But Jeneba is here now — an ocean away from her village. The cotton fields where she now works by day are owned by a man who says he owns her. There are no griots here, no songs of her history. When she was only about ten, she and her two older brothers were snatched from their parents, their village, their ancestry, their motherland, as they were drawing water from the banks of the Niger. They were tied and gagged and forced into the hold of a stranger's boat bound for the sea, then sold, separately, into slavery. Jeneba doesn't know where her brothers are; she hasn't seen them since then. By now, they are men.

Her memory of the long, dark voyage has gone blank, as has the place in her heart where joy once lived. Every day, with a leaden heart, she asks herself: Will I ever see my mother's face again? Will my son ever hear her stories?

With many others, more than she can count, she picks cotton all day. Many of the field workers are from the former Kingdom of Mali, where the people have grown cotton since Sundiata's time. These Africans remember the griots' songs of praise for their Lion King who was the first to introduce cotton cultivation and weaving to his mighty kingdom. This was at a time when only European royalty could afford to wear garments fashioned from this white gold.

These Africans know cotton the way they know their families, their ancestors, their histories; the way they know the sun and the moon and the stars. They are experts in every aspect of cotton's cultivation — from preparing the soil for planting, to celebrating the cloth its threads create. Their culture is entwined with cotton, like spun fibers.

Yet here in this new world, the African field workers are treated like ignorant draft animals — less than dogs. If the cotton pickers take too long on the rows, for example, wondering, "Is this boll ready to pick? Is this the right moment?" the owner, sitting high on his favorite stallion like some kind of king, snaps his sharp whip on someone's shoulders and sends his beloved dogs to bark and growl and bare their long teeth, forcing the work-

ers to move faster along the row. To the owner, this white cotton is yellow gold, and the pickers are merely his diggers.

In the evening, by pine light, Jeneba sits at her table and sews. She sews pieces of cloth together, as though sewing her life back together. Her owner's wife taught her how to make things for their family — shirts and trousers for her husband, dresses for her two daughters and herself, quilts for their big beds in their big, cold, stone house. She tells Jeneba that she is a talented seamstress, that Jeneba has "a gift" with a needle and thread. But Jeneba says nothing in response. She doesn't tell the owner's wife that this "gift" springs from her blood. She doesn't tell the woman her history, her story.

Jeneba knows the owner's wife, a frail and pale woman with a whispering voice, tries to be kind. (She never turns to peer into the cradle to look at Jeneba's son.) She allows Jeneba to keep the remnants of her fine, imported fabric for herself. Jeneba likes to see the way these colorful scraps become something new and useful, sometimes even beautiful. Their beauty for her lies in their silent messages, like the ancient, secret, celebratory symbols her mother painted on the mud cloth. With these jagged patches of multicolored fabric, Jeneba makes seditious quilts that shout wordless stories, like traitorous griots with severed tongues.

At night Jeneba sleeps beneath her quilts and dreams she is free. She dreams she is back in Mali, drawing water from the Niger in a calabash she carries on her head like a crown. During the day, she hangs her quilts out to air, to allow the others in the quarters to hear her silent griots sing.

From time to time, when the moon is high and the owner's wife and daughters are sleeping soundly in their big, stone house and he has had too much to drink, he staggers to Jeneba's cabin and wakes her. Fumbling and cursing, he tears her quilts away, unbuttons the front of his trousers, and forces himself into her, pinning her shoulders down with his rough hands. He leaves his work clothes on — the trousers and shirt Jeneba herself has sewn by hand, sometimes from fabric woven from the cotton she herself has helped to pick — as if this clothing will protect him, like thick armor, from his own Christian guilt and shame, as if the part of him that he pushes inside her is not him at all but a separate being he cannot control the way he controls all others.

What hurts her most is having to breathe his odor, the acrid odor of his sweat mixed with whiskey. She is choked by it, as though choked by sobs. But she never allows herself to cry when he is here. Instead, she tries to hold her breath. But she finds she cannot do so for long. When he lifts his body off of her, she gasps for air. She knows she must keep breathing, go on living — if only for the sake of her son.

In his drunkenness — an abomination to Allah — he calls her Jemima, as though he himself was not the one who wrote her true name in his record book when he bought her. He calls the pale-brown baby sleeping in the nearby cradle, whom Jeneba straps to her back when she works with the others in the fields, Beau. He told her — and this is a secret she must keep or he will take his whip to her — that he listed this child in his record book as "James Beaufort Wilson," after himself, because this child is his only son. His wife has become barren, he says. He claims she is a meek and sickly woman who never looks in his record books and never asks him questions. He tells Jeneba he plans to treat their son well — send him North to college, leave him an inheritance when he dies. He is rich, he says; he has land, cotton, slaves. He is rich in "black gold."

He calls himself a Christian and says he intends to convert all of his "heathen" slaves to his superior ways. But the black-suited minister he sends to convert these slaves preaches loudly of a meek Jesus, King of the Jews, who rode on a lowly donkey and never carried a whip. So what is a Christian, the "heathen" ask among themselves?

This man, her master, Mr. Wilson, tells Jeneba she is lucky to be the "beauty" he has chosen for his "secret" midnight visits. She is lucky to be here on his plantation, he says, rather than back "in darkest Africa." She says nothing. She looks away, thinking: He doesn't know what he is saying. He lives in darkest unknowing. He has never been to my village. He has never watched the handcrafted boats with cowhide sails float like low-lying clouds along the wide, glass-smooth surface of the Niger at sunset. He has never heard a griot singing.

There is no returning. There is no escaping. Those who try are caught and whipped or even hanged. Jeneba heard whispered that an African man named Denmark Vesey, who had bought his own freedom but remained filled with rage over slavery, tried to organize a slave rebellion in Charleston just this year. His plot, involving thousands of slaves, failed. He was betrayed by one faithful house slave. Vesey was hanged last June, and more than thirty of his followers quickly followed him to the gallows.

Jeneba knows she cannot risk being hanged. No, she must live, if only for the sake of her son.

Her owner's smell lingers long after he has gone. She pulls her quilts back over herself, shivering. Then in the morning she airs her quilts out outside her window to let the silent griots weep.

- - - - - - - - - - - - -

"The Patchwork Project is a good project of development.
It is a project that can succeed here because
Malian textiles are very rich.
It will also permit women to have money,
which will make them economically independent."

— FATOU SOGOBA, Patchwork Project graduate
(translated from the French)

Puppets and Primers

ANOTHER REASON I'D BEEN DRAWN TO SÉGOU had to do with puppets. While I was still in Gabon, wondering where in the world to go next, my friend Marty sent me a photo she'd taken in her travels to Mali. The photo showed a Malian shopkeeper wearing a blue-and-white skull cap and a purple, flowing *boubou*, and holding up a carved, wooden puppet that he had for sale. In Mali, Marty informed me, the people use puppets (*marionnettes*) in their storytelling traditions, unlike most other African countries where mostly masks are employed. On the back of this photo Marty wrote: "Marionette from Ségou. I think you'd love this town."

Puppets? I'd been in love with puppets all my life, ever since I'd been entranced by the fifties kids show "Kukla, Fran, and Ollie" on TV. I loved my first puppet, a Peter Pan marionette, because it was I who could make him fly. I especially loved the five hand puppets I'd created in Gabon for giving health presentations, in skits and songs, for the elementary school children of Lastoursville.

"Chantal Chanson" (*chanson* means song in French) was the star of my handmade hand puppet theatre troupe in Gabon. There was something about her that the children adored. Was it her purple yarn bob that swooshed when she sang? Her chipmunky face and wide eyes turned eternally heavenward? Her sweet bow mouth, always open to a song? Her clapping green-felt hands and indefatigable energy? Her lilting singing voice, so different from my own?

Among the little ones of Lastoursville, Chantal was something of a rock star, and her signature song, *"Lavez les Mains,"* shot to the top of their charts. Sometimes little children would stop to serenade me with this song when they saw me walking in town.

"Pour avoir la bonne santé" (to have good health), Chantal belted out, head bobbing, purple hair flying, green hands clapping manically, *"lavez les mains a l'eau et au savon!"* (wash your hands with water and soap). To avoid intestinal worms, her hit tune continued, wash your hands with water and soap. After using the toilet, she rhapsodized, wash your hands with water and soap. Before preparing a meal, she crooned, and the children jumped in to complete the refrain, *"lavez les mains a l'eau et au savon!!!"*

The little children in her audience had obviously never seen anything quite like Chantal before. To them, it seemed, (and not just to me) she was alive. Their wide eyes were so focused on her performance that they didn't notice me at all. It was Chantal's voice they heard, not mine. She was the one with charm and charisma, not me.

Little girls in frilly dresses watched her, awestruck, their hands over their mouths. Little boys in faded T-shirts and shorts, who were usually on the wild side, were well behaved, enthralled by the show. Within minutes, everyone knew all of the words, and they were singing and clapping along with sunny Chantal.

Then, after Chantal took a few bows to the kids' applause, I brought out two more puppets who put on a Punch-and-Judy-style performance. There was "Yvonne Savon" (*savon* means soap), whose head was carved from a big block of blue soap and her dress made from a hand towel, and her archenemy, "Mick Robe" (the French pronunciation of *microbe*, or "germ") who was decidedly ugly. Mick's papier-mâché face was birdlike, beaky, green, and mean, with a down-turned mouth and slitty eyes. His green yarn hair was braided in rastas that stuck out all over his head. I'd made his robe from a brown and beige African print that looked vaguely like microbes seen under a microscope. He was the puppet the kids loved to hate.

Mick opened his act with an earnest, Pavarotti-style rendition of his theme song, *"Si tu aimes les maladies…"* which, translated, was: "If you love being sick, you love me — Mick Robe! If you love diarrhea, you love me — Mick Robe! If you love filth, you love me — Mick Robe! If you love being sick, then I, Mick Robe, will be happy to make you sick!…" At first, the children were aghast, but, as they got the joke, their smiles grew. Yvonne Savon then appeared on the scene and saved the day, overpowering Mick with the magic of her soapsuds.

My puppet shows closed with "Renee Repas" (*repas* means meal), a big-mamma of a puppet with a yellow plastic plate on her head (filled with handmade fruit and vegetables), who gave a Julia Child-like lecture on the importance of eating well every day to keep from falling ill. Renee explained dramatically each of the three food groups depicted on a poster pie chart: "This group, called Protection," she warbled, "with all the nice fruits and vegetables in it, provides vitamins and minerals which protect us against illness. This Energy group — which includes such foods as rice, and bread, and manioc — gives us strength to run and jump and work and play. And this one, Construction, includes foods that offer body-building protein, like peanuts, dried beans, eggs, meat, and fish."

In Gabon when I asked Youssef about puppets' use in Mali, he remembered that every year in a village called Markala not far from

Ségou the Bambara people hold an enormous *Fêtes des Marionnettes*, which has become world-famous. The puppets they make for this celebration are larger-than-life-size, he said, representing both mythic animals and symbolic people, who, through accompanying drums, dancing, and singing, tell stories of the people's origins and their relationship to the animals and the earth.

"Have you ever been?" I asked him.

"Pas encore" (not yet), he said, adding, "but we must go when we get to Mali."

That clinched it. Malians love puppets, and I love puppets. *That's where I belong,* I said to myself. I could feel a strong pull, as though I myself were a puppet on strings.

- - - - - - - - - - - - -

According to a legend that circulates in the region of Ségou, which is the center of puppetry in Mali, the use of puppets originated with a Bozo fisherman by the name of Toboji Canta, who one day was abducted by some genies of the forest. While in their captivity, the genies taught Canta the art of puppetry. Upon returning to his native village, Gamitogo, Canta commissioned local craftsmen to make two kinds of puppets: *Sogow*, animals, and *Manin*, little men. The people of Ségou have employed such puppetry in their festivals ever since.

Mali's use of puppetry actually dates back many hundreds of years. Ibraim Battuta, an Arab visitor to the court of Mansa Souleymane, then king of the Mali Empire, which at that time encompassed most of what we know today as West Africa, is believed to be the first to document, in 1355, Malians' art of using masks and marionettes in their performances. To this day, intricately handmade puppets of all shapes and sizes draw locals as well as some adventuresome tourists to annual festivals in the Ségou region. There is the new *"Festival sur le Niger,"* held on the banks of the Niger River in Ségou at the beginning of every year, promising a long weekend filled with "tales and legends, music and dance, masks and puppets." And there is the world-renowned *"Masques et Marionnettes"* Festival held in Markala, about 35 km outside of Ségou, every year just prior to the rainy season — late May or early June.

Elisabeth den Otter, a Dutch anthropologist who specializes in musical cultures of the non-western world, is one of the few Westerners who has done in-depth studies of the puppetry of Mali. Her stated aim was to "study and document the traditional masquerades of the Bamanan [also known as Bambara] in the area of Ségou: the history, function and meaning of the puppets/masks, as well as the accompanying music, songs and dances, from an anthropological perspective." In so doing, she says, "some of the mystery of Malian puppetry was revealed to me."

Describing the festival at Markala, den Otter says:

> … large puppets in the shape of mythical animals (*sogow*) are made to dance by puppeteers that are hidden inside. Some of the animals carry small rod-puppets on their back (*manin*, literally "little people"), which "dance" as well. They alternate with masked dancers, equally representing mythical animals and symbolic persons. These hidden dancers express the character represented by the puppet or mask, through their movements. There are visible dancers as well: the guide who accompanies a *sogo* or a mask, and dancing with it, often in unison, and the members of the youth association, who perform circle dances and have jumping contests. Moreover, individuals from the public may dance with a puppet or mask to show his or her respect or admiration.

This "total theater" — enveloping music, song, dance, drumming, costumes, masks, and puppets, traditionally created and organized by the youth associations of Mali — is designed to express the values of Malian society and transmit them to the next generation. Through amusing skits, evocations of history, and reenactments of everyday life, the festival participants play an important cultural role. This theater, says den Otter, "is a way of continuing tradition, and an important means of cultural identity.

"Puppets and masks may be seen as two sides of one coin," she says. "Manipulated by man, they are located in the magic field between illusion and reality, connecting the invisible world of the supernatural and the visible world of the human." Within the framework of the masquerade, the people of Markala celebrate their origins and their relation to the animals of the land and the water.

- - - - - - - - - - - - -

In late May 1999, Youssef and I traveled to Markala by taxi-bus to attend at least one day of this three-day festival. We left our house in Pelangana a little before noon and arrived in Markala at 2:00, having been delayed by the taxi-bus driver who'd refused to set off from Ségou until his vehicle was filled to overflowing with passengers. Once in Markala, we found a shady spot by a sheepherder's hut near the river to have our picnic lunch, then we walked back along a dusty road to the festival grounds in the town square just before the show began.

The crowd had already gathered, filling the bleacher seats six rows deep, around the perimeter of the plaza. Mine was among only a dozen or so white faces in a gathering of many hundreds of Malians — men, women, and children of all ages. Some smart ones had found seats in the shade of a few tall neem trees; but most of us, including Youssef and me, felt lucky to have found seats at all, despite their being in the scorching sun.

What followed remains a multicolored blur set to Malian music in my memory, aided by only a few still photographs: a hushed, respectful audience; the tense sense of anticipation in the air; drumming that made the dusty earth tremble; call-and-response singing that required no translation; dancers wearing feathered headdresses, costumes made of cowry shells, and various footwear — plastic sandals, espadrilles, high-top basketball sneakers — dancing in a tightening spiral; ingeniously made puppets, twice-life-size, dancing, twirling, bowing, acting out; a wooden puppet-person riding an immense horse-puppet with two strong men hidden inside it; a bird puppet even larger and more comical than Sesame Street's Big Bird.

Each puppet, Youssef explained to me as the spectacle unfolded, has a specific name and symbolizes something larger than itself. The big bird, *"Mali Kono, le grand oiseau du Mali,"* symbolizes Malian independence from colonial rule, he said. *"Bamba le Crocodile"* symbolizes fair-mindedness. *"Sogo Djan la Girafe"* symbolizes tolerance. *"Banikono la Cigogne"* (Stork) symbolizes generosity.

In one skit we saw, there were two toweringly tall female Peule puppets, both with long wooden faces, large gold hoop earrings, darkened mouths, bared breasts, and matching pink-and-white flowing gowns, fighting over one poor man. *"La femme Peule,"* Youssef told me, *"est toujours la femme fatale."*

The angry white puppet, *Tubabu Kun*, dressed in a French colonial uniform, needed no explanation; he represented the oppressor, the exploiter.

Unfortunately, Youssef and I were not able to stay for the night performances because there was no food or overnight accommodation left in Markala, and there would be no available safe transportation back to Ségou later that night.

The night puppets, I had read in *Marionnettes du Mali,* are different from the daytime puppets in that they are generally smaller, humanlike figures, with broken mirrors for eyes — to reflect the outdoor firelight, create a mysterious atmosphere, and mesmerize the audience. In addition to singing and dancing, they talk a lot. Their primary job is to teach people, especially young people, life's hard truths.

I was disappointed to miss the night puppets, but Youssef assured me we could come back again "next year." I looked at his face for deeper meanings, but he had looked away. Our love had been steadily fraying. He spoke often of leaving Ségou on his own to find his fortune elsewhere. "Okay," I said in an effort to be agreeable, gathering up our things.

- - - - - - - - - - - -

It was this Markala trip that inspired me to also teach puppet making in my Benkady classes. The five hand puppets I'd created for my children's health and hygiene lessons in Gabon were small fries compared to the puppet I made for Benkady after seeing the outsized puppets perform in Markala. This new puppet, whom I named *Jelimuso Jeneba* (or Jenny the Storyteller), was life-size — and to me, almost alive.

I formed her papier-mâché head over a large, inflated balloon supported by a cardboard tube anchored into a chicken-wire frame that shaped her shoulders, upper back, and chest. I made long, life-size arms of stuffed cotton, complete with elbows, wrists, and fingers — all encased in dark nylon stockings. I made a puffy-sleeved dress for her out of ample, brightly colored African fabric, the kind that my Benkady women friends liked to wear. I made her head wrap out of tie-dyed fabric, knotted at one side so the ends resembled a butterfly. I gave her large, round, plastic earrings, and painted a face with wide eyes and an open smile. This Jeneba would tell only happy stories.

Her first performance, in late June, from the steps of my front porch for an audience of five Benkady teachers sitting in chairs in my courtyard, appeared to be a success. With the help of Marie, one of the women there who was attempting to teach me Bambara, I used the big puppet to tell a short and happy story in their language, which I'd spent weeks rehearsing. The women in the audience clapped and giggled among themselves. Was this Jeneba really funny, or was it my hopeless mispronunciations of their tricky, tonal language? I never found out because my Benkady friends were too kind and polite to discourage my efforts. Instead, they told me that they planned to follow my lead and make similar papier-mâché puppets to sell to *"les jardins d'enfants"* (kindergartens) in town for them to use to instruct and enthrall the little children.

- - - - - - - - - - - - -

EVERY WEDNESDAY AFTERNOON little girls from my *quartier* would come to my home to crochet. As Aminata and her friend Bintou and I had agreed, we called it "Club Crochet," and it was only for girls. Those who chose to join in — as many as thirty Malian girls between the ages of eight and twelve — were happy and proud to belong. I gave each of them her first crochet hook and taught them all the basics. Our "yarn" was free and plentiful, since it consisted of recycled plastic bags.

Although Mali is economically poor — one of the poorest countries in the world, in fact — Malians themselves, I was quickly learning, are exceedingly rich in such intangibles as creativity, dignity, and determination. These little girls were no exception. Although none of them owned a watch and only a few knew how to tell time, they arrived at my house punctually at four, wearing their best, pressed, prettiest dresses. They greeted me — as all Malians do, because duly acknowledging other human beings is an integral aspect of their culture — with a handshake and a slight bow. They removed their shoes (flip-flops), a sign of respect when entering anyone's home, at the bottom of my front terrace.

And there, protected from the unremitting African sun, in the 115-degree heat, sitting on straw mats spread out on the cool tile, we would crochet.

Plastic bags, in a rainbow of pastel colors, feather-light and fine as silk, are, as everyone who has traveled there knows, everywhere in Africa. In places where municipal garbage pickup is unheard of and Nature's talent for biodegrading matter has been counted on for countless centuries, carelessly discarded plastic is a problem. It doesn't biodegrade. These pretty plastic bags are so pervasive in Africa that many have taken to calling them "African flowers," as if they were local varieties of roses or bougainvillea. These "African flowers," are tossed by winds and scattered everywhere. They litter streets, get caught in fencing, and choke hungry animals to death as they graze in open fields.

Club Crochet provided a small, informal, and local solution to this problem. Its band of enthusiastic, energetic members collected these ubiquitous bags as if they were indeed bouquets of flowers. We then washed them like laundry, dunking them in buckets set up on my front lawn, and hung them on my clothesline to dry. Then we set to work: folding and cutting each bag, magically transforming it into one continuous ball of "yarn." This process is tricky, but the girls were quick to get the knack. Within no time, they were pros.

They began by crocheting small change purses from the colorful, silky strands. Their hands worked quickly and confidently, never missing a stitch. When the body of the change purse was completed, I gave each girl the closure — a zipper in a matching pastel color that she painstakingly sewed across the top. Some of the older girls became more ambitious, fashioning lovely, multicolor "evening" shoulder bags, which they proudly modeled, strutting across my porch to everyone's delight. One girl surprised us with an elaborate backpack she'd created on her own that must have taken dozens of plastic bags.

What each girl made she sold at the *marché* to earn money for school books and supplies — things few Malian families can afford, particularly for daughters. Instead of taking their hard-earned money home, where it might disappear into the hands of an impish sibling, they preferred to entrust it to me, their "banker." I kept careful records for them, which they enjoyed inspecting regularly: attendance noted with gold star stickers, and columns of numbers beside each name. They knew they could withdraw their money at any time, but most preferred to watch her bank account grow.

Pricing was an issue we tackled democratically (but my vote counted most). When a girl finished her project, she held it up for all to carefully inspect. Quality was paramount: Were the knots sufficiently hidden? Was the zipper securely sewn? *"Cent francs!"* one girl might say, and the rest might agree; but I would shake my head and raise my palms upward. They had yet to learn their own worth and the worth of their work.

I still couldn't speak their language, Bambara, and only a handful of them knew a little French, but we managed to communicate nevertheless. They all knew *"oui,"* and *"voilà!"* and *"très bien!"* and the universal language of smiles, nods and applause.

- - - - - - - - - - - - -

FOR A TREAT I SERVED THEM Kool-Aid and cookies, of which they were careful to take only one until everyone had had one. For entertainment, I played cassette tapes of Malian music, especially their favorite singer, Salif Keita, the albino who rose from rejection by his own family to international fame. Once, just for a change, I played a Pavarotti tape and asked the girls' opinion in another word they all knew: "Okay?" Aminata's pal Bintou wrinkled her brow and told me earnestly, *"Il peut chanter!"* (He can *sing!*)

At the end of our two-hour sessions, if we'd all worked hard and "stuck to our knitting," we put down our crochet hooks, scissors and plastic bags for the last ten minutes and danced. The girls thought it amusing that I, an American *toubob* grandmother, development worker, would have such fun dancing their traditional line dances with them. They would laugh and clap and urge me on with something in Bambara that roughly translated to, "You GO, girl!"

- - - - - - - - - - - - -

THE WALLS OF MY ONE-ROOM, Upper West Side apartment in Manhattan were lined, floor-to-ceiling, with built-in bookshelves filled with well over a thousand books in a broad range of subjects — from history, philosophy, literature and poetry to cooking, crafts, gardening and travel. These books to me were friends and family; surrounded by them this way, I knew I would never feel lonely or at a loss. They were always there, just an arm's reach away, to guide, enlighten, uplift, entertain, comfort, or teach me.

So the fact that I had chosen from among my crafts books *The Quilting Primer* by Dorothy Frager to take with me to Mali was fortuitous, because, once settled in Ségou, I found I needed it to teach myself how to quilt.

"Technically," my new primer said, "a quilt is a bed covering that is made of two layers of fabric with a thin interlining between. This is all held together with rows of stitches passing through the three layers — the face or show-off side, the backing, and the batting. The face or 'top' layer is designed in an artistic manner and shows the originality and personality of its maker. ..."

- - - - - - - - - - - - -

The day that the core group of Benkady teachers had stopped in my living room to study the quilt I'd hung on the wall, and I'd gamely promised Ami Sylla I would try to teach them how to do patchwork quilting, I had no idea how I would go about it.

The truth was I didn't know the first thing about quilting. I had not come from a family of quilters. My father's Scottish mother, who died when I was two, had, I'd been told, knitted practical woolen socks and sweaters as protection against the Northeast winters. My mother's German mother busied her hands, I observed when she visited every Christmas, crocheting lace-like doilies incessantly. And my mother had, as the spirit moved her, made machine-sewn sock dolls and sometimes pretty little matching Easter dresses for my two sisters and me when we were small. But none of these women nor any of the women I knew growing up were quilters.

My first stab at patchwork quilting, then, while I was in the Peace Corps in Gabon, was like playing darts in the dark. I had no idea what I was doing. And, frankly, it didn't matter. Who would see it? Who would judge? Hand-sewing triangular pieces of colorful African fabric into pinwheel designs, then bordering these pinwheels with wildly patterned African fabric strips, became just one of the many projects that occupied my hands and mind while I was living alone in the Central African rainforest so far from anywhere with nothing better to do.

I had no TV — nor sewing machine, washing machine, telephone, computer, or any other kind of modern convenience or appliance — and only a few books at my post in Lastoursville. But I did have scissors, needles, thread, straight pins, and access to all sorts of African-print cotton fabric. Most of all, I had the luxury of time. I had enough free time, in fact, to hand-sew a whole, child's bed-size patchwork quilt as I sat in my study in the evenings listening to the Voice of America on a battery-operated shortwave radio.

Each piece of scrap fabric I used in that quilt added to the story of my two years in Lastoursville. One triangle, for example, with yellow umbrellas on it, represented the ferocious rain there — rain like I'd never experienced before. A red strip of fabric with babies printed on it stood for the maternal-infant clinic where I taught health and nutrition every weekday morning. Another strip, printed with blue fish swimming nose-to-tail, represented my young post mate, Morgan, who was in the Peace Corps fish program.

Without originally intending to do so, I used this quilt to tell the whole story of my Peace Corps experience in wild, kaleidoscopic patterns and colors; and the fact that the end result was far from perfect or pristine became not only part of its charm but also a true reflection of those two years. So I hung this rough-and-tumble, humble quilt, like folk art, on my living room wall in Ségou out of sentimentality, not out of pride of workmanship.

It became, though, as I began to study my *Quilting Primer*, a helpful guide on how NOT to make a quilt: Do not (in the future), I lectured myself, sew bold-patterned pieces side-by-side like this; the result is a muddy-looking mess. Allow for wider borders, a better balance between the design blocks and the outer frame. Use smaller quilting stitches, and make those quilting stitches part of the overall textured design. Do not use an old, frayed bed sheet for the backing; it won't hold up over time. Don't just sew loops at the top for hanging; make a proper "sleeve" on the back instead.

Many times a day, as I passed by this amateurish quilt hanging limply on my living room wall, I was reminded of how much I had to learn before I could begin to teach quilting. So, because the women at Centre Benkady were eagerly waiting for me to give them lessons, I threw myself into a self-taught crash-course. From virtually quilting in the dark with my first patchwork project, I now needed to become an instant expert — or at least come as close as I could.

In Ségou, though, I knew I had some advantages that I hadn't had in Lastoursville: I had a quilting book at my fingertips, a larger variety of better quality fabric in the town market to choose from, plus a sturdy sewing machine. For the equivalent of $50 I'd bought a Chinese-made, old-black-Singer-style electric sewing machine in Ségou, which Youssef fitted with a device that allowed me to hand-crank it, so I could sew even when the town's electricity was cut.

I started small. For my first relatively easy quilting project, I chose to make a patchwork-quilted checkerboard — which could actually be used as such, with found soda-bottle caps for playing pieces and a matching carry bag with drawstring tie — that the Benkady women might consider making to sell in their *boutique* to tourists passing through Ségou.

I cut a perfect two-inch square from a sturdy piece of cardboard and used it to trace with pencil onto designated sections of African-pat-terned remnants I'd cadged from local Malian tailors. I cut 72 squares from these exuberantly colorful swatches, then 72 more from locally made natural muslin, then sewed the squares together with military precision, alternating plain with patterned, forming long strips. I then sewed the strips together, matching the points obsessively. I bordered and backed this checkerboard face with deep red *bazin* (damask) fabric and quilted it by machine along the seam lines ("in the ditch," as my primer called it). The result made me proud.

This quilted checkerboard became the model for my first quilting lesson at Benkady. Through it, I hoped to show my eager students that the quilting process can be applied to all sorts of things, not just bed coverings (*"couvre-lits,"* as they called them) and wall hangings. I wanted them to begin with the simplest geometric design (squares) and proceed from there.

Seeing the women's enthusiasm bolstered my own. From patchwork blocks made from squares, we graduated to triangles, and from triangles to eight-pointed stars. From the checkerboard quilt project, we moved on to a baby blanket. As a group, they made a baby blanket of six star blocks, plus backing and bordering fabric in baby pink. I gave them a piece of batting and showed them how to "sandwich." They were well on their way.

- - - - - - - - - - - -

I SELDOM GAVE MUCH THOUGHT to my distant past, especially while in Mali, which was so far away from it all. But at times, when I was alone in the evenings sewing in my study, that past would creep up on me.

At the bottom of my deep need to keep creating and recreating a reason for being — by being of some service to others — I realized, was the memory of my father's drunken, belligerent words to my siblings and me, "Get off your no-good asses and DO something useful around here! Justify your existence!"

It had never been enough for me to BE; I'd always had to DO — make things that weren't there before: words on blank paper, bread from my oven, now colorful fabric remnants stitched together to make something beautiful and new. In Mali, especially, I found that the joy these creations brought was healing. Wounds, it appears, can be patched. Torn hearts can be sewn.

I began work on a new quilt project in the evenings — a star quilt wall hanging, which I hoped would be 100 percent more handsome than the one I'd made in Gabon. This new quilt would tell the story of my new life in Ségou: I chose adobe-brown fabric to represent Mali's soil and traditional architecture; dark-green fabric for the myriad mango trees' foliage; light-green *bazin*, a gift from Centre Benkady; a burgundy-yellow-and-green floral print to represent my home and garden in Pelangana. I laid these out in a patchwork design of stars, to depict the actual starry sky as well as the Muslim religion, and blocks for the grid-like layout of the town.

I worked on this new wall quilt every night in my study, while listening to French language tapes. The tiny, precise quilting stitches taught me patience, as life in Africa in general teaches patience. I hoped to have this wall quilt finished before the new millennium.

Hand quilting, I soon discovered, is far more than mere sewing: It's a story, a statement, a commitment, a legacy. Making a quilt is actively committing to life, one small, breath-like stitch at a time. *This is what I'm doing*, I said to myself, *I'm committing to the patchwork quilt of my life, and Africa is teaching me how.* My new Ségou wall quilt, then, became an emblem of my passion and purpose.

A South Carolina Plantation, 1833

Mr. Wilson favors Beau above all the other children. He takes the boy on his horse with him as he oversees the daily work on the plantation. Sometimes, from the corner of her eye, as she is bending low along a row of cotton, Jeneba can see the two of them sitting high on the stallion, Wilson's left arm wrapped protectively around the slender brown boy in front of him, while his right arm snaps his whip on the shoulders of slow workers. Jeneba watches the whip crack like lightning in a dark thunderstorm and the struck worker jump and yelp in pain. Then, with a shiver, she hears the boy laugh and cheer, as though this were a game and he were on the winning side.

The other children on the plantation are both jealous and afraid of Beau. They never include him in their made-up games. Jeneba observes her son from a distance: on his own, head down, walking alone, kicking stones out of his way along the dusty road leading from the slaves' quarters.

In the evening in their cabin, Beau tries to chase after his two younger sisters and whip them with a long, thin switch he has fashioned of willow. His sisters, too, are afraid of him. They run to their mother, squealing, for protection. Slowly, Jeneba puts down her quilting, rises up and approaches him.

"Give me that stick," she tells him, reaching out her hand.

"No," he says. "I don't have to listen to you."

"Give me that stick now," she repeats, frozen with fury. She feels the ancestors shudder at his disrespect. She wants to shout, "Who are you?" and "How did you get this way?" But she knows he doesn't know the answers to these questions. He doesn't know what is in his blood. He is not to blame. He is only a child — about the same age Jeneba was when she was taken from her village. He has never known such a village.

Jeneba takes the stick from his hand, and he backs away, fearing, perhaps, she might whip him for the first time. She knows she cannot do this; he would only tell Mr. Wilson, his protector, the man he does not know is his father. He would show this man his welts, and then Jeneba would suffer for it. Wilson would whip her with a real whip for disciplining his only son with a willow stick.

"Go to bed," she tells the boy, as she bends the branch of willow until it snaps in several places. She tosses it into the hearth, where it crackles and smokes because it is green.

Before she tucks her two little girls into their small, shared bed, she tells them a story, one of her mother's stories, about the king who tried to force his subjects to spin cotton into gold.

- - - - - - - - - - - -

Mr. Wilson's wife is very ill now. She seldom leaves their big, stone house; but when she does, Jeneba can see from a distance that she has gone gray and grown bone-thin. She never comes to Jeneba's cabin anymore to bring her the imported fabric she has so carefully chosen for Jeneba to make their clothing and quilts. The last time she did, after Jeneba's first daughter, Amelie, was born, it was clear to Jeneba that Mrs. Wilson could see the baby's strong likeness to her own daughters. Truth, Jeneba saw, stabbed the woman's heart like a long spear. She clutched her chest, drew in her breath, and reeled in place before gathering her genteel Southern composure.

"Why! My word! She truly is a beautiful baby," she said softly, with her right hand still flat against her thin chest. "Why, yes, Jeneba, she looks just like you.

"Here," she added, placing the bolt of fabric on Jeneba's wooden table and turning to leave. "You know what you need to do."

Since then Mrs. Wilson has had someone else bring the fabric to Jeneba — either Annie-Mae, the old cook, or Samuel, her buggy driver, on their way home to their cabins. They hand over the package with this message: "Jeneba, you know what to do."

- - - - - - - - - - - -

Although Jeneba was still young when she was kidnapped from her motherland, she could remember that in Mali a rich man is allowed to take several wives into his compound. The first ones initially resent the newcomers; but in time, these co-wives grow close, almost like sisters, acknowledging and accepting their familial interdependency. This custom is considered best for the children. All of the children know their one father, whose task is to love and provide for his whole family equally. The man's wives watch over and care for all of the children night and day. And there are always many siblings to play and scrap with endlessly, within the safety of the family's compound.

But here in this New World, Jeneba could see, the truth of men's voracious ways is kept hidden, cloaked in lies, deception, and unreasonable laws, until it erupts in heartbreak, betrayal, and rupture. Wives and children suffer. Sometimes that suffering leads to illness and death.

Mrs. Wilson began to look so ill, Jeneba feared she was near death.

- - - - - - - - - - - -

Perhaps this was why Mr. Wilson no longer came to Jeneba's cabin in the night. Perhaps his frail wife had frightened him so many times with her imminent death that he at last promised himself he would change his ways; he would attend only to her. Or perhaps the reason was that Jeneba's children were too grown and aware now for him to keep his dalliances "secret and discreet."

"The boy might wake and see me here," he said to Jeneba the last time he made a midnight visit. "I don't want to corrupt him."

Or perhaps it was, as Jeneba suspected, that she herself, nearing thirty, having borne three children, and weary from almost twenty years of field work, was no longer of interest to him.

There were few secrets in the slave quarters. Truth was like a full moon on a clear and star-filled night for those whose eyes were open. Everyone knew Master Wilson had found another, younger slave with whom to keep the "secrets" of his marital lies and unchristian lusts. Jeneba didn't want to know who she was. She already knew how she felt.

Now, at last, Jeneba thought, I am free of him — at least at night. I no longer need to breathe his acrid odor and feel the unbearable weight of his guilt on top of me. I can sleep the whole night in peace, except for the children's occasional nocturnal sniffling or whimpering. I can dream of Mali and once again hear my village griots singing.

She could work at her table by pine light — all night if she wished to — making seditious quilts.

- - - - - - - - - - - -

In the slaves' quarters it was whispered that many people both in the North and the South were organizing to abolish slavery. They said that an American Anti-Slave Society was formed just this year. When Jeneba heard this, she resolved not to have any part in these efforts. She knew that where she was, in South Carolina, such abolitionists were hunted down like woodland animals, arrested, beaten, and killed in broad daylight in cold blood. No, she would stay put and stay well out of it — for the sake of her children.

- - - - - - - - - - - - -

*"The Patchwork Project is a very interesting work that helps
in development. It is also very demanding and very meticulous. One
must have courage to complete all the steps. With what I have learned,
I will make things for my religious community. I will teach the women
in the villages where we work. We have already talked with
the village women, and they are interested."*

— PHILIPPINE RAZAFIN, Catholic nun, Patchwork Project graduate
(translated from the French)

The Way God Works

I'D LEARNED OF THE UNITED NATIONS-SPONSORED international self-help effort Clean Up the World in late-1996 while vacationing in Zimbabwe during my first year in the Peace Corps in Gabon. One of its main objectives, I read, was "to bring together citizens from every corner of the globe in a simple activity that will positively assist their local environments"; namely, voluntarily cleaning up the place where they lived.

When I returned from Zimbabwe to my Peace Corps post, both inspired and on fire, I promptly planted the seeds to institute a "Clean Up" campaign there in Lastoursville. It took twenty-one months of nudging to accomplish, but at last, on the third Saturday in September 1998, shortly before my Peace Corps service ended, Lastoursville participated in the international Clean Up the World day, thereby adding Gabon to the nonprofit organization's 120-country world map.

That first clean-up day in Lastoursville was like a *fête*. There was singing and dancing in the streets as people spontaneously came forward to fill the large, heavy-duty, bright blue plastic Clean Up the World-donated bags with side-of-the-road trash. A nearby forestry company had donated eight empty oil barrels to use as garbage cans, which we volunteers had hand-painted red and stationed at critical places throughout *centreville*. In a celebratory speech at the end of the day's clean-up effort, the mayor's representative committed to collecting the accumulated trash on a regular basis.

Along with a write-up on the success of Lastoursville's first-ever clean-up day in Clean Up the World's 1998 annual report was a group photograph taken by Youssef of Lastoursville's participants, pointing to and admiring the novel red object labeled *"POUBELLE"* (garbage can) in the center of the picture. Lastoursville had never seen garbage cans before; there had never been in the history of the town anything resembling municipal trash collection. "This," I wrote to Marty that September, "is one of my proudest Peace Corps accomplishments."

The concept, I learned first-hand, was simple yet infectious. It all began with one man in Australia, a yachtsman named Ian Kiernan, who in 1987 was repeatedly shocked by the pollution he encountered as he sailed around the world. Once back in Sydney, Kiernan enlisted the help of friends and held Clean Up Sydney Harbour Day in 1989, in which 40,000 volunteers removed rusted car bodies, plastics of all kinds, glass bottles and cigarette butts from Sydney Harbour.

The following year Kiernan and his committee mobilized close to 300,000 volunteers to participate in the first Clean Up Australia Day. For Kiernan, then, taking this national effort to the rest of the world was only one step away. After gaining support from the United Nations Environment Programme (UNEP), Clean Up the World was launched in 1993.

- - - - - - - - - - - -

Having fallen in love with Clean Up the World's yes-you-can grassroots program in Gabon, I was keen to bring it to Mali. So I wrote to Australia from Ségou for the necessary materials. In late August I received the requested packet, containing a video cassette in French, 30 posters, plus the "How to Do It" kit in both French and English. On a Thursday morning, I met with Adama Oulalaye, director of the nongovernmental environmental organization ALPHALOG to propose the program to him. Clean Up the World, aka *"Pour un Monde Plus Propre,"* Mali '99, was beginning to look as if it would, *inshallah*, become a reality.

I used ALPHALOG as a base of operations for doing my part — visiting the governor, mayor, director of sanitation, and others, to give out Clean Up the World posters to display in strategic places all over town.

The difference between the cooperation I encountered in Ségou, Mali, and Lastoursville, Gabon, was dizzying to me. In fairness, Lastoursville was only a small town hunkered down in the densely rain-forested interior of the country, ten hours by train from the coastal capital, Libreville. Heavily blanketed by equatorial heat and humidity year-round, everything moved painfully slowly there — transportation, communication, as well as cooperation, I found.

Ségou, on the other hand, was relatively sophisticated and savvy. The VIPs I met with in town government seemed eager to aid the Clean Up cause because they could see the benefits — for themselves personally and politically, as well as for the community and the environment in general. Each man I met with was attentive, interested, appreciative and gracious, promising to throw the full weight of his office behind the effort. What had taken nearly two years to push through in Lastoursville took only about six months in Ségou.

My Clean Up colleagues and I decided to launch a poster contest in Ségou's elementary schools for a drawing depicting environmental stewardship that we could use on a T-shirt to be given to participants at the September 18th Clean Up the World event. By the end of August, the semifinalists had been chosen, and the final judging took place on my living room floor. I was one of three judges, and our choice was unanimous: The grand prize went to a young boy's drawing of a sparkling clean village scene with adobe houses, a mosque, palm trees, a blazing sun and a baby blue body of water. Clearly, a cleaned-up world.

(From the Clean Up the World annual report, 1999)

First Year 1999 — Mali

On Saturday morning, 18 September, in the Darsalam quartier of the city of Ségou, the Republic of Mali (West Africa) participated in the Clean Up the World global effort for the first time. Government groups involved included the Director of Health and Sanitation and the Governor/Mayor's office.

A grammar school had been chosen for the site because of the students' enthusiastic response to a poster contest to raise awareness about environmental protection. Armed with brooms and rakes brought from home, 230 students and teachers joined with various community leaders to clean the area, loading debris into waiting donkey carts....

A festive fête included the humorous antics of the troupe de theatre who, via their skits and songs, communicated the importance of each person doing their part to keep Ségou's corner of the world clean.

Three local radio stations interviewed the major participants in the day's events and recorded in full the speeches given by the Director of Health and Sanitation and the Mayor of Ségou during the ceremony.

Throughout the following week, the radio stations repeated the Clean Up the World *("Pour Un Monde Plus Propre")* program, spreading the message far and wide.

In October I made a trip to the U.S. and France to see family and friends and to set the wheels in motion to sell my Upper West Side studio apartment in Manhattan. This tiny apartment had been my home since I was a student at Columbia University twenty years before. When I moved into it in 1978, the monthly rent was $125. When the building went co-op in 1987, I bought it at the insider's price of $22,000, using some of the small inheritance my mother had left me.

Now, after living in Africa for three years, I was faced with the co-op's firm rules: either return to the apartment to live (I had been subletting while serving in the Peace Corps in Gabon and after moving to Mali, and I was nearing the maximum number of sublet years allowed) or sell it. I felt I could not return to the city to live, especially after having lived in spacious homes with lush, sunny gardens in Africa for three years, so I decided to sell my New York studio.

The question then became, though: Where would I, could I, should I go next? Remain in Mali, where I felt happy and fulfilled? Emigrate to France, where I had kind friends and where I could at last perfect my wobbly French-speaking skills? Return to the United States, but to a simpler, sunnier region, where I could begin a new life, from scratch?

This trip became a fact-finding, answer-seeking mission for me.

Within days of my arrival in New York, it was clear to me that I could never live there again. The city made me nervous — too much stimulation, too many options. After having adapted to life in Mali, life in Manhattan felt too-too fast for me, the pace too inhumane. Everyone on the street appeared stressed, pressed. No one seemed to have time to do the simple, pleasurable things I had time for in Ségou, such as relax, visit with friends, sew, or write letters. I felt like a foreigner. An African.

I visited my daughter and celebrated her thirty-fourth birthday with her and her family. Dressed up in a flowing, pale-green Malian *boubou* and matching turban, I gave animated talks on life in Mali at both my grandson's and granddaughter's elementary school classes. All of the children seemed interested. My daughter sat in on both presentations and took photos. One of the teachers sent me a hand-written note afterward, thanking me for telling the children about "life on Maui."

My daughter was understanding and supportive of my need to return to Mali, at least for the time being, to work with the women there. She took me shopping at a local JoAnne's sewing center, where I bought sewing and quilting supplies — rotary cutters, cutting mats, heavy-duty plastic geometric cutting forms, quilting thread, good-quality scissors and sewing kits — for myself and for Centre Benkady. As a gift, my daughter bought me a large wooden hoop to use for lap-quilting.

At the register, we chatted with the store's genial manager and I told her about my new economic development project in Mali, in which I would be teaching Malian seamstresses patchwork quilting, even though this craft was new to me.

"Be careful," the manager warned me, as my daughter and I were about to leave the store.

"Why is that?" I said. Was she referring to the usual — malaria and cholera, wars and corruption, venomous snakes and wild predatory animals — that most people automatically associate with life in Africa? Was she assuming the worst, as most people do? If not, what else could she mean?

"Addiction," she said, smiling. "Quilting becomes an addiction."

- - - - - - - - - - - -

In Paris I spoke French to people in whole sentences for the first time in my life, and I actually understood what French people were saying when they responded to me. The last time I'd been to Paris, four years before, when I told my French friends (in English) about my hopes of joining the Peace Corps and serving in a Francophone African country — and finally, *finally!* achieving a lifelong goal of learning to speak French — my French friends nodded politely. Now, four years later, they were impressed.

"Your French is good!" my friend Marie-Laure said, surprised. "You don't have an American accent — or even an African accent. *Très bien!*" My French, I knew, was still barely passable. Marie-Laure, a dear, long-time friend, was only being kind.

As on previous trips to Paris, I spent whole afternoons walking, admiring this, my favorite city, on foot, taking it all in at my own, solitary pace. This time, though, I also treated myself to a haircut at Marie-Laure's favorite coiffure, Jean Noel; and I shopped at the grand department store, Samaritan. There, in the sewing department, I bought a large picture book on quilting written in French to give to the women at Centre Benkady.

- - - - - - - - - - - - -

Youssef met me at the airport in Bamako, the way he'd always met my train when I returned from Libreville to Lastoursville in Gabon, with a wide, welcoming smile and a warm embrace. A three-week separation was what we had needed. He told me he'd missed me.

The women at Centre Benkady were overjoyed at my return. Perhaps they'd known of other development workers who left for their homelands on holiday and never returned to Mali. Their obvious delight and relief at seeing me again filled my heart with joy. When I presented them with the gifts I'd brought — sewing supplies for the center and for each of the women a pair of artisinal earrings that I'd bought from a street vendor in Paris — the women broke out in spontaneous cheers and applause.

"You are too good to us!" Ramata, the president of the center said. "You have a good heart."

"*Regardez,*" I said. I gave them a quick demonstration of the workings of their new, razor-sharp rotary cutter, cutting through several layers of fabric at once on the special cutting mat, following the contours of a five-inch square plastic form. "*C'est pour le bon patchwork!*" You would have thought I'd performed a magic trick. "And this quilting book," I pointed out, "is in French! I bought it in Paris, just for you."

- - - - - - - - - - - - -

I was extremely happy to be back in Ségou, back in my home, working in my garden, sharing my sun-filled life with my Malian friends. I had a sense of belonging there, which I simply didn't have elsewhere.

I finished my Ségou stars quilt wall hanging. I sewed a sleeve on the back of it, and Youssef and I put it up in the living room. We thought it was gorgeous. I immediately began work on a new one, which I called "Autumn in New York and Paris." The Lastoursville, Gabon, quilt had taken me six months to make; the Ségou quilt wall hanging took six weeks; this new one, I realized, could take as little as six days, if I did it all by machine.

Every evening, after I accomplished everything else on my to-do list, I worked on this new quilt project until my eyes gave out from fatigue at about 10:30. The colors, designs, textures, symbolism — all aspects of it — thrilled me. *Yes,* I had to admit, *I've become addicted to quilting.*

Then I got an inspired idea: to formalize my quilting lessons and create a larger, more structured project that would allow me to stay in Ségou. I would design a teacher-training program and write a proposal seeking support for it from an American aid organization. With their imprimatur and blessing, I would be able to renew my Malian work permit so I could legally extend my stay. I even came up with a name for this plan: "The Patchwork Project of Ségou, Mali." *Yes,* I thought, *quilting will keep me here.*

- - - - - - - - - - - - -

"MILLENNIUMS COME AND MILLENNIUMS GO," I blithely noted in my journal at the tail end of the twentieth century, "and very little changes on this continent." At a time when most others — at least those in the First-and-Fast World — were losing sleep and chewing fingernails over possible terrorists' attacks, Y2K computer catastrophes, or other end-of-the-world cataclysms heralding the New Millennium, I was experiencing only a low-grade, faith-shaking anxiety over the glacial progress of my Patchwork Project in Ségou, Mali. Would I get funding for it? Would I be able to stay in Mali and fulfill my dream of making this economic development project come true? Should I stay in Africa? Should I go somewhere else? If so, where? These and other unanswered questions continued to linger and gnaw as January 1, 2000, loomed.

One aspect of my life that *was* changing dramatically, however, was my love for Youssef. In the course of the past year in Ségou, he had become someone I hardly knew, someone I didn't even like at times. And it was clear to me he regarded me similarly. The look of love I once saw in his eyes was gone, replaced by a look of anger and resentment. When his anger occasionally erupted into uncharacteristic rage, and I suggested it was time he went his own way, he would only go out for the night and return full of remorse and apologies the next day. Then stay.

"I think Youssef will be leaving," I noted in my journal, unable to make my usual New Year's resolutions because so much in my life was uncertain. "Our romance is long dead. It's better that he leaves before our friendship dies too. Sooner, rather than later, in this New Millennium."

- - - - - - - - - - - - -

On New Year's Eve, 1999, Youssef and I left our house in the guardianship of our next-door-neighbor Camara the *forgeron*, whom I paid to stay on our terrace while we attended a party given by our friends Vivica, a Peace Corps volunteer, and her Canadian fiancé, Sylvain. Camara, to my surprise, brought over a tall metal spear, taller than himself, as well as a warm woolen blanket, which he'd folded and tossed over one shoulder. Our neighborhood was peaceful and the night was mild, but

Camara, looking like a Masai warrior standing at attention there on our terrace, gripping the spear by his side, seemed prepared for the worst — marauding tribes, perhaps, and maybe even a blizzard.

Youssef and I walked for nearly an hour under the vast, dazzling, diamond-studded sky to get to Sylvain's home, taking the back, unlit, dirt roads through freshly mowed millet fields. The walk was glorious. I held Youssef's arm to keep from stumbling in the darkness in my dressy heels, and he held a flashlight in his other hand to point the way. It was the first time in a long time I'd felt this physically connected to him, but he seemed miles away.

"Regardes les étoiles!" I kept remarking at the star-filled sky, like a school child on recess or a grown woman who didn't get out much — which in fact was true. Without a car or any extra spending money, Youssef and I seldom went out at night.

He didn't respond or look up. His eyes were focused on the stony path ahead, or at least the part of it that he could see directly in front of us illuminated by the flashlight beam.

It was indeed a memorable party. Vivica had invited a few of her fellow Peace Corps volunteers; Sylvain had invited some fellow Canadians as well as Malian colleagues from his work. Vivica's divorced mother and younger brother were there, visiting from Maryland; Sylvain's eight-year-old daughter was visiting from Quebec City. We all danced under the myriad stars on Sylvain's expansive, oval terrace; then we watched CNN in the living room — first, an extravagant fireworks display from the Eiffel Tower at 11 p.m. Malian time, followed an hour later by even more spectacular fireworks from London Bridge at midnight.

Outside, Sylvain set off his own modest fireworks from the rooftop of his grand house, while we guests watched and cheered, toasting the New Millennium with French Champagne. All of the couples kissed, clinked glasses and wished *"Bonne Année!"* Except Youssef and me. What had happened to the love we'd had in Gabon? I couldn't help but reflect and mourn:

In the equatorial heat, in the closeness of the thick rainforest that blocked the night sky, in the solitude of my ovenlike cinderblock house on the hill in Lastoursville, our differences had melted away. Alone together there, Youssef and I were reduced to our essences. The externals evaporated. We became virtually ageless, colorless, nation-less, language-less. The fact that Youssef was Malian and had never been beyond western Africa; that he was born when I was twenty; that he spoke barely one word of English with a confident smile ("yes!"); and that he had had to drop out of high school due to crippling illness, was background, not barrier. We connected at the core, and at that core, we were two solitary human beings with like hearts, souls, and minds.

Despite the fact that we came from different worlds, we found ourselves standing on the same patch of earth in Gabon, far from our families and countries of origin. Despite our diametrically different backgrounds, we held harmonious values and worldviews. We both believed in one Great God, one human family, one beckoning globe filled with potential adventure. We both retained — despite some measure of adult disillusion and world-wisdom — a childlike sense of wonder. And we both were sufficiently brave to embrace the unknown.

Youssef never asked for anything. We shared everything. We shared clothes; we wore the same size jeans and baggy T-shirts. We shared house and garden chores. We shared a bed and made love, uncomplicatedly, as though we were cooking and eating a good meal together. Yes, sex for us was like good food — healthy, necessary, and delicious. And it was deliciously free of encumbrances, such as guilt; or *accoutrements,* such as sexy lingerie; or perversions, such as pornography — none of which had ever held any appeal for me. Our lovemaking was as natural as breathing.

- - - - - - - - - - - - -

Love and death and the death of love became burning issues for me in the first few months of this new year that marked the new century. This was the year I would turn 55; and although I'd learned a lot about life in that span of time, the secrets of success in the realm of romantic love were still complete mysteries to me. What kept couples together "until death do you part"? I wanted to know. What was the magic, the glue?

Where was the script for this particular drama, the rules for this strategic game? How did others do it? Why had I never learned? *What was wrong with me?*

I studied the love-relationships among my women friends at Centre Benkady.

Ami Sylla, the head *formatrice*, was happily married to a sweet, bearlike "doctor" (nurse practitioner) who was selfless enough to even make house calls. They had two teenage children. By all appearances, Ami's husband adored her. She carried herself with the calm, unwavering bearing of a woman who is completely secure in her husband's and her children's love. Her home life was like an enormous baobab tree with immeasurably deep roots. I envied her.

Sali Traore, treasurer of Centre Benkady, too, had the same bearing for the same reasons, it seemed to me. Her husband, a prosperous *commerçant* in Ségou, was her "rock," she said. He encouraged her efforts to learn and grow. Although they had five children, Sali was not tied down by household chores. All of her children were in school, and she had a full-time, live-in servant, a young woman from a remote village who sent her earnings home to help support her family. Sali's love-fueled *joie de vivre* gave her a distinct, sunny beauty, which I also secretly envied.

Funny thing about love, I thought, as I observed my friends' love-relationships, *when a woman is loved and she knows it and feels secure in that knowledge, she has a special kind of beauty that shines from within. When I felt that Youssef loved me, I could see flickers of that beauty in myself in the mirror. No more. Now he looks at me as though I'm a dried-up, brittle, old white woman. Which I guess I now am. That's life. Things change. Relationships die. And people die, too, of course.*

- - - - - - - - - - - - -

My Benkady friends and I traveled to Markala to pay our respects to Hawa, our Benkady-sister, a few days after her fifty-six-year-old husband's sudden death from a stroke. We made the one-and-a-half hour trip on an exceptionally cool morning in a pickup truck rigged up like a covered wagon. A dozen of us women sat in the back of the pickup, huddled together, bent over against the cold, and wrapped up in shawls.

When we reached Hawa's in-laws' compound in Markala, we filed into the courtyard, covering our heads with our shawls or scarves, respectfully. We greeted the older family members sitting on mats and chairs lining the entryway. All of the women in our group then entered the room where Hawa and her two co-widows sat side by side on a straw mat against one wall, all three dressed identically in royal blue mourning gowns that looked to me like nightgowns with hoods.

The three widows appeared dumbstruck. They sat silently, close together — Hawa in the center because she was the second wife — listening to what seemed to be an inspirational tape recording in Bambara that played repeatedly. Their pain was palpable but also dignified. There were no tears, no empty words, no needless motions.

We women from Benkady filled the room, sitting shoeless on the woven-mat-covered floor. The spokeswoman from our delegation spoke only a few words: a few soft words of greeting, a few words of condolence, and then, after about ten minutes, a few words of farewell. Ramata, the president of Benkady, conveyed my condolences in Bambara to Hawa. "Thank you, Bonnie," Hawa said to me in French, which touched me deeply because these were the only words she spoke while we were there.

According to custom, I learned, Hawa and her co-widows had to remain secluded in their husband's family compound for four months. Her involvement in the affairs of Benkady would have to be suspended. Her plans to participate in my hoped-for, upcoming Patchwork Project teacher-training course would have to be cancelled. She and her co-wives were widows now, but they were not free.

- - - - - - - - - - - - -

Ramata, too, was a widow bound by Muslim custom. Her first husband had died in an automobile accident eight years before. So, according to religious law, she was obliged to marry her husband's brother. Fortunately for her, this man lived in France with his first wife, to whom he remained faithful and with whom he had two grown sons.

His only husbandly obligation toward Ramata was to visit her once a year and to support her financially.

I met Ramata's second husband, Omar, at a *fête* held at her house in early January. It was the feast marking the end of the month-long fast of Ramadan; and the food that Ramata's niece, Fily, prepared was delicious: lamb stew with couscous-like *fonio*, fried plantain chips, mixed-greens salad, and fresh fruit (papaya and watermelon slices). As we ate outside together in the shade of an arbor, Omar, a quiet, dignified man who must have been close to sixty, told me in perfect French:

"I've lived in France for the past thirty-six years. I could never live in Mali again. The climate is too hot, the medical care is too awful, and I have too many lazy family members — maybe fifty or sixty of them! — who would look to me to support them." He shook his head and laughed mirthlessly. "No, as a retired person, in poor health myself, I could not afford to be drained like that. *Pas du tout.* No, I'll just come to Mali to visit Ramata once a year — briefly."

- - - - - - - - - - - - -

Youssef would be gone for long stretches, and I never knew where he'd gone or when he would return. Sometimes when he returned late he went straight to the guest bedroom, which had become his bedroom, to sleep. At other times, he was angry and wanted to argue.

"If you are so unhappy here," I told him calmly, though my stomach was in tight knots, "you're perfectly free to leave. We are not married. You have no obligations toward me. Please, just leave."

But he stayed.

After these blow-ups, I would sometimes go for long bike rides in the opposite direction from town to regain a sense of calm and equilibrium. It was always an exhilarating ride, along the smooth, flat, paved road toward Mopti, all the way to a village called Dialabougou, at least 10 kilometers away. The landscape, with its patches of scrubby trees, occasional winding dirt paths leading from the *goudron*, the towering baobabs and balanzins here and there in the distance, was pure Africa. The sight of the slanting, sinking sun and the smell of dried hay in the baking fields always made my heart sing. On the surface, I knew well, I was a rootless stranger here; but deep down, I felt Africa loved me. I could feel the ancestors' embrace.

- - - - - - - - - - - -

At times I tried to reason with Youssef.

"Why are you so angry at me?" I begged him to tell me. "What have I done to make you so angry?"

"I'm not angry with you," he said. "I'm angry with myself."

I'll never in this lifetime understand men, I thought. *I would need another millennium.*

"Then why do you take your anger out on me?"

He shook his lowered head; he didn't look at me. I let him continue without interruption after he'd found some words: He explained that he was frustrated by the fact that his photographic career hadn't taken off in Ségou; he felt he might have better success elsewhere. He said he was also under pressure from his Malian friends and family members in Ségou to live a more "normal life," to follow custom and time-honored tradition. They worried that his *toubob* (white) lifestyle was making him *gâté* (spoiled) and *gonflé* (puffed up). They urged him to attend Friday services at the mosque in *centreville* with the other men, find a nice young woman and marry her, have children, become a good Muslim husband and father.

"I never thought I would say this," Youssef said to me, "but I think it's time I had a family of my own now."

"Bien sur," I said. *"C'est normale,"* I assured him. I always knew this day would come. I remembered the very moment when I had predicted it:

One day, as Youssef and I were walking up the hill to my home in Lastoursville together on our way home from the *marché,* he'd asked me to marry him. He said I was the only woman he'd ever asked, the first woman other than his mother he'd ever loved. He said he wanted to spend his life with me.

"Quoi?" I said, not sure I'd heard him correctly. He repeated his proposal.

"Are you just looking for a passport to the States," I asked him laughingly, trying to make light of the moment, "like all the others who want to marry Peace Corps volunteers?"

"I would never want to live in the USA," he said, seemingly hurt by my glib response. "I could never be happy living in a place where I would be treated like a second-class citizen." My mind flew back to something my English boyfriend, Melvyn, had said in Rhodesia in the early '70s when we were contemplating marriage: "I'd never live in the States," he said. "It's full of bloody Americans."

"That's true," I told Youssef. "You're right. The U.S. is indeed racist, still. That's the ugly truth."

Youssef lifted his head and raised his chin. He often spoke of dignity, which in French sounded to me like "DEEN," something he prized more than money. Dignity and pride were his treasured possessions, which no one could take from him. He would not stoop to second-class status for anyone.

We walked silently for a while, both of us carrying bags of produce from the *marché,* both of us sweating in the late-morning equatorial heat. The scar from my burn accident still hurt — it was as if a large sheet of leather in the shape of Idaho had been Superglued to my left thigh, and every step I took pulled the newly knitted skin tissue nearly to the breaking point — so I walked slowly, like a much older woman. Youssef, ever patient, slowed his pace to keep pace with me.

"I am much too old for you," I said matter-of-factly. "I'm old enough to be your mother. We can never get married. One day you'll wake up and decide you want to have a family; you'll want a younger wife who can bear you children."

"Africa has enough children," he told me firmly, for the first, but not the last, time.

"Yes, but you might change your mind someday. I don't want to stand in the way of that. I think we must be together *jour par jour*, on a day-to-day basis, as if we had no future, only the present. Our lives are intersecting now, but we may well go in different directions in the future. Please don't speak of marriage again."

Saying these words to him at that time made me feel, fleetingly, noble and selfless. The truth was, deep down, the very human me wished we could be together forever.

"You are young and free to go your own way," I said to him that evening in Ségou, "and I only wish you well."

But he stayed.

- - - - - - - - - - - -

Here is a simple, universal truth: Love can surely die. I wasn't alone in this realization, I knew. Another of my Benkady "sisters," Mah Coulibaly, was experiencing a love-death of her own at the same time: Smilau, her businessman husband, to whom she'd been married ten years, for whom she had borne three children, and whom she still loved deeply, had decided to take a new wife. Mah was visibly stricken by this news, as though shot through the heart.

When the wedding day came, Mah, according to custom, had to play gracious hostess at the wedding celebration, which was held at their home. She looked beautiful, almost bridal, in a fancy white dress. She also wore a broad smile, the forced look of happiness, which we Benkady women knew masked great pain. We were attending the wedding at her request, to be her "support group," to help her get through this ordeal.

"Isn't this unbearably difficult for her?" I asked my Benkady women friends naively, as we sat together, barefoot, on the floor of a side room, under a languid ceiling fan, sharing a large, round communal platter filled with heaped rice smothered with lamb-and-vegetable stew.

"Oui, vraiment," they agreed. *"Mais, il faut supporter"* (one must endure).

"Ah, the men here…" Delphine added with a sigh. "How we suffer…" Unlike the other Benkady women, Delphine was Roman Catholic. And unlike the other Benkady women's husbands who were Muslim and therefore nondrinkers, Delphine's, being Catholic, drank. "See this finger?" she said, displaying the badly deformed middle finger on her right hand. "He broke it in a drunken rage. He has beaten me and made me cry so often, I've run out of tears. When my neighbor's son was struck and killed by a car recently, I couldn't even cry. I have no more tears…"

Delphine and her husband had long since stopped speaking to each other. Their love, clearly, had died. But Delphine, the mother of their five children, could not leave them or divorce him.

I wanted to tell my Benkady friends there and then, as we reached into the central platter of rice and sauce with our right hands, that one of the reasons I was so enthusiastic about the potential of our Patch-work Project was that it could one day provide the women with some independent income. If they could learn to make top-quality quilts that could be sold over the Internet to well-off women in colder cli-mates, especially African-American women who might see them as "ancestor" quilts, then these Malian seamstresses could earn good mon-ey, which in turn could allow them to break free of abusive, dependent relationships.

But I said nothing. There were too many unknowns — "ifs" and "coulds" and "mights" — in this ambitious equation. And I couldn't find the correct conditional verb tenses to express myself adequately in French. Even if I could, would it have made a difference?

Also, this was neither the right time nor place. When Mah came in to our room on her rounds as gracious hostess, the women brightened. They made jokes in Bambara to make Mah laugh. Although I couldn't understand their words, I understood the meaning beneath them. We were there to show solidarity, to buoy our sister lest she sink in despair.

I became determined to make the Patchwork Project work. I girded myself for a long, slow, uphill climb. I prayed for patience and toler-ance — and money to live on, to see this dream through.

- - - - - - - - - - - - -

As Youssef's anger and frustration escalated, he became more threaten-ing. One morning in late February, behaving as though he had sudden-ly lost his mind, he made a scene in our courtyard as I was watering the garden. This time it was Camara's turn to stare in rigid disbelief from across our courtyards' divide. Youssef shouted at me in Bambara (as if for Camara's benefit), shook his fist in my face, and then said in French, "I could KILL you!"

I stared at him, speechless and horrified, thinking, *What has brought us to this place? How could this be the same man who saved my life in Gabon?*

My mind returned to that time:

Youssef had had malaria — *le palu*, the Africans called it — when he arrived unexpectedly at my house in Lastoursville the day before Thanksgiving, 1997. So I led him to the spare room I called my office, with the makeshift desk — a wide wooden plank laid over empty, freshly painted oil barrels — at the window, overlooking the river and the forested mountains in the distance. I'd made a rudimentary daybed for the room too, from a Peace-Corps-hand-me-down, narrow, single mattress resting on boards propped up by NIDO cans and an assortment of colorful pillows against the wall.

"Please lay down here," I told him, and then I covered his shaking body with a blanket. He complained of fever, chills, painful joints, headache, dizziness, and weakness. I took his temperature, which confirmed a high fever, gave him some Fansidar from my personal, Peace Corps-issue medical kit (which I knew was against the rules, but I thought this costly medicine would cure him quickly), and told him I'd make him some chicken soup for lunch.

Before Youssef's arrival, I'd been preparing for a Thanksgiving dinner I was having at my house the next day. I'd invited a handful of people — my Peace Corps postmate, Morgan; my American missionary friend, Bev; my Chadian neighbors Dr. Djimet and his wife; Madame Nimba, a local Camaroonian restaurateur and her husband, a retired Gabonese *fonctionnaire* (beaurocrat); plus Youssef, who was going to take keepsake photographs. For most of the guests, including Youssef, it would be their first traditional American Thanksgiving dinner; and I wanted to make it a memorable event.

Already the poultry stock was gently simmering in a huge stockpot on the front burner of my new, small stovetop and filling my home with its homey fragrance. Chicken stock, I used to tell my cooking school students in New York, is "liquid gold" in the kitchen because it adds a rich flavor to everything made from it, especially soups and sauces.

My menu for the next day's feast included pumpkin soup as a first course, roast turkey breast, mashed potatoes and gravy, canned peas (fresh or even frozen peas were unavailable), fresh carrots and salad from my garden, and my homemade, healthy bread.

I had plenty of stock bubbling on the stove, so I knew I could spare some of it for Youssef's healing soup. It was lunch time, midday on the Equator, unbearably hot and humid, as usual. I was wearing only a tank top and tennis shorts, which I could get away with in the privacy of my own home but not in public in Gabon; and, as always in my house, I was barefoot.

Youssef's long, slender frame beneath the blanket on the narrow daybed shook like a tree limb in heavy winds. His normally gentle, smiling face looked clenched. His semisweet-chocolate color skin looked ashen.

"Stay here," I told him, smoothing my right hand over his short-cropped hair, "and try to rest. I'll make you some good soup and come right back."

"D'accord," he said, nodding weakly.

I walked down the hallway toward my kitchen at my usual, brisk, Manhattan-pedestrian pace. When I turned the corner hurriedly, into the kitchen, I didn't see that something had spilled on the floor. Water? Oil? Whatever it was, it was slippery on the terra cotta tiles. The heel of my right foot skidded on it. I lost my balance. I reached wildly for something to grasp to catch my fall. My left hand fell on the handle of the tall stockpot sitting on the stovetop at the entryway to my kitchen. Without knowing, without thinking, without seeing, I pulled the heavy pot toward me, pouring the boiling liquid down onto my bare left thigh, knee, shin, and foot. ...

When my mother was dying of cancer, I sat at her bedside and listened to her slow, soft moaning. There are sounds that women make, I thought then, that have a vocabulary all their own. Baby-girl squeals, schoolgirl giggles, lover's sighs, childbirth cries, heartbroken sobs, death's moans — all fall within women's wide, wide range of wordless emotional expression. But the sounds I made that day in Gabon, as the boiling poultry stock, the burning liquid, molten gold, melted the skin on my left leg as though I were made of candle wax, were unlike anything I had ever heard before. Unlike any sound I had ever heard myself make.

I was on the kitchen floor, rocking and screaming from the unutterable pain when Youssef appeared at the kitchen door, wide-eyed, shaken.

"Qu'est-ce-que se pas?!" he said as if he couldn't believe his eyes. Or ears. We had always been so quiet together. He had never heard me raise my voice, much less scream. I myself barely knew who was screaming.

"Get the doctor," I begged him. "Please get Dr. Djimet!"

Youssef found Dr. Djimet at his house, farther up the hill from mine, directly across from the hospital, having lunch with his wife and teenage son and daughter.

When the two men returned, they lifted me up and carried me gently as if I were a bird with a broken wing. They put me between them in the cab of Dr. Djimet's pickup truck, and rushed me to the hospital's surgery room, where Dr. Djimet treated my burn. Youssef stood beside me. He gave me his hand, and I squeezed it with all my strength, to counteract the pain.

"Youssef *a le palu*" (Youssef has malaria), I told Dr. Djimet, gritting my teeth, trying to be brave, as brave as I imagined an African would be under the same circumstances, as I laid there on the operating table and Dr. Djimet tore the layers of burned and blistered skin from my thigh. But he was concentrating on the task at hand. He ignored my words. The Fansidar, though, must have worked its magic on Youssef. His *palu* had seemingly vanished.

In the days that followed, my condition worsened. I had a violent allergic reaction to the mercurochrome Dr. Djimet had used liberally to dress my wound. I experienced high fevers, cold chills, and gushing sweats for days. I received excellent outpatient attention at the Lastoursville hospital (where I chose not to stay because my home was cleaner), but getting there, on foot, taking baby steps the whole way, was excruciatingly painful; and having the enormous bandages changed there every day, without anesthetic, was like being skinned alive. I couldn't keep from screaming. I tried to be quiet and courageous, to show the African nurses attending me that thin-skinned white people can be brave too, but the screams escaped against my will.

Youssef never left my side. He cared for me, night and day, doing everything he possibly could to comfort me and ease my pain. He fed me, took me to the toilet, changed my drenched shirts and sheets, washed my face, brushed my hair.

When I asked him, "Why are you doing this? Why are you so good to me?" his only response was, *"C'est normale."* But no man in my life had ever been this kind to me. This was not "normal" for me.

One night, when I was delirious with pain and fever, I thought I saw two women — one white and resembling my mother, the other black and unknown to me — reaching out to me from the next life. I wanted to go with them. I wanted so much to go. Wherever these women were, I knew there would be no pain.

"I want to die," I told Youssef, who was sitting beside my bed.

He stretched his long, slim body out next to mine on the bed, gently, careful not to disturb my heavily bandaged left leg, and he spoke softly into my ear: "God has sent me to tell you, you cannot go now. *Pas encore* (not yet). This is not your time. You have more work to do, *ici, en Afrique.*"

Yes, I thought, accepting Youssef's words as if from the voice of God, *Africa needs me. And I need Africa even more.*

When my Peace Corps postmate, Morgan, arrived by motorcycle a few days later from her village, Manna-Manna, and saw my worsening condition and Youssef's exhaustion, she swung into action. She found a phone in town that actually worked and eventually got through to the Peace Corps Medical Officer in Libreville, who arranged for my evacuation on the next scheduled flight to Libreville out of Lastoursville. I asked that Youssef fly with me, and the Peace Corps agreed.

News traveled fast among the American expatriate and Peace Corps communities in Libreville, and I began to get visitors. People wanted to see me, the burn victim, now amazingly gregarious, thanks to morphine, but also Youssef, the hero of the dramatic story they'd heard. This was the man who had risen from his own malarial death bed to get the doctor, just in time; the man who saved the life of a Peace Corps volunteer posted in a remote town in the middle of rain-forested nowhere; the man who'd flown with her to Libreville and never left her side — even to the extent of sleeping in a chair beside her hospital bed for three whole weeks.

These visitors showered me with flowers, books, and stationery; and they surprised and embarrassed Youssef with thank-you gifts and praise. When the Peace Corps director in Gabon came to visit me, he gave Youssef a black cotton T-shirt with the profile of an African woman's face outlined in white on the front. The T-shirt read in French, "Teach a woman and you teach a country." Youssef accepted the T-shirt humbly and wore it proudly.

The Peace Corps doctor wanted to send me back to the States for a skin graft, but I rejected his suggestion because it would have meant terminating my Peace Corps service. "Don't worry," I told him, "I'll keep this ugly scar well hidden. I won't be modeling any swimsuits." I chose, instead, to remain with the Peace Corps and return to Lastoursville with Youssef. I knew I wasn't ready to leave Africa — or Youssef.

But now in Ségou, Mali, the Youssef I had known then seemed to have vanished, only to be replaced by this enraged stranger threatening to do me harm.

Soon after that outburst in our courtyard, as I was biking past the police station in town on my way to *La Poste*, my heart told me: "Tell them." So I went in and talked privately with a young police officer. I explained the situation briefly, saying I was threatened, and if something should happen to me, Youssef should be their prime suspect. This policeman seemed sincerely concerned. When I said Youssef hadn't actually *done* anything yet, he countered, "He's threatened you. That's doing something."

"I've been to the police," I told Youssef calmly the next time he returned to the house. "They say you should leave."

"*D'accord*," he said, offering no resistance. It was as if he welcomed this outside force, forcing him to finally make a decision. He packed up what few things he owned, and by March 4th he was gone. He didn't say where he was going, and I didn't ask. I locked the metal gate behind him, and I walked back into my house. March 4th, march forth.

- - - - - - - - - - - - -

In the days prior to his final departure, though, Youssef's words to me had been harsh. He told me I could never live in Mali alone, without him. Mali was not like the United States, he said, where women were free to live alone, do as they pleased. With him gone, he claimed, I would have to leave Mali also.

I took these words as a dare. *I'll find a way to stay*, I thought to myself. *Just watch me.*

But when I visited my friend Mariko and sat with him in the shade of his arbor, I wept. Doubts and fears assaulted me, and I needed his wise counsel.

"I can't leave now," I told us both. "With all the planting I've done, I feel as if I've planted myself here. I feel rooted."

"No, you can't leave," Mariko said with a deep, sure voice that sounded to me like it came from God. "You will be more useful here than you would be in the United States."

Useful, I thought. *That's the magic word. I must be useful to justify my existence.*

That day I bought a small flamboyant sapling from Mariko and planted it on the other side of my front courtyard. For the duration of my stay in Mali on my own, however long that might be, I was determined to watch this graceful tree grow.

And along the narrow alleyway between the bedrooms and the cement wall, I planted a row of papaya trees from seeds. Farther forward, in the rock garden, along with the cacti and other succulents I'd planted earlier in large terra cotta pots, I added an ornamental cassava, banana trees, ginger plants, and, in between, a low-lying, flowering creeper, which Mariko called *"couvre sol."* In no time, I knew, the rock garden would become full and lush, the papaya and banana trees would bear welcomed fruit, and the flamboyant sapling, with its fine, out-stretched branches covered with delicate, feathery leaves, would grow taller than my house.

ON MARCH 8TH, International Women's Day, *"La Journée Internationale de la Femme,"* which is widely celebrated in Mali, thirty of my Club Crochet girls arrived at my house early in the afternoon. We'd made a date to walk together as a "women's group" to Centre Benkady, where an International Women's Day *manifestation* (event) was to be held.

It would be a women's-only gathering with dancing and singing, so the little girls, aged eight to twelve, had dressed for the occasion in their best lacey, satiny dresses. Instead of their usual flip-flops, some wore plastic sandals with low heels. Their mothers or older sisters had done their hair in braids, bows, and barrettes. Some of the girls even wore lipstick.

We walked the mile to Benkady holding hands and singing a marching song I'd just made up: *"Nous sommes les femmes et nous sommes FORTES!"* (We are women and we are STRONG), stopping to stamp our collective feet when we got to the word *"FORTE!"* Aminata's best friend Bintou translated the words for her. Aminata shot me a conspiratorial smile. She knew what I was up to.

What a sight we must have been to the people we passed: thirty lively little African girls in party dresses, led by a tall, thin, middle-aged white woman, all laughing, giggling, singing, holding hands, swinging arms, marching and stomping our way down the dusty roads of *quartier* Pelangana. Most of the people we passed, I knew, wouldn't know the words of our marching song because they probably didn't speak French. So they smiled and waved at us benignly as we paraded by, as though we were just having fun, playing a game. The girls seemed to know, though, as we marched forth, that this was much more than a game. I was leading a mini-revolution that, I hoped, might grow as these girls grew into strong women.

- - - - - - - - - - - -

After Youssef left, silently walking out our front gate, carrying all of his belongings in two plastic satchels, I bought a new bed and put it on the roof of my house. I wanted to sleep alone safely under the stars. It was an inspired move, I felt, and it came about this way:

One afternoon, on the way home from teaching a class at Centre Benkady, I stopped at a metalworker's atelier to ask whether he might make an iron ladder for me that could be attached securely to the front terrace of my house, allowing me to have access to the flat roof. The man, Mr. Dao, agreed, and within a few weeks the sturdy, narrow ladder was installed.

Then, as if heaven-sent, I saw, one Monday morning on my way to the *centreville marché* but not yet far from my home, a Malian family from an outlying village conveying on their donkey cart a new, hand-made traditional bed frame made of smooth sticks tied with cowhide to be sold at the market.

"Arret!" (stop!) I called and motioned to the father frantically, even though I knew he likely didn't speak French. But just at that moment a tall, turbaned, and long-robed man crossed the road and offered to translate for me.

"Is this bed for sale?" I asked through the interpreter.

"Oui."

"How much are you asking for it?"

"3,250 CFA."

"Could you follow me to my house not far away and deliver it for the same price?" That price came to the equivalent of $6.50.

"Oui."

Once on the roof, this narrow bed provided me with a private sanctuary, a refuge, a solution to the confines of my oven-like bedroom, a new love affair with the night sky. With strips of rubber inner tubing, I attached tall bamboo poles at each corner, forming a four-poster bed, to support my mosquito netting. Thus protected from the ever-present threat of malaria, I felt ready to face the elements, braced to take on the encroaching *saison chaude.*

And not only that. This rooftop getaway renewed a sense of child-like wonder in me. I felt like a kid, climbing, unafraid, up the narrow ladder to her own secret "hideout." Once on the roof, it was as if I'd reached a mountaintop, where nobody could see me but I could see everything, especially the sky, the countless diamond-like stars and the fat, bright-as-day moon.

"Blessed is He who decked the sky with constellations and set in it a lamp, a shining moon" (Koran 25:61), I noted in my journal not long after Youssef's departure. "It's as if a whole new world has opened up to me," I added. "I don't think I've ever slept under the moon and stars before. What pure joy."

And what a celestial show. Before falling asleep, I would study the stars dotting the jet-black sky surrounding me. Some of the stars were bluish, some orangey-yellow; some were fat rounds, others tiny pinpricks. Some seemed to jump, while occasionally one would fly, leaving me to wonder whether I'd seen an airplane, a satellite, or an actual shooting star.

When *la saison chaude* arrived, I was ready for it. Sleeping on the roof, I enjoyed a slight, treetop-level breeze. Though the days were typically punishingly hot, the nights became blessedly tolerable. I no longer perspired all night. I slept well, as if on a cloud, beneath a glorious canopy of stars.

One morning in May after a good night's sleep up on the roof, I read in the Koran, "It is He that has created for you the stars, so that they may guide you in the darkness of land and sea" (Koran 6:97). Although I was on my own in Mali now and my future there was uncertain, I wasn't afraid. I would march forth boldly, with at least a trillion twinkling stars to guide me.

YOUSSEF AND I HAD BEEN friends and partners — equals, in my view. Surprisingly, even to me, our obvious significant differences in age, race, religion, nationality, language, education, family background, and life experience seemed to melt away for a time, due to our deep spiritual and emotional connection. As a proud Malian who spoke the native language and who navigated easily in this new to us milieu, Youssef had been my bridge to life in Ségou. And, at least initially, as we had in our first year together in Gabon, in Mali we complemented and cared for one another in equal measure. Both of us were strong-willed, independent, wounded individuals, who allowed ourselves to be interdependent for a while, out of mutual respect for and faith in each other.

But I always knew we would reach a crossroads one day, and I knew I could go on alone. I had lived alone most of my adult life, including twenty years in my studio apartment on Manhattan's Upper West Side. I'd lived alone in Lastoursville, Gabon, too, during the year before I met Youssef there. I knew how to take care of myself, even as a single white woman in Africa.

But when I told my Benkady friend Ami Sylla that Youssef had moved out, she became alarmed.

"You must get a guardian," she said, in her characteristic, no-nonsense, headmistress tone.

"Why?" I asked. "I'm a big girl."

"Women don't live alone here," she said firmly. "It is not done. You must have a guardian at your house, and that guardian must be a man."

"But I don't know anyone I could ask," I said. *And I don't know where to begin to look,* I didn't add.

"We'll find someone for you," she said.

The women of Benkady then mobilized to help me. Abandoning whatever sewing or crafts projects they were working on that day, they immediately canvassed the *quartier* on their motorbikes, and within what seemed like no time at all, returned with a likely candidate for me. Pierre Coulibaly was a short, slightly built, sweet-faced man in his early forties with an innocent, childlike smile. He was, Ami informed me, a church-going Protestant Christian, a *celibataire* (bachelor), who could speak some French and happened to be free to work nights.

Feeling pressure from my Malian women friends, I sensed I had no choice but to hire their find, Pierre, as my night guardian.

Pierre was to arrive at 9 p.m., three hours after sunset, sleep on a chaise lounge on my front porch, water the gardens and trees in my courtyard after sunrise, and leave by 7 a.m. For these responsibilities, I would pay him 15,000 CFA a month, which was, I learned, what the Peace Corps volunteers in Ségou paid their requisite guardians.

At first, things went well. Pierre seemed to be contented with his new job, and I was relieved that Youssef had gone for good. *Things change*, I told myself. *I've changed. Youssef changed. Circumstances changed. That's life. Get on with it. End of Youssef story.*

The best part of my new story in Ségou was the love and solidarity I felt from my Benkady women friends. They'd come to my rescue, they said, because if I lived alone my security would be at great risk, and if something bad were to happen to me, I'd have to leave and they'd lose me. They made me feel loved and appreciated in a way that I needed — and maybe everybody needs.

For the moment, all was well.

That moment, however, didn't last long. Pierre, I soon found, tested my tolerance; and I felt I was failing the test. He turned out to be a filthy man, ignorant to the point of imbecility, and irresponsible as well. His presence in my home, in my life, made me question everything, especially the cultural barriers too high for me to climb. He tried my patience beyond its limits; he made me want to run away, screaming. Youssef's words, *"You won't be able to live here without me,"* echoed in my mind.

But my stubborn response remained, *Oh, no? Watch me.*

As the days and weeks went by, I noticed that Pierre never changed his shirt and pants nor washed with soap. Seeing this, I gave him a few of my clean T-shirts, a bath towel, washcloth, and a new bar of bath soap. Thinking he might never have used a modern shower, I showed him how to turn on the hot and cold shower knobs in the guest bathroom off the front porch. But every morning after he left, I'd see that he hadn't availed himself of the shower, and the bar of soap was dry.

When he arrived for work at 9 p.m., he knocked on the metal front gate, and I would walk out into the darkened courtyard to unlock the gate to let him in. He would extend his right hand to me in greeting, and, knowing it is highly impolite in Mali to refuse to shake an outstretched hand, I would cringe and take his filth-encrusted hand in mine.

Ninety percent of Malians are Muslims and most are exceptionally clean, I'd observed. Their long, flowing, damask *boubous*, often in light colors, were always pressed and spotless, even in the extended, dusty dry season and the shorter, muddy rainy season. Observant Muslims washed their hands and face at least five times a day, as part of their before-prayer ritual. Their hands offered in greeting could be counted on to be clean. Cleanliness seemed to be a hallmark of their religion and their sense of pride and dignity.

Youssef, a non-practicing Muslim, was exceedingly clean and fastidious — more so, even, than I. The first thing he did upon waking, as he'd been forcibly instructed throughout childhood by his devout-Muslim father, was to perform his ablutions. In this way, he approached each new day and everyone in it with a pleasant, freshly shaved face; a clean, sweet-tasting mouth; and a clean body dressed in clean, sweet-smelling, freshly ironed clothes. It had surprised him at first that my early morning priorities were so different from his own: Showering came third for me, long after drinking a potful of tea and spending time alone quietly writing in my study.

Unlike the majority of Malians, however, Pierre wasn't Muslim. He was among Mali's small minority of Protestant Christians, and good hygiene didn't appear to factor into his personal religious tenets. In fact, he seemed to follow, unwittingly at least, the ancient practice of *alousia*, "the state of being unwashed," which, according to Katherine Ashenburg, in her fascinating history of cleanliness, *The Dirt on Clean*, was chosen by hermits, monks and saints in early Christendom as a "badge of holiness."

Ashenburg goes on to quote Charles Gerba, a microbiologist at the University of Arizona who is known as "Dr. Germ," who claims that the hands are the only parts of the human body that really require washing for serious health reasons. "His mantra," she says, "is an ancient one — clean hands, clean hands, clean hands."

As my hand puppet Chantal Chanson used to sing to the little children in Gabon, *"Pour avoir la bonne santé* (to have good health) *lavez les mains a l'eau et au savon!"* (wash your hands with water and soap). This had been my message, my credo, part of my mission as a

Peace Corps health volunteer in Gabon — to teach the importance of clean hands to good health.

How could I, I asked myself, *knowing what I know, believing what I believe to be true, shake Pierre's hand every night at nine? How could I touch this filthy little man? Where had his hands been all day? Certainly nowhere near soap and water. How many thousands — or millions — of sickening microbes did they harbor? Will his germs make me sick?*

After letting him in to my courtyard, I excused myself, wished him a *"bonne nuit,"* and rushed to my bathroom to scrub my hands anxiously with antiseptic soap before climbing the ladder to my rooftop bed.

- - - - - - - - - - - -

And Pierre smelled. His odor was rank, foul, as bad as the worst bag person's in New York. But in the twenty years I'd lived in the City, I could quickly walk away whenever I encountered such a foul-smelling person, as if he or she wasn't a person at all but rather a pile of filthy, tattered, malodorous rags. With Pierre this wasn't possible. He spent his nights in my space. He was in my employ.

When I was a chef and caterer in New York for ten years, I had trained my nose to pay attention. With several dishes cooking simultaneously — an apple tart baking in the oven, a white sauce simmering on the stove, and sole fillets under the broiler, for example — I needed a nose sensitive enough to send me important signals. I learned to tell just from the fragrance whether or not a dish was finished cooking. "The nose," Katherine Ashenburg says, "is adaptable, and teachable":

> The scent of one another's bodies was the ocean our ancestors swam in, and they were used to the everyday odour of dried sweat. It was part of their world, along with the smells of cooking, roses, garbage, pine forests and manure.

I had taught my nose to aid me in my culinary career, but I was unable to adapt it to life with my new guardian, Pierre. Although I took to lighting matches and burning candles to fumigate the space he'd occupied, his odor lingered in my overly sensitive nostrils.

- - - - - - - - - - - -

117

In the mornings, when it was time for him to leave for the day, I walked Pierre to the front gate so I could lock it tightly behind him. Normally he carried a Bible in one hand and, I noticed one day, a racing form in the other. But one morning he also carried a plastic bag with something round and seemingly heavy in it. When I asked him what it was, he told me it was a dead rat, which he'd killed in the courtyard during the night with his slingshot and a small stone. He seemed proud. I asked what he planned to do with the rat. He told me he would cook it and eat it.

That evening when he returned, I asked Pierre whether he'd eaten the rat. He smiled his childlike smile and nodded broadly.

"*Oui,*" he said, "*avec le pain*" (with bread).

"*La peau et tout?*" (Skin and all?)

"*Tout,*" he replied, smiling and patting his stomach. He added that the rat he'd killed and eaten was part of "*un couple,*" and he planned to hunt down the second one and kill it with his slingshot that night.

I wondered what my mother and grandmother would have made of Pierre. "You can judge a man's character by his fingernails and his shoes," my mother used to say to my sisters and me when we were young. By this measure, Pierre was devoid of character. Her German mother, the original Mrs. Clean, who taught me the rigors of house-work and made me conscious of every speck of dust on the furniture and every unguarded cough in the vicinity, would have no words for Pierre and his revolting ways. She would be speechless with horror.

- - - - - - - - - - - -

Malians are social people, I observed; far more social than I. Aloneness seemed to be unknown and unacceptable to them. My Malian friends, perhaps taking pity on me, would drop by my home if they saw that I was alone there, to "*dit bonjour*" (say hello), sit and pass some time, "keep me company." In frenetic New York, friends made appointments, as if with the doctor or dentist, to get together; but in slower-paced Ségou, such friendly visits were all impromptu. So to carve out the time I personally required for solitude, to replenish my relatively small social reservoir, to read and think and write and pray, I woke early and holed up in my study.

From the open window above my desk, I could watch the dawn gently bring my flower-filled courtyard to light; I could listen to neighbors' roosters crowing, donkeys braying, and goats bleating. I could hear the rhythmic thump-thump-thump-thump-thump, comforting heartbeat sound of women pounding millet for their family's breakfast porridge. I could admire my little green parrot, Irwin, strutting in circles in his cage in the front mango tree. This time alone restored my soul and helped me to retain some measure of equilibrium.

Unlike Youssef, who had always understood and accepted my need for morning solitude, Pierre could not. Each morning Pierre stood right in front of my study window, blocking my morning view, his benighted face almost pressed against the screen peering in, as he watered the flowers in the window box and the plants below.

"Bonjour," he said amicably. *"Il fait beau aujour'hui, n'est-ce pas?"*

"Yes," I said, clenching my teeth, "it's a beautiful day," *but you are not a beautiful sight.* "I think these front flowers have been given enough water by now. How about watering the papaya trees on the side of the house?"

In those moments when he stood there woodenly, studying me from the other side of my study window, he made me feel like a caged animal. I had to grip the edge of my desk tightly to keep from clawing the window screen.

- - - - - - - - - - - -

I NAMED THE YOUNG, green parrot Irwin, after his original owners who gave him to me before they left Ségou. American missionaries in their fifties, the Irwins had worked in Mali for nearly twenty years and were more than ready, they told me when I first met them in *centreville* one day, to go back home to the States. The unhappy-looking couple appeared to me to be burnt out by their Christian mission work, flattened and exhausted. Their spirits seemed shriveled by Mali's merciless heat and entrenched Muslim culture. They confessed to chronic homesickness for Texas. They yearned to be near their young grandchildren.

Although their house on the other side of Ségou from mine had all the comforts and conveniences of any home they might have in America — including air conditioning, plush living room recliners, modern kitchen appliances, and high-tech communications equipment in one of their spare bedrooms — they couldn't pack to leave Ségou fast enough. They'd had enough. They told me they'd found a good home for their outdoor guard dog, Jake, and their two skittish house cats, Salt and Pepper; but they'd yet to find a place for their unnamed, young, green parrot.

"He's nasty," the wife told me. "Ever since my husband and I had his wings clipped to keep him from flying away, he's been in a foul mood."

No wonder, I thought. "I'll take him," I said.

- - - - - - - - - - - -

In Gabon I'd had a pet rooster, whom I named *Dîner* (pronounced DEE-nay), the French word for both "dinner" and "to dine." The first time I saw him, strutting over to my house, I thought I was looking at a free meal.

"Yooo-hooooo! ... cluck-cluck-cluck! ... *viens ici, mon petit Dîner!*" I would call to him sweetly, all the while thinking homicidal thoughts. "I have a nice slice of homemade bread here for you to peck at! What you need is a little fattening up…!" But the closer he got, the more my attitude changed. I started to see *Dîner* differently. I experienced a change of heart. Proximity, like timing, I found, can make all the difference in this world.

Funny things happened to Peace Corps volunteers living alone in far-off places tourists seldom see, on the other side of the globe from Fairway on Upper Broadway and Balducci's in the Village. Some volunteers were known to sit and stare at one wall of their hut for hours on end. Others spent whole days deep frying beignets. I seemed to have become emotionally attached to a neighbor's rooster.

When I asked myself how this crazy thing came to be, I could come up with a couple of fairly sane answers. The first was I didn't have any pets in Lastoursville. I'd left my beloved Himalayan cat, Sweet Basil, at home in New York in the care of my friend and next-door neighbor, Marty. I missed him. *Dîner* had begun to fill Basil's shoes, so to speak. Another reason was that *Dîner* was a first for me, and the novelty of our relationship was oddly appealing. He was the first living, crowing rooster I'd ever gotten that close to in the feathered flesh. Since I hadn't grow up on a farm, poultry for me had always been something encountered only in a cold, plucked, gutted, raw, lifeless, ready-to-roast form in a grocer's or butcher's refrigerated meat case.

Eat this rooster, *Dîner?* I soon realized I couldn't think of it. He was too beautiful, too elegant, too utterly regal. Below his bright-red crown, his widening body was covered by a feather-cape the color of the polished copper pots hanging on the kitchen wall of my New York apartment. His haughty, black tail feathers reminded me of my favorite, shiny black silk pants (in storage), the pants I knew I'd have no use for in the rainforest.

Dîner was dignified, too, and proud. I loved the way he strutted around my house — kingly head held high, copper chest puffed way out — like he owned the place. And what a voice! Vibrant, piercing, ear splitting, in fact, at close range. When he hopped up on my front porch and serenaded me at dawn every day, I found the sound of his commanding cock-a-doodle-doos strangely comforting.

The thought of another feathered pet in my new life in Ségou appealed to me. So I brought Irwin home to Pelangana and found the perfect spot for his artisan-made, globe-shaped cage in my courtyard — in the crook of the central branches of the young mango tree directly in front of my study window. This way I could watch him primp and preen and pace in his cage as I sat at my desk in the early morning. And he in turn could watch me as I wrote and read and prayed. He and I could commune with the dawn in our respective ways, together.

Irwin, with his gray, characteristic curved beak and yellow-rimmed, beadlike eyes, was the same pale green color; tapered, oblong shape; and roughly eight-inch length as a young mango leaf. So he was perfectly camouflaged in the mango tree. In fact, to make him happy, I tied together several of the branches of the nearby mango trees to his tree, so he could stroll along this aerial walkway when I let him out of his cage during the day, in lieu of flying.

Whatever bitterness and resentment he had harbored toward the missionaries for clipping his wings, he promptly forgot soon after coming to live with me. His daily strolls — more like military struts — from mango tree to mango tree seemed to delight him. He whistled, chortled, laughed and sang what sounded like freedom songs as he swaggered among the high branches. Some of the words to these distinctive, squawky songs seemed to be, "Look at me! I'm FREE! I'm no longer in a cage! I can do as I please all day!" Secretly, I applauded.

Then, just before sunset, at about 6:30 every evening, he'd head back down to his cage purposefully, knowing I had his dinner — fresh water and freshly shucked corn-on-the-cob — waiting for him. Once he was inside his cage and happily attacking the corncob, I closed the cage door behind him, locking him in for the night.

Irwin, I would later learn, was a Senegal Parrot of the subspecies *Poicephalus senegalus senegalus*, whose native range includes southern Mauritania and southern Mali. According to a report on the European ban on African bird exports, the Niger River makes Mali one of the most biodiverse and bird-rich countries in Africa. "Along the banks of the Niger River," the report states, "the birds are so thick that dozens can be captured in a morning with nothing more than a simple net and patience, and the quick wrists of men who have been catching birds for several generations."

The Senegal Parrot, which has only recently been bred in captivity, has become the most popular Poicephalus parrot in aviculture. Hand-reared Senegal Parrots, which cost from $250 to $700, depending on whether bought from a breeder or a retail store, are said to make excellent pets, because they are curious, comical, acrobatic, and generally sweet. Wild-caught Senegal Parrots, on the other hand, do not make good pets because they do not become tame and they will always remain frightened of humans.

Irwin, surely a locally caught wild Poicephalus, must have been the exception to this rule. He showed no fear toward me. When I opened his cage in the morning, he would cock his head quizzically, as if to say, *"Where have you been?"* then puff out his chest and stroll slowly out his front door, past me, into his mango-tree kingdom. I was merely the gatekeeper, there to do his bidding.

In time, my courtyard became a haven, a true sanctuary, for all sorts of birds. Birds of all sizes and colors and songs — pigeon-like birds, bluebird-looking birds, tiny red birds, yellow weavers — all came (but not at once) to drink and bathe at the birdbath I positioned in the center of the courtyard, beneath the branches of Irwin's mango tree. It was a joy for me, as I sat in my study, to watch them, listen to them, and know that they felt safe coming to my house, that it was as much an oasis for them as it was for me.

As I observed them, I began to understand how people could become avid bird watchers. Birds are natural performers, dazzling the earth-bound with their envious abilities to swoop through the air, float on a thermal current, perch on a branch far above the fray, *fly*. Irwin, sadly, couldn't fly, but he had the power to attract other performers to his stage. Wild green parrots, even more beautiful and majestic than Irwin, with their bright red hooked beaks and long turquoise tails (could they have been males and Irwin, in fact, *female?* — the thought briefly flitted through my mind), would occasionally swoop by Irwin's cage to visit early in the morning before I'd opened his door.

These visitors usually arrived in two's, screeching and flapping and circling, then sitting for long moments on the sturdy stick that extended from Irwin's cage — facing him, beak to beak, as if kissing. As their loud (but not angry) parrot-to-parrot conversations continued, I tried to conjure a translation. Were they saying, "Let us in (to share what's left of your corn-on-the-cob)"? or "Please come out (to hunt/play/eat/make love) with us"? Whichever, they ultimately tired of having their requests denied, so they took off — WHOOSH — two streaks of green against the morning's azure sky.

After these visits, my funny little plump parrot looked deflated and downhearted sitting there alone in his cage. Instead of his standard freedom plea — "Come and let me out of here so I can take my daily stroll!" — he became uncharacteristically quiet. Was he sad that he couldn't fly off with his newfound friends? He seemed to mourn the truth of his clipped wings.

In time, like an errant lover, Irwin sometimes failed to return, and I'd be left to worry, the way I used to worry when Youssef didn't come home. At sunset, I would wait for Irwin, then call to him, and look for him among the high branches. I'd leave his cage door open, with his waiting dinner inside, just in case his absence was voluntary and he might change his mind. If, at dawn, I saw that he was safely back in his cage, my heart would sing and I'd forgive his errant ways.

But in mid-April, 2000, Irwin was gone for days. At one point I could see him, his small, leaf-like body silhouetted against the clear blue sky, at the top of the tallest mango tree in my courtyard. What could he be living on, I wondered — green mangoes? Isn't he thirsty? Why is he staying away?

"Irwiiiiiin," I called to him sweetly, "come hoo-ooome. I've got nice corn and water for you here!"

He wouldn't budge. The tree was too tall for me to climb. I didn't have a net. I couldn't get to him or recapture him. I could not enforce my will on him, force him to come back to me. He was free to choose his own destiny.

Two days later, after watering the courtyard garden, Pierre brought me Irwin's body. Pierre had found him, already dead, clinging to the top of his cage. He turned Irwin's body in his filthy outstretched hands to show me there was no sign that Irwin had been attacked by predators. Pierre's theory was that Irwin had died of dehydration: He'd waited too long to come back to the water bowl in his cage.

I felt as sad as a small child at the death of her favorite pet. But the stubborn, independent grownup in me understood: Irwin had chosen liberty; he simply refused to be caged.

- - - - - - - - - - - -

I was determined to stay in Mali, to work with Ségouvian seam-stresses, to teach them the patchwork quilting they wanted so much to learn. The problem was, however, that I didn't know how to go about turning my burning determination into a viable reality. My temporary work visa in Mali was about to expire, the sublet of my New York apart-ment — which was the source of my small monthly income — was about to end, and I had no one I could turn to for financial backing. Would my country, I wondered, help me? Would it, could it, renew my visa and provide the support I required to make the Patchwork Project a reality? Would it aid my efforts to teach these Malian women the Amer-ican craft of quilting, which could prove potentially profitable for them? I took my time and wrote a long letter to the American Embassy.

"Patchwork quilting," I stated in my request for support, "is an art and craft born of necessity and practicality by American pioneers. Like these American pioneers, clever Malian women are determined to use every available scrap and remnant possible to create better lives for themselves and their families."

I explained to the U.S. Embassy that I was an American develop-ment worker and recent Peace Corps volunteer (Gabon, 1996-1998) who had been working with women artisans in Ségou for the past year. "Among other projects, I teach senior members of a women's sewing center — *Centre de Formation Feminin Benkady Coupe Couture*, Pelen-gana — once a week," I told them. "These talented women, after having seen the patchwork quilts I've made, which hang on my living room walls here in Ségou, are extremely interested in acquiring this addition-al skill and are anxious for me to teach them as soon as possible.

"Though I cannot claim to be an expert," I confessed, "I am indeed passionate about patchwork quilting and would like nothing more than to spend my time teaching the women at Centre Benkady. The reality is, however, that quilting is a painstaking craft, rather compli-cated to teach, and requiring a commitment of time I am not at the moment in a position to make.

"Since completing my Peace Corps service, I have been living in Ségou on my own funds in order to continue the gratifying work I'd started as a secondary project at my post in Gabon — teaching crafts and cooking at women's centers. Although, thanks to my Peace Corps experience, I've learned how to live simply in Africa — on little money, with no car, no telephone, and so on — my funds are nevertheless dwindling, and I cannot continue to deplete them.

"Rather than leave Mali and abandon the worthwhile work I've begun here, I am now seeking support in my efforts to help Malian women artisans. Specifically, I would like a sum presenting one year's basic living allowance, roughly the equivalent of $5,000, which will allow me to stay in Ségou another year (Jan.-Dec. 2000, at least) and devote my time and energy toward creating a quilting project which will show tangible results by the end of next year.

"Ségou, in the heart of habitable Mali, is also at the heart of Mali's cotton textile industry," I continued. "With so much colorful African fabric to choose from, and with the determination of these able, industrious Malian women, I am sure we can produce quilted items — in all sizes and price ranges, from tote bags and baby quilts to bed covers — that combine both American and Malian pioneer ingenuity and that will attract appreciative buyers both near and far.

"To the best of my knowledge," I concluded, "patchwork quilting has not been done in Mali. I would like very much for our Centre Benkady in Pelengana, Ségou, to be the first. Could you please help?"

This is the way God works, I thought to myself as I biked the several miles in the broiling heat to Ségou's post office in *centreville*, dodging potholes and pedestrians the whole way, with my letter to the American Embassy safely tucked inside my backpack. *God plants an idea for something positive, creative, helpful, or useful in a willing person's mind and heart and then provides the means and methods for making it happen. Faith is trusting that God will make it happen, knowing that it will indeed happen if it is God's will. "Inshallah,"* as Malian Muslims say about all future plans: *If Allah wills, it will come to pass. The Patchwork Project will come to be,* inshallah.

The post office building, one among the many visibly aging, colonial-era buildings in Ségou that line the Niger, is more spacious than its present needs require. Few people, it appeared to me when I visited it regularly to get my mail, used its services. Postage for outgoing mail was more costly than most Ségouvians could afford, and few among them relied on written communication anyway. Theirs was an oral tradition.

Packages that arrived at *La Poste* were held hostage; one had to pay dearly to claim them. Most of the mail I received reached me months after it was sent, and almost all of it had been tampered with. The envelopes showed clear signs of having been steamed open and resealed sloppily with glue or tape, or both.

"This is against the law in my country," I said testily in French one day to the one sleepy clerk on duty, as I pounded an angry finger at the evidence of smeared glue on the back of the envelope. In addition to being irritable, I was also hot, tired, thirsty, and dirty from my four-mile bike ride in the midday heat.

The clerk looked at me coolly as if to say, "Then go back to your own country," and shrugged her shoulders.

"I am not blaming *you*," I added quickly, realizing the powerful hold she held over my mail, my lifeline to the outside world. "I'm sure this tampering takes place in Bamako."

Youssef had told me that he suspected there were pros at the main post office in Bamako who supplemented their salaries this way. They scoop up incoming mail, especially from "rich" USA, going to "rich" Americans living in Mali, Youssef had claimed, hide it in a satchel, take it home, steam each one open, reap whatever harvest they can in terms of worthwhile (especially monetary) enclosures, reseal it with messy glue, then take it to work at the post office the next day — or whenever they get around to it — and send it on its way.

Despite its drawbacks, I was dependent on the Malian postal system and grateful for the mail I did receive. Although the World Wide Web, still in its relative infancy, was growing exponentially elsewhere in the world, it hadn't yet enveloped me. I didn't own a computer, and although it was rumored that a cybercafé was to open soon in Ségou, "soon" seemed like a long way off.

The day I mailed my letter to the American Embassy, I had to trust that they would in fact receive it, read it, take my request seriously, and reply to me promptly — and, I hoped, affirmatively. This took all the hope and trust I could muster.

- - - - - - - - - - - -

On the days I received mail or, especially, packages from friends, it felt like Christmas morning to me. Books, in particular, reached me without a hitch because who at the Bamako *Poste* would want to steal a *book*, much less one written in *English*? One day, when I opened a package I'd just paid to receive, I saw a newly published book, sent by my friend Paul in New York, who knew of my hopes to teach quilting in Ségou. The book was *Hidden in Plain View: A Secret Story of Quilts and the Underground Railroad*, by Jacqueline Tobin and Raymond Dobard. I couldn't wait to bike home and begin reading it.

This book, I soon learned, proposed a controversial theory: that antebellum slaves used quilts as maps indicating routes to Canada and freedom. According to quilt scholar Cuesta Benberry in her Foreword, authors Tobin and Dobard establish "a significant linkage between the Underground Railroad effort, escaping slaves, and the American patchwork quilt." The Quilt Code, which this book deciphers, was, says Benberry, "a mystery-laden, secret communication system of employing quiltmaking terminology as a message map for black slaves escaping on the Underground Railroad."

This revelation struck me like a dazzling epiphany: For my Patchwork Project quilting classes I could teach the same patchwork designs that were used in the Underground Railroad Quilt Code, outlined in this book. We could come full circle — making "freedom" quilts for Americans that would in turn help provide economic freedom for these Malian women.

Controversial theory or not, the Quilt Code felt right to me. I could see Harriet Tubman, the escaped slave, who was herself a quilter, leading more than three hundred other slaves to freedom along the Underground Railroad. I could see this courageous, latter-day Moses enlisting other slave-quilters in her surreptitious efforts.

- - - - - - - - - - - -

A South Carolina Plantation, early 1850s

One sunny Sunday afternoon in autumn, while her grandchildren were playing outside and she was inside sewing, there was a knock on Jeneba's cabin door. The woman Jeneba saw there was a stranger to her, small of stature, dressed completely in black as if in disguise. The woman wore a wide-brimmed black bonnet, tied under the chin, which hid her face, and a long-sleeved black satin dress, cinched at the waist, that reached to the dusty ground. Only her small, brown, leathery hands folded together in front of her proved she was African.

"Yes?" Jeneba said, wondering who this could be and what she might want. Jeneba was unused to visitors on a Sunday afternoon, when most of the others were resting at home in their beds from their weeklong field labors. Was the woman in black a missionary from somewhere, here to convince Jeneba to attend her church services? Jeneba wondered, Who could have told her I don't go to church?

"I saw your beautiful quilt airing in the window," the woman said, looking up at Jeneba with small, brown, piercing eyes. "It called to me. May I come in?"

The two women sat together at Jeneba's table and talked for a long time. At first, they talked about quilting. The woman told Jeneba she too was a quilter. When she said she admired Jeneba's quilting skills, Jeneba opened an old wooden trunk and showed her the multicolored quilts she'd made for herself over the years.

"They are my griots," Jeneba told her. "They speak for me. They tell my story."

"What is your story?" the woman asked, leaning forward and pinning Jeneba with those eyes. "Tell me in words."

No one had ever asked this of Jeneba before.

"I come from the Kingdom of Mali," she said. "My village was beside the Niger River. I was captured when I was just a child and brought here. I was bought by Mr. Wilson, the rich man who owns this plantation. My children are his."

As Jeneba spoke truths she had never shared with anyone, the woman listened as though she had nothing in this world better to do. Jeneba felt compelled to continue. "My firstborn, Beau, has gone North. Mr. Wilson sent him North for an education, and now he works as a cotton merchant in New York City. My son is a free man now — and rich, I'm told. He writes to Mr. Wilson but not to me. He knows I cannot read. I fear he is lost to me — and to the ancestors — forever.

The woman nodded as if she understood. Her eyes begged Jeneba to go on.

"My daughter Amelie was sent away when she was only fifteen. Wilson gave her as a wedding gift to his eldest white daughter when that daughter got married and moved to Texas. My Amelie was a seamstress like me. She learned it all from me. That quiet little girl was always by my side. Wilson said to me, 'Every plantation needs a fine seamstress like you, Jemima!' before he pulled her away from me. The day he took her away, he took the last fragment of my heart.

"My youngest child, Carolina, is here. She is married and has two little children. I care for Carolina's children when she is out working in the fields."

Jeneba could not go on. She sat back in her chair and shook her head, exhausted by the words she'd had to pull up, as if out of a deep, old, abandoned well.

Then the child-size woman in the long black dress told Jeneba her own story: that she was a fugitive slave from a place far north of here called Maryland, and that her life's mission had become to escort other slaves to freedom on the Underground Railroad. She was here, she told Jeneba in a whisper, on such a mission now.

Jeneba watched the woman's wizened face and listened to her earnest words, but her mind could not make sense of all that she was hearing. A railroad without wheels or iron tracks? Underground, yet through the woods, streams, and cotton fields? What kind of mission was this? Was this woman in the smooth black dress, sitting stiffly at Jeneba's rough wooden table, touched in the head, or even a witch?

Jeneba had seen with her own eyes what happens to runaway slaves. In the many years since she was brought to this plantation, she'd witnessed a handful of attempted escapes. Each of them were unbridled young men without a plan who had taken off on their own at night on foot — without so much as food to eat or a blanket against the cold — and who were tracked down by patrolmen with guns and bloodthirsty dogs and brought back within days. Each time, everyone in the slaves' quarters, even the children, were forced to watch the returned runaway's punishment: He was tied, naked, face-forward to a tree and whipped by Mr. Wilson personally, until the young man's back and buttocks and legs were no longer recognizable as parts of a man's body. They were raw, red meat.

The last time this happened, when Beau was just a boy, Jeneba had tried to shield his eyes and pull him into her skirt with the other little ones, but Beau stepped away. He kept his eyes fixed, not on the boy being whipped (that boy was only in his teens), but on the man doing the whipping. Beau watched transfixed, it seemed, by the man's strength, the snap of his right wrist, the righteous determination on his flushed face, his holy admonitions, "You must obey me! I am Mister Wilson, your Master!" That whipped teenage boy never again disobeyed. Just weeks later he died of infection caused by his wounds.

"People here don't speak of running away," Jeneba told the woman at her table. "We are too afraid of our owner, Master Wilson. Or, if some do talk among themselves about escaping, they don't tell me. They know he is the father of my children…"

"But you can help me help others," the woman in black said. "I know you can keep the secret."

Then the woman got up from her chair, took a charred stick from the hearth and used it to draw geometric designs on Jeneba's wood plank floor. As she did so, she asked Jeneba boldly: Could you piece these designs into patchwork blocks and use those blocks to make a quilt face? Could you display this coded quilt face outside your cabin window, the way you display your own quilt creations? Could you let another griot sing?

Her intensity frightened Jeneba, and her words confused her. What could quilts have to do with a railroad? What story would these griots tell? And what were the risks to her and her children of getting involved in this madwoman's scheme?

This woman, this former slave in her fancy-Sunday-dress disguise, was clearly courageous, though, if, as she said, she traveled into treacherous territory seeking to blaze escape routes for slaves to follow to freedom in Can-

ada. Jeneba knew she herself was not as brave. Her world stretched only as far as the nearby cotton fields. She had no strength left to venture farther.

"Your coded quilts will show others the way," the woman said, as if reading Jeneba's doubts and fears. "You need not do or say or know anything more. Your quilts will tell the 'passengers' that they are on the right track. This star," she pointed to the eight-pointed star design she'd drawn on Jeneba's floor, "this north star will point the way. You will be a silent 'agent' on the Underground Railroad."

In all this urgent talk, the two women had not even introduced themselves. The woman's given name, she told Jeneba, was Araminta, but she later took her mother's name, Harriet. "My full name is Harriet Tubman, but people call me Moses," she said with a slight smile. It was the first time she'd smiled the whole afternoon. Jeneba smiled back at her.

"All right, Moses," Jeneba said. "I will let your griots sing."

- - - - - - - - - - - - -

"The Patchwork Project is a source of development in Ségou…
to help us to fight poverty. I believe that if we create an association,
we will be well organized to continue this art, to teach new people,
and to work in a timely manner on the orders that come in."

— KORO TRAORE, Patchwork Project graduate
(translated from the French)

Pioneers

WHEN THE RAINY SEASON ARRIVED, I sometimes woke to find Pierre robotically watering the garden.

"Pierre?" I called to him trying mightily to suppress my irritation and frustration. Pierre = Peter = stone. I felt I was addressing a stone.

"Oui?" he answered me sleepily.

From the screened window of my study I watched the raindrops drip down his childlike face and drench his filthy, tattered T-shirt as he watered the flowers and plants in the window box below the window.

"Il pleut" (it's raining), I said with forced composure.

"Oui."

"Ce n'est pas necessaire a arroser" (it's not necessary to water).

"Ah, bon?" (Oh, really?)

"Oui. Dieu arrose pour toi" (God is watering for you). I pointed to heaven and made hand movements as if accompanying the children's "Teensy-Weensy Spider" song: *Down came the rain and washed the spider out.*

"Ah, bon! D'accord" (Oh, good. Okay), he said as the rain pattered on his head.

Dear God, I prayed, *how can I wash this spider out?*

- - - - - - - - - - - -

Pierre had become a hot topic in my letters home. I wrote about his frequent watering-in-the-rain episodes and the time I returned from a two-day trip to Bamako to find that my "guardian" Pierre had not bothered to show up. He'd left the house "in God's care," he told me, the same God, presumably, who had done him the favor of watering the garden. I wrote, too, about the time Pierre fell asleep with a lit kerosene lamp perched precariously beside him on his bed. When I, who slept far less soundly than Pierre did, saw this and woke him, he jumped up, accidentally knocking the lamp over, nearly causing a fire.

In a letter to my friend Marty in New York, whose tolerance in such matters would be even more scant than mine, I wrote, "I know what you're thinking: *Get another guardian, for God's sake!* In fact, I've tried. The reality is that younger, stronger, smarter, cleaner, nicer-smelling guys here have more exciting things to do with their nights than guard *toubobs'* houses. They don't want these jobs. They wouldn't show up half the time." Pierre, at least, showed up almost all of the time.

- - - - - - - - - - - -

In my heart, though, I grappled with deeper, darker issues that haunted me. Didn't I *love* Africa, especially Mali? Wasn't I a good person who tried to see the best in everyone? Hadn't I learned by this time how to surmount cultural differences? I began to seriously doubt all of these things. I berated myself for my rigidity, lack of tolerance, revulsion toward filth, and impatience with stupidity.

I vented on paper: "Pierre makes me mad. Seeing this lazy, stupid, dirty, smelly man first thing in the morning upon waking puts me in a foul frame of mind. His laziness and stupidity make me angry, but instead of blowing up at him, I just get knots in my stomach. I wish he would go. Just go."

At times, I attempted empathy. Where did Pierre spend his days? Did he have family? Did anyone feed him decent food, the kind most Malians ate at midday every day — rice with tasty gumbo sauce and chunks of sweet potato and meat or fish? Did anyone care for him, love him? Coulibaly was a common name in Ségou. Surely he had family. Why did he seem so lost? Was he mentally deficient? A castoff in his own society? That couldn't be. Malians are noted for their tolerance toward all fellow human beings; tolerance is written in their laws, sung in their national anthem, part of their national pride. They would never reject him.

Perhaps Pierre was just uneducated. Although public primary education in Mali was now free of charge and compulsory, this may well not have been so when Pierre was a child. Maybe he, like a large percentage of adults in this economically disadvantaged country, had never been to school. Perhaps he'd never learned how to question, how to think.

I tried to imagine what it must be like to have had no formal education, to be illiterate — not brain-dead but brain-empty. When I thought of my own schooling and all the books that had filled my mind and shaped my life and my worldview, all of the teachers who had influenced me, all of the discipline involved in learning how to learn, and I compared that with the majority of Malians who had had none of this, I couldn't even imagine that void.

- - - - - - - - - - - -

Despite my best efforts in dealing with Pierre, my resentment toward him grew. When he asked for the night before Easter off to attend an all-night church service, and I used my life-size, storyteller puppet, Jelimuso Jeneba, as my "guardian," covering her body with a blanket in the chaise lounge on my front porch, knowing she would sleep through a break-in just as well as Pierre would, I briefly considered hiring her for the job.

I began to wonder who was guarding whom. Was Pierre really guarding me? Physically, I was bigger and stronger than he was and quite possibly more fearless. I'd always felt, since early childhood, watching my father attack my mother in a drunken rage, that if any man ever tried to attack me, *he'd* be the one with the most wounds.

And what was there to guard? The only thing I owned of value was my bike, the Specialized Hybrid I'd bought in New York ten years before for $400, which I kept chained to my bed and locked in my bedroom when not in use. How could anyone take that?

What was the worst that could happen? Would someone want to kill me? Well, then, let him. I've never been afraid to die. And when you're not afraid to die, you're not afraid of much at all; you're less vulnerable than most are to potential predators.

In the time I'd lived in Mali, I had always felt safe. Even when the U.S. Embassy sent out warnings about a Muslim fanatic by the name of Osama bin Laden, who was encouraging African Muslims to murder Americans, I scarcely paid attention. The vast majority of the people I met in Mali were remarkably kind, polite, law-abiding, alms-giving, non-drinking and God-fearing citizens. But perhaps that was because I'd had Youssef to shield me from those who might do harm. Perhaps he'd been my guardian after all.

"There are evil spirits here," the rebellious teenage son of one of my Benkady friends said to me ominously one evening when I visited her home some time after Youssef had left.

"There are evil spirits everywhere," I countered. "But I believe the spirit of goodness is stronger."

- - - - - - - - - - - - -

By September, six months after Youssef left Ségou, I began to think that he might have been right. Maybe I wouldn't be able to live in Mali without him. Maybe one day soon I would have to go. But not right away. Before that day came, it would be Pierre who would go.

I walked out into the courtyard early one morning in mid-September as Pierre was preparing to water the plants, handed him a 5,000 CFA note, and asked him to pack his things.

"*D'accord,*" he said quietly with a bow, as if that were just what he was hoping for all along.

- - - - - - - - - - - - -

MY HOPES REMAINED HIGH that the American Embassy would respond positively to my impassioned request for support and provide the Patchwork Project with material aid under their established Self-Help program. *How could they possibly refuse?* I optimistically believed. *After all, this is* American *patchwork I'm hoping to teach for the economic betterment of the women of Mali; it's an ideal link between our two countries.*

In November 1999, I had traveled to Bamako to meet face to face with the *Coordinatrice de Projets* (Project Coordinator) at the U.S. Embassay, a tall, handsome, middle-aged Malian woman named Alice Adjibi. When I showed her the patchwork samples I'd brought with me — the wall hangings, tote bag, pillow covers, and quilted checkerboard — and reiterated the points I'd made in my support request, Alice seemed genuinely impressed. She appeared to see immediately the value and suitability of the project for Ségou's talented seamstresses. She explained in a mixture of French and English that I'd come at a good time — "*un bon moment!*" — because she was preparing for next year's budget to be submitted to the U.S. Congress in January, and she felt that my Patchwork Project was indeed a worthy idea.

The catch was, she said, that they don't give money, especially to individuals to live on; they give material aid only. My task, she explained, was to list all our material needs and provide the embassy with pro forma receipts — proof of prices from specific vendors in Mali. "If the project is approved" — and Alice gave every indication she thought it would be — "the embassy will buy the materials listed and give them to your project," she said.

For the duration of my short stay in Bamako, then, I plodded along the overcrowded, dusty, pot-holed streets of the labyrinthine city in over 100-degree heat, gathering the requisite pro forma receipts from willing shopkeepers in tiny, out-of-the-way shops — for sewing machines, fabric, sewing supplies, and even batting — to give to Alice. Modern quilting supplies, such as rotary cutters, heavy-duty plastic rulers, and cutting mats, were not available in Mali, I knew, so I would have to request them directly from friends in the States.

The German government, I came to learn, was more disposed toward helping artisinal projects with financial aid that the U.S. government was. So on another trip to Bamako, in early December, I met with the *Conseiller Technique* of the German nongovernmental organization FNAM *(Federation Nationale des Artisans du Mali)*, Dieter Gagel.

Sitting across from him as he sat behind a dented metal desk in his hangar-like offices at the outskirts of town, I listened carefully while he explained in fast French the history and purpose of FNAM. This ONG, he told me, was created in 1989, to assist what was then only nineteen associations of artisans from Bamako as well as other regions of Mali. "Today," he said, "we're proud to help hundreds of artisinal associations throughout the country."

I smiled and nodded, filling with hope that my project would meet their criteria. I showed him the patchwork samples I'd shown to Alice Adjibi, but his eyes failed to light up as hers had. I explained to him the appeal of patchwork quilts to the American market and the genesis of the Patchwork Project in Ségou. But this tall, slim, balding, fair-skinned German man registered no emotion.

Feeling I had nothing to lose, I came close to begging. I told him I needed financial help in order to continue the project, and I needed an ONG's backing in order to renew my work visa, otherwise I would have to leave Mali early next year.

He studied me, silently. I filled in the silence with desperate prattle.

"I'm half German," I said, grasping to make a connection. "My mother's parents left Germany for the United States at the turn of the century. My German grandfather was from Bremerhaven. He was a sailor in the German Navy under Kaiser Wilhelm. I never knew him; he died when I was two--"

"I'd like to see a budget," Gagel said. "And a syllabus for your course. And your résumé. Maybe we can help you. But I can't promise." He told me to come back in late January, after he returned from his Christmas holidays in Germany, at which time he might have an answer for me.

- - - - - - - - - - - - -

In late December, I mailed Gagel all that he'd requested — a proposed budget, including a half-year's salary of 700,000 CFA (about $1,100), my résumé, plus a lesson-by-lesson outline for the sixteen-week Patchwork Project *formation des formatrices* (teacher-training course) I hoped to offer twice in 2000 — from February to May, and from September to December. At the same time, I wrote to Alice Adjibi at the U. S. Embassy, providing her with my résumé and course outline, too, in addition to all of the *factures* pro forma she'd requested.

"Well, here it is," I announced cheerily in my letter to Alice, "everything I've been able to gather for your Self-Help program. I'm writing this letter in English for the sake of your Self-Help committee — made up mainly of Americans, I assume — to better communicate the importance of my Patchwork Project and the urgency of its receiving assistance as soon as possible." Then, in single-spaced type, I listed the points I hoped Alice would share with her fellow-decision-makers at the American Embassy:

• The art and craft of patchwork quilting, which is now enjoying great vogue in the United States and Europe, has not, to the best of my knowledge, been done in Mali.

• Mali is a leading producer of cotton, and cotton is the fabric used in patchwork quilting. Lively, vibrant, African-print cotton textiles used in patchwork quilted items made here would be enormously appealing to the many quilt lovers and collectors of the world.

• There are many Malian women artisans here in Ségou who are extremely anxious for me to teach them this art and craft so that they might make beautiful items that they could sell on the world market (via the Internet, for example).

• The course I have designed, if followed strictly, would prepare these Malian women not only to do patchwork quilting but also, ideally, to teach the craft to other groups of interested Malian women artisans.

• This course will take 16 weeks. Realistically speaking, it must begin in February 2000, because the months of June through August are unproductive here (that is, there might be a severe drop in attendance when families go off to plant their fields); plus, the weather then is too uncomfortably hot to be working on quilts. The same 16-week course would be offered again beginning in September.

• I have been working in Ségou for the past year as an independent volunteer, living on my own funds. (For the previous two years I was a Peace Corps Volunteer in Gabon.) By February of this coming new year, however, my savings will have just about been depleted. If I do not receive outside help in time, I may well not be able to afford to stay in Mali and continue this important project.

• After the first year, when the course graduates — the best of whom, ideally, will have become *formatrices* — have perfected this new craft and are making and selling world-class patchwork-quilted items, the women should be in a position to use the profits from their sales to replenish the stock of fabric, batting, and other quilting necessities that were provided initially by your Self-Help program. In other worlds, the project is designed to be entirely self-sustainable.

144

• I can envision the day, in only a few years from now, when the women artisans of Ségou, Mali, will be *célèbre* for their beautiful, colorful, creative patchwork. And the American Embassy's Self-Help program will have made it possible.

- - - - - - - - - - - - -

In late January 2000, I made another trip to Bamako. Dieter Gagel at FNAM was, his secretary told me, in a conference all week; but he had come through. He had approved my project, giving me a one-year contract; he had signed the documents that would allow me to renew my Malian visa, and he'd issued a check to me for 700,000 CFA for me to live on.

When I went to the U.S. Embassy to see Alice Adjibi again, she assured me there should be "no problem" in getting the Self-Help aid. It was just a matter of waiting, she said — for the U.S. Congress to decide on a budget, and for the higher-ups at the Embassy in Bamako to decide how their portion of the budget should be spent.

I continued to wait. And hope.

- - - - - - - - - - - - -

"Greatly begin!" the 19th-century poet James Russell Lowell admonished. His urging wafted back to me from some long-past poetry class as I prepared to plunge ahead with the first, formal, sixteen-week patchwork-quilting course for the senior members of Centre Benkady. I couldn't remember Lowell's whole poem, but the ending came to me: "Not failure, but low aim is crime."

I was aiming high, I knew, but I was committed and determined. Failure was not an option. Dieter Gagel of the *Federation Nationale des Artisans du Mali* had already given me a six-month salary of roughly $1,100 to teach a carefully structured, professional-level, teacher-training course; and I felt I could not let him, his German organization, nor the Malian women of Benkady down. Although I was still waiting to hear from the American Embassy about their material aid, I knew I had to forge ahead with my weekly lessons on faith.

As I wrote to my sister Heather, "I'm hopeful the Self-Help program of the U.S. Embassy will come through with the equipment (tables, chairs, sewing machines, fabric batting, etc.) we've requested for my Patchwork Project, but my classes will start this month, equipment or no equipment.

"It should be challenging to teach a craft I've only just learned — in *French*, a language I can still barely speak — to a group of women who've never been to school and who prefer their own language (Bambara) to French!

"The Koran says, 'Allah is with those who are patient' (2:154). When I think about teaching my patchwork course, I think about how much patience I'll need to bridge the culture gap. But I have high hopes. Didn't D. H. Lawrence say something about human beings needing only two things for happiness — love and a crusade? Well, this is my love-crusade."

- - - - - - - - - - - -

On the morning of February 18, 2000, the first official day of my Patchwork Project, there was a power outage and therefore no electricity, so I couldn't iron the pretty cotton outfit I'd planned to wear. The bottled gas for my oven had run out the night before, and I had no way to replace it, so I had to try to bake cookies and cornbread in a big marmite over a wood fire outside. *One must adapt*, I told myself, trying to stay upbeat; *at least there is water, so I can bathe and brush my teeth*.

In most ways, I felt prepared: I'd made lots of notes, rehearsed my "lecture," gathered all my examples. I hoped to make a *fête* out of our first class — serve tea with my homemade cornbread and oatmeal cookies, play Malian music on the radio (if and when the electricity was restored). I didn't know what else to do besides pray that it would succeed. I repeated to myself a passage from the Koran: "Fortify yourself with patience and prayer..."

"Vous êtes les pionnieres!" (you are pioneers!), I told the eight women who attended Lesson 1 held at my home. "You are the first to take this course in patchwork quilting, which will train you to teach other women artisans how to make beautiful patchwork items that will be appreciated, marketed, and acquired both near and far!" The women, elegantly dressed for the occasion in multicolored, flowing *boubous* and matching head wraps, sat on my living room sofa and chairs, bare feet crossed at the ankles, and listened respectfully as I tried my best, in faltering French, to outline what lay ahead for them and solicit their commitment.

Already I could see a potential pitfall: attendance. For Malian women, I'd learned, the first and biggest commitment they have is always their family. Domestic demands supersede everything else in their lives. For this, our first lesson, I had expected eleven women; but only eight could make it. Three were missing, due to circumstances beyond their control.

Hawa, recently widowed, was still under the religious stricture of a four-month seclusion. Mah, whose husband had recently taken a second wife, had to drop out at the last minute due to both complications from a miscarriage she had just had, plus a sick child. Delphine had planned to attend our first lesson but had a last-minute emergency at home: Her maid had seriously injured herself while chopping firewood that morning and had to be rushed to the hospital.

For the most part, the eight who came — including Ami Sylla, Sali Traore, Fily Diallo, Marie Diarra, Tennin Traore, Ami Keita, Sara Diarra, and Ramata N'Djaye — seemed to be following what I was saying, despite my imperfect spoken French and their uneven understanding of a language they essentially disliked (because it was the language of their colonizers) and seldom had reason to use. Sara Diarra, a new member of Centre Benkady who was new to me, and Ami Keita, who'd shown herself to be a bright and earnest student in previous crafts classes I'd given at Benkady, sat with their new babies in their laps. Sara's baby daughter, Fatimata, and Ami's baby son, Modibo, slept soundly throughout my speech. Tennin looked at me with sleepy, half-closed eyes, her mouth partially open. Ramata, whose humingbirdlike energy made it impossible for her to sit still, whispered to the others (perhaps translating some words into Bambara?) and fidgeted in her seat while I spoke.

"Le patchwork est une oeuvre, comme l'art, qui est façonné de differentes morceaux de tissues, cousu selon un dessin," (patchwork is an artistic production made of different pieces of fabric sewed according to a design), I read from my notes in French. *"Le «quilting» est l'operation qui permet de fixer les trois epaisseurs du «sandwich» — la «face» en patchwork, le molleton interieur, et le «dos» — par coudre à la main ou à la machine sur les traits predessines.»* («Quilting» fixes the three layers — the patchwork «face», the interior batting, and the backing — by hand- or machine-sewing along pre-marked lines).

These women, I knew, had never even seen a bed-size patchwork quilt, much less used one to keep themselves warm at night. Like its days, Mali's nights, too, were punishingly hot most of the year. Even the season Malians generously called "winter" didn't call for bedcovers at night. Most people slept outdoors on straw mats under millions of stars, hoping for an occasional breeze, in the safety of their walled-in compounds, year-round. So listening to me extol the warm-and-comforting virtues of patchwork quilts to people living in cold climates required of these women both imagination and trust. They had never known truly cold weather. They had to take my word for it.

"Les produits en patchwork sont très recherchés dans les pays froid, commes aux États-Unis et en Europe" (Patchwork items are much sought-after in cold countries, such as the United States and Europe), I told the women; and they listened, seemingly intrigued. *"Surtout, les couvre-lits en patchwork quilting — de bonne qualité — sont de grande valeur* (Patchwork bed quilts — *of good quality* — are especially valuable). *On peut demander environs 150,000 CFA pour un couvre-lit en patchwork quilting — de bonne qualité — fait ici au Mali"* (One could ask about $250 for a patchwork bed quilt *of good quality* made here in Mali). This price, perhaps reasonable by American standards, represented an enormous sum to these women — more than many Malians earned in a year — so their attention became riveted. *"Cette formation-ci vous prepare a faire les choses en patchwork de bonne qualité"* (This course will prepare you to make things in patchwork *of good quality*). I could see from their positive expressions, their wide eyes and occasional nods, that they clearly saw the value of this opportunity to themselves and their families.

I gave each woman an eight-page booklet I'd made for them, hand-lettered in French, including the "Ten Steps in Patchwork Quilting," which we would be following in our sixteen-week course. In it I also included a page illustrating the quilt code patterns purportedly used as "maps" in the Underground Railroad, and I briefly explained the symbolic and historical significance of each — such as the "Crossroads" pattern, or the "Bear's Paw," "Log Cabin," "Hour Glass," "North Star," and "Sail Boat" — in the American slaves' quest for freedom.

I also gave the women a list of the items they would be making for their individual homework assignments — a pillow cover, tote bag, wall hanging, and baby quilt — in addition to a larger class project requiring a team effort.

"This will be an American-style course," I warned them. "That is to say, it will be demanding." In order to receive a certificate of completion, I added, each student had to attend every class, participate in the satisfactory completion of all class projects, and submit a "personal, creative assignment" — a baby quilt of her own, original design.

Undaunted, the eight women present agreed to participate. Since I would be offering the same class twice a week — on Tuesday and Friday mornings from nine to noon at Centre Benkady — the women divided themselves into two groups, according to the day that best fit their personal and family schedules. If a woman could not, for whatever reason, join her own group one week, she was free to take that class with the other group.

Only after the women flew off on their *motos* at 11:30, looking like colorful birds with their *boubous* flapping behind them in the wind, was I able to exhale. I felt physically drained but spiritually exhilarated.

- - - - - - - - - - - -

Among the handful of friends and family members who supported my efforts in Mali was my cousin Jean in New Jersey. Jean, ten years older than I, was the only daughter of my father's only sibling, his sister Edythe. Jean and I had become estranged after my parents' divorce when I was in high school, but in recent years we had reconnected. She seemed proud of my humanitarian work in Africa and happy to help in any way she could.

In a letter thanking her for the gifts I'd received in the mail from her — a new Dritz rotary cutter with extra blades, a check for $100, and a lovely quilting book, *Montana Star Quilts* — I said:

"I just read the book you sent from cover to cover. I learned that in the late 19th century, when the Sioux were settled on reservations, buffalo became scarce, so the Native American craftswomen were forced to use imported textiles instead of buffalo hides. The Ladies Aid Society of the Dakota Presbyterian Church is said to have introduced quilt making on the various Indian reservations. Montana stars became the most popular quilt design among the Sioux.

"Believing as I do in the God of Art (as in folk art) and Culture (as in all kinds of cultures), I feel as if I've become a missionary for quilting, and I'm setting out to do for the women of Ségou what the Presbyterian ladies did for the Sioux. I wonder whether their mission seemed as daunting to them at first as mine does to me now?

"Last Friday was Lesson 1; this morning was Lesson 2, to be repeated to another group on Friday of this week. Lesson 1 was held in the comfort and relative luxury of my living room. Lesson 2 was at the women's center, where my classroom is a sort of hangar, where the wind blows through pane-less windows, scattering my notes and examples everywhere, knocking over the feeble blackboard and spewing dust on everything. I keep telling myself, *patience, patience, patience!*

"The women were attentive and certainly patient with me, but when I showed them the examples of the amazing Montana star quilts in the book, their eyes rolled. Yes, I have to admit, those star quilts look a little tricky to do. I've yet to attempt diamonds. I think we'll stick with the beginners' level 'variable star,' which uses squares and triangles only.

"Jeanie, did you know that this eight-pointed star is an ancient talismanic symbol, meant to provide protection against evil forces? The things quilting is teaching me!

"Once we get the material 'promised' by the U.S. Embassy's Self-Help program, which I'm hoping will be soon, we will set about making, as a class project, a mini-quilt wall hanging as a gift of thanks for the Embassy. The quilt I'm envisioning will be entitled 'Stars and Stripes Forever' (in French: *Les Etoiles et les raies pour toujours*) and will use this eight-pointed star design, plus various stripes of borders, all in colorful African-print fabric. I'm hoping to have each woman sign the star block she's made. ..."

- - - - - - - - - - - -

Subsequent lessons followed a predictable pattern: First, I took attendance, giving each woman who managed to arrive on time a gold star sticker next to her name in my attendance book. Then we reviewed the previous lesson and their homework from that lesson. Every woman who'd done the homework correctly received another star. (The woman with the most stars at the end of this first semester, they knew, would receive a special prize at our graduation ceremony.) Then I gave a lecture and demonstration for that day's lesson, after which the women practiced making what I'd demonstrated.

Each week we walked through one of the ten steps outlined in their teacher-training booklet. *"Donni-donni"* (Bambara for "little-by-little"), I explained to the women how to:

1) Make a plan: Draw your design on graph paper first; decide on the item's purpose, dimensions, and colors. *"Avant que vous touchez le tissu, il faut faire un plan!"* (Before you touch the fabric, you must make a plan!), I stressed.

2) Choose and prepare your fabric: Choose 100% Malian cotton fabric; wash it (discarding any fabrics that bleed), iron it, and trim off all selvedges.

3) Following your design, cut pieces for the quilt face, allowing for quarter-inch seams. *"Découpez vos morceaux avec beaucoup de soin!"* (Cut the pieces with great care!), I urged them.

4) Sew your pieces into patchwork-design blocks, following the patterns given in your booklet. *"Cousez-les doucement et soigneusement avec une marge de ½ cm"* (Sew them slowly and carefully, with a seam allowance of one-half centimeter), I said.

5) Sew the blocks together; add borders.

6) Make the "sandwich" — patchworked top, batting, and backing — cutting the batting and backing slightly larger than the face.

7) Baste the "sandwich" together, using large, running stitches radiating from the center.

8) With chalk, mark the face with your chosen quilting design.

9) Quilt the item — by hand or by machine. *"Le quilting est un element decoratif qui contribue largement à la beauté du quilt"* (The decorative quilting stitches largely contribute to the beauty of the quilt), I said.

10) Finish the edges with bias binding. *"Est voilà! C'est fini!"*

- - - - - - - - - - - - -

To illustrate for the women the type of person who might want to commission a quilt from them, I wrote a letter as if from an African-American prospective customer whom I named Sally Jones. I pretended the time was two years hence and the letter had just arrived in the mail. I tried to put this imaginary letter into context, explaining how bereft African-Americans were for their roots, having descended from people who had been kidnapped — cruelly uprooted from their motherlands in Africa and brought to the U.S. to be sold as slaves — generations ago. I pulled the make-believe letter from my backpack, unfolded it theatrically, and translated from my typed English original into serviceable spoken French:

123 Fourth Street
Philadelphia, PA 19144
February 18, 2002

Dear Benkady Women:

Hello! My name is Sally Jones. I'm 24 years old and single. I live in Philadelphia, where I work as a nurse in a big hospital. I learned about your patch-work quilting on the Internet, and I'm interested in having you make a quilt for me.

I am African-American. I think my ancestors may have come from Mali. I would like very much to visit Mali; but it's so far away, and it costs so much to go there. Maybe if I marry a rich doctor one day we'll be able to travel to Mali together!

Anyway, since I can't afford to get there now, I thought you might be able to make a quilt for me that makes me feel that Mali has come to me – a beautiful, colorful quilt that makes me feel (when I'm in my big, cozy bed) that I'm being embraced by my ancestors.

Please choose fabrics, colors, and designs that you think are typical of Mali. The dimensions for the quilt should be 95"x 95". My bedroom is painted pale yellow, but I love bright colors!

I have a good salary and could pay up to about $250 for a good-quality quilt that I will cherish forev-er and maybe pass down to one of my future children. Please send me your design and fabric samples as soon as possible. I look forward to hearing from you.

Just think: If you make this "ancestors quilt" for me, all of my friends will want one too!

Sincerely,
Sally Jones

Inspired by Sally's letter, the women spent the rest of that class period drawing possible designs for Sally's quilt on the graph paper I provided, coloring in the blocks with crayons. We discussed among ourselves the colors that would best represent Mali: mango-leaf green, cloudless-sky blue, burning-sun yellow, clay-earth fawn-brown; maybe some streaks of wild-bird turquoise and sunset red. The fabric we would choose, the women decided, would primarily be *bazin* (damask), which they would hand-die to depict these specific, symbolic colors. And the overall design? Each woman drew what she thought Sally might like. Most of their designs contained eight-pointed stars, representing Mali's star-filled nights.

As I wrote to my sister Heather in a letter thanking her for the rotary cutter she'd just sent to us, "The women really got into planning Sally's quilt. It was exciting to see them at work at it. Who knows, maybe this Sally Jones really does exist, and this order-fulfillment could one day be a reality! This is my hope, my dream, my fantasy."

- - - - - - - - - - - - -

Two mornings a week I walked the mile from my home to Centre Benkady (and back) along *quartier* Pelengana's dusty roads, in 110-115 degree heat, weighted down by four bags of equipment and supplies too bulky to hang on the handlebars of my bike. I carried a few of my most colorfully illustrated quilting books, a big cutting board, the two rotary cutters my sister and cousin sent, several plastic rulers, large scraps of cotton fabric I'd collected in all sorts of colors, a long clothesline, a bag of plastic clothespins, a box of detergent, a box of colored chalk for Benkady's blackboard, a small box of crayons, a pad of graph paper, a supply of pencils, a jar of pushpins, and another jar of straight pins.

It was too risky, the women told me, to leave these things at Centre Benkady; they might mysteriously disappear one day. Even if they were to be locked away in a storage closet between my patchwork classes, chances were the person with the sole key to the closet would not be there when I arrived to teach. Besides, these were my own supplies, which I needed for the patchwork projects I worked on at home, addictively, every evening.

The classroom at Centre Benkady contained about a dozen old-fashioned treadle-type sewing machines in various states of disrepair and one rough-hewn parsons-type table, which, if it had been used for dining might have seated six people. The center had thread and scissors, and each woman brought to our classes as many fabric scraps as she could gather (which also earned her a gold star).

While I tried to teach my Tuesday- and Friday-morning groups, there were constant interruptions — young students streaming in to use the machines for other sewing projects or to ask questions, visitors stopping by to *"dit bonjour"* (say hello). It was hard at times to keep my Patchwork Project students focused on the task at hand.

In fact, the challenges mounted.

When I tried to explain that in patchwork quilting *"L'exactitude est crucial,"* I discovered that the concept was essentially untranslatable. The women looked at me blankly, as if I were speaking gibberish. Even when Ramata, Benkady's flighty president, tried to translate my words into Bambara for the whole class, the women seemed not to grasp it. *Exactitude?* The idea of *precision* seemed foreign to them in any language. *Crucial?* Nothing beyond God and their loved ones was of truly *critical* importance to them.

After several weeks of practicing the nine-patch design — *"le carré a neuf cases,"* also known as *"le carré magique,"* and *"le carré d'Allah,"* which they had made for their homework — I asked the women of Group 1 to draw the nine-patch design on graph paper. It took them ten minutes, and only two women in that day's five-member group got it right. Sleepy Tennin, instead of drawing a square divided into nine equal-size squares, drew a long rectangle containing twelve wobbly squares.

When, in a pop quiz, I asked Group 2 what the first step in patchwork quilting is [making a plan], none of them got the answer right, even though we'd reviewed all the steps on a regular basis. In another class, when we were calculating dimensions before cutting some fabric, I saw that no one could divide 24 by 3 or 65 cm by 2. I became more than a little discouraged; I became sad.

I found it difficult at times to be patient and tolerant when the women seemed so muddled and the simplest math was too hard for them. I had to force myself to step back, reflect, and remember that even in the better-educated United States many women would have difficulty designing their own original patchwork projects. These Malian women had never been given a firm educational foundation, and their lack of education clearly handicapped them in some ways. In many other ways, though, they possessed skills that I lacked. I had yet to learn, for example, how to be a more outgoing, sociable person — something Malian people excelled at. Try as I might, I could not change my introverted nature.

To boost my own morale as well as theirs, I sometimes gave pep talks, encouraging the women to think ahead to the day when orders for quilts would come in from the Sally Jones's of the world. How will you fulfill the orders if you don't have enough well-trained women? I asked them. How could you expect anyone to pay you well for the quilts they order from you if those quilts are not of good quality? I tried to be loving and encouraging: "God has given you the talent, the intelligence, the *capacité*." I said sincerely. "You must use these gifts; apply them to this course now."

I showed them a colorful patchworked *pagne* (wrap skirt) I'd found at the Ségou *marché* and bought for the equivalent of $1.50. I held it out, like a bullfighter's red cape, then turned it dramatically to show its flip side. "*Vous voyez*" (you see), I said, pointing out the higgledy-piggledy, slap-dash, mish-mash workmanship that had gone into making it, no doubt by a village tailor trying to hastily capitalize on discarded, misshapen scraps. "*Le patchwork? Oui. Mais, de bonne qualité?*" The women shook their heads like seasoned critics, and we all agreed, "*non!*" In fact, they told me I'd paid too much for it.

"*Il n'y a pas le developpement sans le changement*" (There is no development without change), I stressed. "The Patchwork Project is an *economic development* project. If you want to make real money making patchwork quilts, they must be made with great thought and care."

Did they understand the ramifications of what I was saying? Was I right in pushing for change?

At times — when only a few students showed up for class and not even on time — I became so discouraged I was tempted to throw up my hands. I wrestled in my heart and mind. *Perhaps, my thinking went, patchwork quilting is not for Africans. Maybe Africa is so underdeveloped because Africans are incapable of doing what it takes to "develop" in the Western sense — that is, change old behaviors, attitudes, and habits. It seems to me they like their way of life — the easy, slow, sociability of it — and they don't want to change. Fine. I'm not here to change people, only to offer a means by which these women could, possibly, earn good money by making patchwork quilts and selling them worldwide via the Internet. If it's not for them, and, God knows, patchwork quilting is not for everyone, at least I can say I tried. I must simply keep trying to do my best. As the Koran says, "Life is a test … do your best."*

- - - - - - - - - - - - -

And then there were days when my heart sang and danced: when all of the women arrived for class and proudly showed me their homework — each more colorful and creative than the next. Despite the fact that we still lacked supplies, and the women had to rely on their own resourcefulness and ingenuity — mostly at home where their husbands and children gave them little space and time — they managed to produce remarkable work. They were particularly proud of the nine-patch-design shoulder bags they'd made for themselves, as well as their large, eight-pointed-star wall hangings. When I told them that this star design, *"L'étoile a huit branches,"* was an "ancient talismanic symbol of protection against evil," they said they looked forward to hanging it inside their homes, where it would protect their families from harm.

"I just finished teaching Lesson 13 this morning," I wrote to my sister Heather in mid-May. "My students (who have dwindled to six, unfortunately) are showing enormous progress and ability, doing more than I ask of them for homework, to earn my praise and applause. Given the less-than-ideal conditions they must work under at home

— no tables, no lights, dull scissors, dirty little children's hands into and on everything — I'm impressed by what they proudly show me they've done. I give them lots of positive feedback!

"After reading the wonderful book *Hidden in Plain View: A Secret Story of Quilts and the Underground Railroad*, I made a sheet for my students containing the patchwork designs said to have been used by American slave quilters as maps to freedom. Wouldn't you know it, my students took the sheet home and made almost all of the designs — in one week — to surprise me. These women are really trying hard, doing their best. It's so admirable."

By the time we were ready to work on our class project — the red-white-and-blue, stars-and-stripes wall hanging I hoped to present to the American Embassy when they gave us their Self-Help aid — the women were adept at making perfectly precise eight-point-star blocks. Each of the six remaining women in the class — Ami Sylla, Sali Traore, Fily Diallo, Ami Keita, Marie Diarra, and Delphine Dembele — made a ten-inch-square block with a blue square center and red triangular points on a white background. The border and sashing fabric was in blue-and-white stripes, with solid red squares at the corners. The women took turns in class quilting it by machine, "in the ditch," along the seam lines, to save time, because we expected to hear from the Embassy at any moment. We made a sleeve for the back so it could be hung somewhere in the Embassy's Bamako offices, with pride, because it was so beautiful.

So when I learned through a local Peace Corps volunteer who had close ties with people at the Embassy that the new U.S. Ambassador, Michael Ranneberger, was planning his first trip to Ségou soon, and "he would like to meet" me, I was overjoyed. In my exuberance I immediately envisioned it all: The Ambassador would drive to my house in Pelengana in his chauffer-driven Embassy car; I would show him my house and gardens, serve him tea, tell him personally about my exciting Patchwork Project, then graciously accept his confirmation of our "well deserved material aid." He and I would then drive in his car (I would remark on its refreshing air-conditioning) to Centre Benkady, where my students, dressed in their best *boubous*, would be waiting to *fête* him and present him with their magnificent "Stars and Stripes" wall hanging. Someone would take photographs with my little Olympus Stylus camera of this day-to-remember: me standing next to the tall, well-dressed, stately Ambassador, flanked by the Patchwork Project "pioneers" happily displaying their handiwork in the foreground.

I flew into a frenzy of preparation for the Ambassador's visit: I scrubbed and swept every inch of my house, raked the entire courtyard of fallen leaves, trimmed the front hedge, fluffed all of the plants in my gardens, and generally turned my home into a showplace, a veritable American quilting museum, with every patchwork-quilted item I'd ever made on display.

I biked to town and told everyone I knew — Youssef's family, with whom I was still close, my friends at the nongovernmental organization ALPHALOG, the owner of the stationery store where I'd bought some supplies for my patchwork classes on credit, my favorite merchants at the *marché,* my new friend Abdoulaye Djiabate at the Department of Education, the town librarian, whoever would listen — "the American Ambassador is coming to my house in Pelangana! He's going to help my Patchwork Project!" Everyone I told smiled at my childlike excitement and nodded knowingly, the way my mother used to do when she would tell the child who was me, "All right. Well. We'll see."

- - - - - - - - - - - - -

In Mali, unlike in most parts of the United States, older people, especially older women, are revered. The attitude of respect and admiration shown toward women who have lived long lives and, presumably, gained wisdom along the way permeated Mali's culture like a golden thread woven throughout the social fabric. I marveled at it, reveled in it, and only wished the same could be said for my country. Relinquishing youth, beauty, and sexual appeal for wisdom, reverence, and respect seemed like a healthy tradeoff to me.

In Mali, as a woman becomes older, especially after her children are grown, she takes on regal status. She sits in a prominent chair in the family's compound, for example, and gives directions to the younger women on what needs to be done and how best to do it; all of which the younger women readily and reverently obey. During *fêtes*, the older women wear more dazzling and dramatic traditional dresses than the younger women do. And in line dances, it is the older women who lead the procession, keeping the beat, initiating the dips, claps, and steps, while the younger women follow their every move.

Perhaps one reason older women are revered, I thought, is that they are so rare. At that time, only about 3 percent of Mali's population of close to 12 million people reached the age of 65. Life expectancy for women was 51 (for men, 47). Retirement age, 55.

I reached my mid-fifties in Mali, so I felt the subtle benefits of being an older woman there. I felt respected, not because I was white (a dubious distinction in formerly colonized Africa) or because some might have seen me as "rich" (which I was far from, by American standards), but because I had managed to live so long and I was still functioning.

It seemed to be an inherent aspect of Malians' nature to respect all elders, and older women in particular. The unspoken assumption was: *You have some things to share, oh wise Older Woman. If I defer to you, will you share them with me?* At Centre Benkady this deference and receptivity had a profoundly positive effect on me. It sparked my creativity, compounded my always-meager self-assurance, and spurred my motivation to share my potentially useful ideas.

When I thought from time to time about returning to the States to live, I doubted my artisinal talents would receive the same reception anywhere there. For the most part, unattached women who are no longer young and beautiful and who never were rich or powerful or well-connected to begin with are at a great disadvantage in a country that places higher values on youth, beauty, and money than it does on creativity or wisdom.

Single older women in the U.S. are too often seen as has-beens; and with time, they become essentially invisible. Not seen at all. I wasn't ready for that. I didn't want to be sidelined by a culture that spends ten times more per year on anti-aging efforts than the total market value of all the goods and services Mali produces annually. (In 2005, Mali's gross domestic product was $5.43 billion; the U.S.'s anti-aging industry earned over $50 billion.) So I resolved to stay in Mali for as long as I could. In the United States my advancing age would be a detriment. In Mali it was only a plus.

In mid-May 2000, when I turned 55, I listed my blessings in my journal: good health, great physical condition (thanks to all the biking), freedom and tranquility, my "new love" quilting, and "faith that God has a reason for my life, even if that reason eludes me."

I didn't know how long I would be able to stay in Mali; there were too many unknowns. Would my health and strength hold up? Would my Patchwork Project take hold? Would the owner of my rental house in Pelengana decide to sell? Would I be able to renew my Malian work visa for another year? The only sane approach I saw was to live in the moment, the way easygoing, good-natured Africans do, take life one day at a time, trust that God has a plan, and go forward day by day on hope and faith.

- - - - - - - - - - - -

For my 55th birthday my young Peace Corps volunteer friend Vivica gave me a precious gift — a beautiful marionette she had made. A recent Smith graduate and accomplished artist, Vivica had, like me, become captivated by Malian puppetry. She and her Canadian fiancé Sylvain had embarked on creating a series of doll-size, Malian-costumed string puppets, which I had greatly admired. So Vivica surprised me with one of them — the one I admired most — as a birthday gift. I had just turned 55, but I was as thrilled as a child.

I named this pretty puppet, dressed in an elegant African ensemble with a matching tall turban, Kadiatou Kouyate, and I used her in my lessons with my Club Crochet girls. As a treat, after they'd worked hard on their crocheting, I put on little puppet shows for the girls. I brought out Kadiatou and had her dance around the terrace, tapping her black bamboo feet to one of Salif Keita's songs on tape.

All of the Club Crochet girls were always wide-eyed and open-mouthed with wonder. Many voiced their appreciation in heartfelt French: *"Merci, Bonnie; merci, Bonnie!"* Kadiatou led the line dance, and all the little girls followed, tapping their bare feet and clapping to Salif Keita's music.

One day I told the girls that Kadiatou would like a black plastic shoulder bag, and she was willing to pay 500 CFA for it. I presented this appeal in the form of a contest: The Club Crochet member who made the best little shoulder bag for Kadiatou would win the prize.

At our next Club Crochet meeting the following Wednesday, eight of the girls submitted tiny black shoulder bags for the contest I'd proposed. I chose the best of the eight and attached the strap of it to the puppet's shoulder. It was perfect, and all the girls agreed, applauding as Kadiatou did a little tap dance of delight. The prizewinner opted for a pair of scissors instead of the cash. I paid the other seven contestants 100 CFA consolation prizes, and most of these girls put their winnings directly into our Club Crochet bank.

I felt grateful to Kadiatou's magic for helping me to teach the girls more than just how to crochet small items with plastic bags. Even more, I felt thankful for the way that life was still, at 55, pulling my strings.

- - - - - - - - - - - - -

I KNOW WHAT "SELF HELP" MEANS. It means fending for yourself, doing for yourself, looking to yourself for all your needs. It means pedaling your own bike in life, baking your own healthy bread, paying all your own bills. It means never leaning on anyone or asking anyone for help, if you can help it.

"Y'er on yer own, kids!" my father used to say repeatedly, as if we his four children were so dim we needed it repeated. "Don' look ta me fer *anything*." Then, for emphasis, he'd wave a huge, drunken hand, as though batting a fly. Yes, we got the message, and it stuck.

In high school I made my own clothes, bought my own shoes, and paid for my own eyeglass prescriptions and doctor and dentist visits with the money I earned babysitting on weekends and working every day after school as a checkout girl at the local Acme supermarket. My father, without intending to teach me anything, taught me self-sufficiency. Also without intending to, he taught me not to follow his path toward self-destruction through belligerence and booze.

So when, after making a firm appointment for a Thursday at 9 a.m., the Ambassador's office cancelled his visit to my house at the last minute ("He had to rush back to Bamako," his apologetic Malian assistant Mr. Koniko told me. *Rush back from where?* I wondered. *Was his meeting with the governor in Ségou held at dawn?* "He's such a busy man!" Koniko hastily added); and when, a short while later, I received a letter in the mail from the American Embassy's new Self-Help Coordinator telling me my request for material aid had been denied because my project was "not community-generated," I didn't fall too far for too long. This blow, in fact, sounded familiar to me: "Y'er on yer own, kid."

But I got up swinging. In response to the new coordinator's curt letter — "...your project ... does not qualify under the definition of 'Self-Help' ... If anyone in the [Malian] community wants to initiate such a project, they are welcome to apply..." — I wrote a two-page, single-spaced, typewritten letter giving the entire history of my Patchwork Project and request for aid. This new coordinator was, I learned from my young Peace Corps volunteer informants, new to the Embassy, new to Mali, clearly out of touch with the reality on the ground in the interior of the country, and obviously unfamiliar with my prior relationship with Alice Adjibi, her predecessor, who had mysteriously disappeared from the scene. With sparks flying from the little Olivetti portable typewriter I'd brought with me from New York, I attempted to set her straight:

"…I will, Ms. Archer, ask someone from the nascent patchwork community here to re-apply for the Self-Help grant — as soon as I can locate someone who is sufficiently literate to be able to fill in the forms you sent, someone who is also sufficiently familiar with patchwork quilting to identify the project's near-future material needs, and some-one who is sufficiently free of myriad household and familial responsi-bilities to hunt down the requisite *factures pro-forma*. This may take a while. In the meantime, please retain the *factures pro-forma* from Bama-ko that I obtained last year; this will save the next applicant a great deal of time, energy, and travel expense."

I knew the likelihood of that "next applicant" coming forward was slim-to-none. Nevertheless, in an effort to leave the door of possibility open even slightly, I tried to close my seething letter on a positive note: "…I hope it's only a matter of time before the American Embassy believes in this worthy project enough to help it along. After all, patch-work quilting is an *American* thing."

I carbon-copied the Ambassador on this letter, but I never heard from him. In fact, I never met him and so never learned whether he was indeed as tall and stately as I had envisioned. I never gave him our "Stars and Stripes" thank-you gift either. The women of the Patchwork Project of Ségou, Mali, kept that beautiful wall hanging for themselves.

"The hell with them!" I wrote to Marty after receiving this bomb-shell from the Embassy. "I'm determined to make this project work. I'll ask my willing friends in the U.S. to each send a roll of polyester bat-ting. I'll ask the Patchwork women here to hunt around town for more tailors' scraps. I'll fill in the blanks out of my own pocket. We'll manage — somehow."

- - - - - - - - - - - - -

Sometimes, a setback can serve to propel a person forward with greater velocity and direction, like a small stone from a slingshot. That's what the American Embassy did for me.

After I picked myself up, I biked to town to explain to everyone to whom I'd spoken too soon that I'd been wrong about the Ambassador's visit and American aid. My mistake entirely. My poor judgment. My misplaced hopes. My African friends, so much wiser than I, listened knowingly. Lives filled with daily struggle and flecked with countless disappointments had taught them never to place hopes too high. For them, everything hoped-for hinged on the conditional, *"inshallah"* — if Allah wills it. God alone decides what the future holds.

But rather than sit back passively and wait for God to do it all — as I'd noticed faithful Malian Muslims tended to do — I renewed my belief that God helps those who help themselves. I resolved to keep barreling ahead on this project without the hoped-for aid, trusting that God would provide whatever it really required. I would do it *my* way, beholden to no one, with no bureaucratic strings attached. Stubborn determination hardened to a spiky burr under my saddle that made me more driven than ever. If it killed me, I would see this Patchwork Project succeed before I left Mali. *Inshallah.*

- - - - - - - - - - - - -

After I wrote to other friends about the Embassy's rejection, even without asking those friends for help, their help poured in.

My dear friend Ron, who had been my sous chef when I had a catering business in New York and who had since begun a successful career in real estate in Los Angeles, sent me a check for $500.

Wendy, an old friend from New York, now retired and living in St. Augustine, Florida, sent $100, plus a box filled with quilting supplies — 14 spools of quilting thread, 10 thimbles, 10 packets of special quilting needles, 10 marking pencils, 2 tape measures, 3 pairs of good scissors — and the book *Quilting for Dummies*.

My friend Marie-Laure in Paris contacted a French patchwork magazine that published a short piece about my Patchwork Project, which prompted a few readers to write to me and send back issues of the quilting magazine, *France Patchwork*, in addition to quilt patterns printed in French.

My cousin Jean and my sister Heather continued their generous support. Ron, Wendy, and Heather even commissioned our fledgling project to make bed quilts for them. The first real quilt we would attempt, I decided, would be the king-size quilt my sister ordered for her newly married son, my nephew Tyler, and his wife Sarah.

But two major obstacles loomed. I knew I needed to widen the circle of students for the fall semester, and I knew I could not teach my fall classes at Centre Benkady. If I had learned anything in teaching the first semester there, it was that I'd exhausted their available talent pool; and their busy, dusty, ill-equipped center was not conducive to teaching patchwork quilting. At the risk of offending my Benkady women friends, who tended to consider me theirs, I decided to seek out additional qualified students from other women's centers in Ségou and hold the fall classes in my own home, which would, among other things, be a more central and neutral setting.

"I'm now in the process of scouring Ségou —" I wrote to Marty, "visiting every single women's sewing center in town, on the back of a friend's *moto*, holding an enormous bag filled with my patchwork quilting samples — looking for the very best candidates to take my course this fall. I find myself telling each group, 'If I must leave Mali next year, I want to be sure I've taught the most capable women the best possible methods under the most favorable conditions (that is, my clean home) so that these well-trained women can then teach many, many other women. When the orders for Ancestor Quilts come in over the Internet (when???), we'll need *a lot* of able women to fulfill them. … This project must not die!…'"

I hand-lettered an announcement, had it copied, and posted it all over town:

- -

<u>Annonce Importante</u>
aux meilleures couturieres de Ségou
qui voudraient Apprendre et Enseigner
le métier Americain
PATCHWORK QUILTING:

« Le Patchwork Projet, »
créé et coordiné par Bonnie Black,
offre une
FORMATION des FORMATRICES
un matin par semaine (9H30 ~ midi)
pour 14 semaines : 21 Sept. ~ 21 Dec.
chez Bonnie
quartier Pelengana

Si vous vous êtes intéressees a assister, laisser l'échantillon
avec Assiatou ou Fatou a ALPHALOG avant 7/2000

- -

[An important announcement for the best seamstresses in Ségou who would like to learn and teach the American craft, Patchwork Quilting: "The Patchwork Project," created and coordinated by Bonnie Black, offers a teacher-training course one morning per week, from 9:30 am to noon, for 14 weeks — September 21 through December 21 — at Bonnie's house in *quartier* Pelengana. If you are interested in attending, leave a sewing sample with Assiatou or Fatou at the offices of the ONG ALPHALOG before July 2000.]

- - - - - - - - - - - -

169

Fatou made it all possible. She arranged the meetings with the other women's sewing centers for me. All I had to do was bike the three miles to ALPHALOG's offices in town, chain my bike securely in their carport, and ride off with Fatou on her *moto*, gripping my big bag of samples with one arm and her sturdy body with the other, holding my breath as she navigated Ségou's back streets at breakneck speed.

Over the course of several days, the two of us covered a lot of ground, visiting places I hadn't known existed. It seemed that every neighborhood, or *quartier*, of Ségou had its own women's center, which served both social and practical functions. The sense of sisterhood and collective betterment I felt at each center was palpable.

By the time Fatou and I pulled up, the women had already gathered in a wide circle of folding chairs set up in the shade of a large tree in their center's courtyard. They watched, wide-eyed, as I pulled my quilted items from the bag and explained the value of patchwork quilting. They listened attentively to my invitation to apply for the next Patchwork Project teacher-training course. In deliberately slow, simple French I explained and demonstrated the application process I'd devised:

"Take two squares of complementary 100% cotton fabric, both *precisely* 9 cm square, and sew them together along one side, exactly ½ cm from the edge, like this…" (I showed them an example I'd made.) "Put this sample in a white business envelope, seal it, and mark it clearly with your name and the name of your *centre feminin*." (Again, I showed them how.) "Then deliver your sample to ALPHALOG's office *before July 1st*." (Fatou told them where.)

Most of the women nodded enthusiastically. Some took notes. "Only 20 women can be accepted for the course," I continued, "so that means I can take only one or two women from each of Ségou's women's centers. I will choose the best applicants based on how well you follow directions…" The women appeared to love the prospect of this competition; it seemed to feed into the undercurrent of rivalry that already existed among the various women's groups.

Six Benkady women, "the pioneers of patchwork in Mali," I explained, had already taken the course and earned their certificates. These women would serve as teacher's assistants in the upcoming classes, which would be held at my home. This December's graduates will become teacher's assistants for the Benkady Patchwork Project teachers, and so on. "This is an American teaching method," I posited. "It won't be easy."

After each demonstration, tearing back to ALPHALOG's offices on the back of Fatou's *moto*, I felt wildly hopeful.

With the money Ron had sent me, I was able to transform the larger of the two guest rooms of my house into a bright, clean, well-appointed classroom, devoted solely to the Patchwork Project. This room had an impenetrable metal door with a strong lock. It had good electric lighting. It was across the terrace from a clean bathroom with running water. Even before I added other amenities, it was better in every way than the classroom I'd had to endure at Centre Benkady.

I had the room painted a pleasing pale blue. I proudly displayed the "Stars and Stripes" wall hanging on one wall, and I made a picture grouping on the opposite wall of four framed patchwork blocks with accompanying calligraphied slogans:

- **Nine-patch block:** *«Il n'y a pas le developpement sans un change-ment.»* (There is no development without change.)
- **Log cabin block:** *«Quand la vie vous donnez les coupons, faites le patchwork!»* (When life gives you scraps, make patchwork!)
- **Eight-point star block:** *«Rien de valeur est facile a realiser.»* (Nothing great is easy to accomplish.)
- **Pinwheel block:** *«Si vous voulez reussir, n'arretez pas d'essayer.»* (If you want to succeed, keep on trying.)

I had a local young *menuisier* (carpenter) make us three sturdy tables, long and narrow enough for us to carry with ease onto the terrace where we could do our cutting and sewing after my classroom lecture. I bought a dozen identical, stackable, white molded-plastic armchairs to comfortably accommodate the three separate groups of students who would be attending. I bought eight matching hand-woven baskets to hold the washed-and-ironed fabric scraps we would gather, each basket for a different family of colors. I made a felt board for demonstrating how patchwork pieces fit together to form blocks. I asked my friend Abdoulaye Djiabate of the Ministry of Education whether he might locate a large, new blackboard for me for the front of the classroom.

In early July I revisited each of the women's groups to announce the winners of my application process. Among the samples that had been delivered to Fatou's office, I chose those by women who had clearly been able to follow my directions in French, had chosen two comple-mentary-colored fabrics, cut and sewn them precisely, enveloped and labeled them as instructed, and delivered them to the right place by the designated deadline. As I'd suspected, at least one and at most two women from each center qualified. When I announced their names, the winners literally jumped and shrieked with joy, as if they'd been accepted to Harvard.

On a Wednesday afternoon in late July, when my Club Crochet girls and I were happily crocheting with plastic "yarn" on my front terrace, Abdoulaye Djiabate surprised me by arriving with the black-board I'd requested. Without my asking, he then installed it for me, as the little girls looked on. With that blackboard filling up its front wall, this spare room was truly transformed into a classroom, and I was now ready for the upcoming semester to begin.

- - - - - - - - - - - -

Abdoulaye Djiabate, regional director of the Ministry of Education in Ségou, a progressive man in his late forties, was having a modern, new house built for himself and his family in the open field across from Mariko's nursery at the far end of *quartier* Pelengana at the time I met him. He was a large, imposing man, nearly 6 feet tall and at least 200 pounds; the size and shape my father and ex-husband had been but worlds apart from both of them in every other sense. Abdoulaye was a solid, centered, gentle man who, I felt sure, would never have raised a threatening or drunken hand. He was a Malian and a Muslim. He had honor and dignity. He didn't drink.

For reasons I couldn't fathom at first, he began to visit me once a week, when he came to Pelengana after work to check on the progress of his new house. Initially I was baffled. Had Mariko sent him? Had he heard about my patchwork classes through his wife or her friends? Was he curious about me? Concerned about my welfare? Or was it simply a sense of Malian neighborliness, in advance of his family's moving in to the neighborhood?

Regardless, I soon looked forward to his rap on my front metal gate just as I was finishing watering my gardens and the sun was setting and the air beginning to cool. My heart warmed to his gentle, shy smile as I greeted him and led him into my courtyard, where he parked his *moto* by a mango tree and lumbered up to my front terrace to sit and talk. We sat side-by-side, but not too close, on the terrace steps, where we could see and be seen. I knew it would have been culturally improper for him, a married man, well known in the community, to visit with me inside my home, since I was an unmarried woman living alone. He was a good man, it seemed to me, who cared about propriety and appearances.

We talked, that's all. Or, I should say, he asked me questions, and I tried my best to answer his questions in my still-limited French. As I talked, he listened, as though hungry for whatever it was I had to say.

And as I talked, I studied him, this big, rock-like man with a large, gentle face, looking at me as if he'd never seen anyone quite like me up-close before.

Unlike my friend Mariko, who generally wore a flowing, traditional Malian *boubou* and sandals, Abdoulaye was usually dressed in Western clothes — long-sleeve cotton shirts, crisply ironed and slightly strained across his middle, striped ties, dark trousers with a firm crease, beige socks, and polished leather lace-up shoes. In his own unstated way, he seemed to strive to straddle two worlds — the world he knew as a proud Malian who had never been out of his country, and the Westernized world beyond Mali's borders he'd like to know better. Perhaps, I thought, I represented for him a piece of the puzzle beyond.

When I looked in his eyes, I saw hunger. Not for food, to be sure, for he was clearly a well fed man; nor for sex or companionship, which I assumed he certainly got enough of at home; nor for power or prestige, which he'd earned in his professional life at the Ministry of Education. But rather for knowledge. He seemed hungry to know more about the world I represented. He wanted my first-hand accounts of life in *les états unis*, especially life in New York City. He wanted to know about my education, my family.

"You've only had *one* child?" he said, astonished. "Why not more?"

"That marriage only lasted a year." I didn't elaborate.

I knew he didn't mean to pry into my past; he simply wanted to know what it was like to be me. It was as if I were the first approachable white woman he had ever known; and he wanted to look closer, into my mind.

Most of all, he wanted to know what had brought me to Mali and what kept me in Mali on my own.

"The ancestors brought me," I blurted out, as though I'd finally learned the answer. "And love keeps me here."

"*Whose* ancestors?" he said, as if he never would have imagined such words coming out of a white person's mouth.

"Mine. Yours. Everyone's. Everyone came from Africa originally."

"You truly think so?"

"Yes. Well, it's true."

"And why do you love Mali? What is it about Mali in particular?"

I waved my right hand in an arc along the darkening sky above us and across the courtyard surrounding us. "I love those stars. You can't see stars like these in New York City. And I love these gardens. I've never had such gardens in my life," I said. "I love the peace-loving people here and my work with the women. I love the sense of purpose I have, the feeling that my life is not in vain."

"How could your life be in vain?" he said.

If I had been African, if I had been younger, if he had been single, if I had better judgment when it came to men, I would have wanted to marry this man and spend the rest of my life with him. He was what I was discovering too late in life to be the definition of a real man: strong enough to be gentle, smart enough to listen, genuinely kind enough to genuinely care. He seemed unshakeable, invincible to me.

At times, as I sat under that canopy of emerging stars and studied him, I was tempted to wrap my arms around him, to hold him in place and prevent him from speeding off on his *moto* to his home, his family and his dinner. But I never did that. And he never touched me.

"More coffee?" I asked him, reaching for his plastic mug.

"*Non, merci*. I must be getting home now," he said, bowing politely.

Was his wife ever jealous, I wondered? Did she question him when he got home, demanding, "*Where have you been?!,*" giving him a piece of her mind? I was sure not. I imagined her to be a wise woman, as solid as he was, who knew her man well. She knew him well enough to trust him.

- - - - - - - - - - -

Abdoulaye was particularly interested in my books: Where did they come from? What did they mean to me? One by one, I showed him my small but precious collection — the few special books I'd brought from my studio apartment in New York, such as N.J. Dawood's English translation of the Koran, which, I told him, I read portions of every day; and the growing number of books sent as gifts from American friends, such as Barbara Kingsolver's hefty new novel *The Poisonwood Bible*, which I'd already reread five times. Abdoulaye's eyes widened at the thought that I, a non-Muslim, could derive spiritual sustenance from daily readings of the Koran. He hung on every word as I summarized Kingsolver's dramatic story of an ill-fated American missionary family in the Congo of the '60s.

He seemed astounded to see that someone, a scholar by the name of Maryse Condé, had written a famous, fact-based historical novel — in English! — called *Segu*; and now I, having read it, might just know more about his hometown's rich history than he did. He was not surprised, however, to learn of the theory found in my well-worn paperback edition of *Hidden in Plain View* that African slaves in the American South used quilts as codes for the Underground Railroad.

"Markings on textiles have always been like words in books for us," he said.

When I showed him my newest treasure — a beautiful, coffee-table book by the brilliant African-American photojournalist Roland L. Freeman, *The Communion of the Spirits: African-American Quilters, Preservers, and Their Stories*, sent to me by an African-American Peace Corps volunteer friend who had just returned to the States after serving her two years in Mali — I was particularly proud. I opened the big book on my lap and turned the pages slowly, pointing out the many vivid photos of black Americans, mostly older women, with their magnificent handmade quilts.

"You see," I said. "African-Americans have learned how to sew their lives back together. They know how to make something beautiful and colorful and meaningful from the scraps life has dealt them."

"And this is why you love your project here," he said.

"Yes," I said. He understood.

He asked about my future plans.

No one else during my stay in Ségou had ever inquired about my past or asked about my future. I'd assumed that for most Malians life was lived primarily in the present tense, the here and now. What was, was gone; what might be was in God's hands. No regrets over what might have been; no anxiety over what might or might not be. Abdou-laye was different in this respect. He had a hunger to know.

"Do you plan to stay in Mali?" he asked me.

"To stay? To go? I don't know what to do," I confessed to him. "I feel very torn. My heart wants to stay, but…"

I stopped to gather my thoughts. Although I'd often confronted this issue in my journal, I'd never had occasion to put my thoughts into spoken words, especially in French.

"To be honest," I said, "I'm a little afraid to return to *les états unis*."

"*Pourquoi?*" he asked, hungrily.

"Well, for one thing, it's becoming too technological, and I have no talent for nor interest in technology. You know, I had a science profes-sor in college who said that one day computers would be able to repro-duce themselves, with mutations, and they would become the next super-beings; the humans who created them would become their slaves."

"You're joking."

"No, this professor wasn't joking; he really believed this would come true. So I can imagine the day when those computer-robot-overlords will kidnap their creators-turned-underlings and whisk them off in rocket ships, to a new life in outer space, abandoning the planet mankind has so successfully degraded. Africans, however, will not be included. They will be overlooked, disregarded — as they are largely now. They'll be left behind."

Abdoulaye leaned into me. "And you," he said. "Where will *you* be?"

"Well, if that day should arrive while I'm still alive, I will opt to stay behind too, with the Africans — banging on drums, dancing, kicking up dust, and celebrating life as we know it right here on Planet Earth."

"Yes, you belong right here," Abdoulaye said. "You must stay."

"I love Africa, I do. I love the fact that I have *time* here. Time to sew and quilt and read and write and think. Time to listen to the Voice of America on my shortwave radio every evening. Programs such as the one I heard the other night about a new study showing how stress levels in the States are rising, causing increased health problems, family prob-lems, depression. 'The social fabric is fraying,' the reporter said, which made me thankful to be here instead of there.

"But the problem is I'm not African. I am an obvious outsider here. I am not a part of your rich, resilient social fabric. I don't speak your native language. I'm just passing through."

"But you could marry a Malian and stay," he said.

Was he hinting that *that* Malian might be him? Was he about to inform me of what I already knew — that Malian men are allowed by law to take up to four wives, if they can afford them?

"You're not the first to propose that solution to me!" I laughed. "Marriage might indeed provide me with a permanent visa, but it would not make me an African."

I quickly changed the subject. "Your new house is being built of cement blocks, *n'est-ce pas?*"

"Yes," he said, "it is."

"This 'modern' house that I'm renting is made of cement, and I must tell you it is way too hot inside. Cement blocks capture the heat and hold it in, like an oven. Cement is better suited to houses built in colder climates. Here in Mali, the old-style, traditional houses made of adobe bricks are better for this hot climate. Sometimes the old ways are best."

No, I thought, this man would not want to be married to me. He would not want that much of my mind.

- - - - - - - - - - - -

When blood tests I'd had taken at the hospital in Ségou came back positive for diabetes, my friend Mariko and I had one more thing in common. To the extent that I was able there, I researched Type II diabetes and followed the authorities' advice. I cut out all sweets and sugar from my diet and counseled Mariko to do the same.

"That means no more sugar in your tea," I scolded him as we visited at his nursery one afternoon at teatime.

"Not possible," he said with an impish smile, revealing front teeth already ravaged by sugary tea. "Sweet tea is a part of our culture. It's the Muslim equivalent of beer."

Deteriorating health due to diabetes was just one of Mariko's weighty concerns. Another was financial — the day-to-day demands of feeding and providing for his immediate family. Two of his grown sons had traveled overseas in search of better economic opportunities, leaving their wives and small children with Mariko and his wife to care for. Mariko's other children, in their teens to early twenties, lived at home and helped with the manual labor required of the nursery. But every day, three times a day, Mariko had close to twenty family members to feed on an educator's pension, plus whatever income he might earn from his nursery business.

By this time, as an independent development worker, I had made significant contacts with people in both local governmental agencies and nongovernmental organizations in Ségou. I knew that August 4th was Mali's annual *"Journée des Arbes"* (Day of Trees). So I came up with a plan: I proposed that in celebration of this day in 2000 — and in conjunction with this year's Clean Up the World effort — the people of Ségou plant flamboyant trees all along the main roads. In years to come, I argued, when the trees were tall and flowering, Ségou would be known as the loveliest city in Mali; tourists would be drawn to its beauty; the economy would prosper. This dream for Ségou was inspired by the memory of my life in then Salisbury, Rhodesia (now Harare, Zimbabwe), in the late '60s, when Salisbury was known as "the city of flowering trees" because the avenues were lined with towering jacaranda trees. I knew a similar vision was possible for Ségou; I wanted to make it come true.

My proposal called for one thousand healthy, young trees. And I recommended where they could be purchased (because I'd urged Mariko to prepare for this day): from Abdoulaye Mariko, the *pipinieriste* (nurseryman) in Pelangana.

ALPHALOG, Ségou's sole ONG (nongovernmental organization) specializing in environmental concerns, agreed to pay Mariko 250 CFA each for one thousand saplings, earning him the equivalent of $1,000, or four times the average annual salary in Mali. I was overjoyed. This windfall would lift, at least for the near future, some of the financial burden from his broad but bent shoulders.

On the morning of the tree-planting, August 4th, about fifteen neighborhood children, mostly Club Crochet girls, arrived at my house at nine and happily marched with me to the main road — carrying a cloth banner I'd made at Benkady, reading *"Aimez la Terre: Plantez des Arbes"* (Love the Earth, Plant Trees) — where the planting had begun. When a fresh supply of saplings arrived on Mariko's *charrette*, I threw myself into helping to plant them — digging a hole with a hoe, removing the sapling's roots from its black plastic bag, placing the tree in the center, covering the root ball with soil, leaving a well-like surrounding area for rain to pool. As I finished planting each tree, the children circled both the tree and me and applauded.

That evening Mariko arrived at my house on the back of a *moto* driven by one of his sons to tell me how happy and grateful he was. Without coming in, he wanted to thank me again for initiating this project. He took my sore-from-tree-planting right hand and gallantly kissed it.

- - - - - - - - - - - -

Weeks later, after I'd returned from a visit to the States to see friends and family, Mariko sheepishly shared the news of his son's wedding. While I was away, Mariko had thrown an enormous wedding party for the young couple. He'd invited friends and family members from all over Mali.

"Many, many people came, and everyone ate very well," he said. "It was a memorable *fête*." From Mariko's confessional tone, I knew there was more to the story and it involved money.

"So you're telling me you spent all of your earnings from the sale of the saplings?"

"Yes."

I shook my head. "But that money was supposed to ease your financial worries for a while. I thought you could put it in the bank and draw on it little by little. You could budget –"

"You don't understand," he said, patting my hand as we sat together in the shade of his arbor, "making such a feast for others is like money in the bank in our culture. In time it will come back to me, *inshallah*. You'll see."

- - - - - - - - - - - -

On the morning of September 21, 2000, eighteen women filled my living room for the combined first lesson of the second semester of my patchwork course. They filled the white molded-plastic chairs I'd bought for our classroom, all of my living room chairs, every inch of my sofa. Their flowing *boubous*, trimmed with white cotton lace and brushing the tile floor, were in every color—tomato red, sunshine yellow, Easter-egg purple, morning-sky blue — as well as solid white and multicolored prints. Their faces were radiant, expectant, and proud. These were the application-contest winners, the chosen ones from Ségou's various women's centers, plus the six Centre Benkady first-semester graduates who would serve as *stagiaires* (teacher's assistants) in this second semester. They all had good reason to hold their regal, turbaned heads high.

Among the new students filling my living room were: Koro Traore, age 36, and Bassam Sacko, 38, from Centre Sinesigi; Mariam Dolo, 49, and Assitan Kane, 39, from Centre Jamajigi; Philippine Razafin, a Madagascan nun in her early forties from Mission Catholique; Nathalie Berthe, 40, from Centre Cesiriton; Rokiatou Bah, 30, from Express Couture; Rokiatou Diallo Ouattara, 26, and Rokia Dembele, 22, from ALPHA-LOG; Mariam Coulibaly, 42, and Fanta Diarra, 33, from Centre Bougoufie; and Fatimata Traore, 38, an independent *couteriere* who had responded to my posted announcement. Six women on my list of those accepted were unable to attend this first class due to illness or family obligations.

Whether or not the women filling my living room had ever met or mingled before, or whether they harbored any historic rivalries, was unclear to me. What was clear was that they seemed supremely happy to be gathered together to celebrate the start of this special opportunity.

I stood before the gathering, wearing my simplest, prettiest dress, hands shaking. Would I be able to fulfill the women's expectations? Could I communicate and demonstrate clearly enough for them all to understand? Could I bridge the cultural divide? Had I learned enough during the first semester's lessons to improve the course this time? As always, as I delivered my explanatory speech, I kept my Who-What-Where-When-Why-and-How notes nearby, to aid my faulty French. I spoke with my hands, too. I forced a nonstop smile.

"This course will be hard work," I told them matter-of-factly (and my Benkady *stagiaires* concurred), but I also stressed the rewards. I showed them the official certificate they would receive upon successfully completing the course in three months. I explained that their class project would involve making a king-size bed quilt commissioned by my sister for her son and daughter-in-law, for which the whole class would be well paid.

"This quilt will be a *grand defi*" (big challenge), I said, "but I know you will be able to do it!" I told them other commissions should follow if this first quilt was done well.

I explained that they would not only learn how to *do* patchwork, they would also learn how to *teach* it, so that they could keep this economic development project alive after I was gone.

I showed them the inflated beach-ball globe Marty had given me when I left for the Peace Corps and which I'd used in my health lessons in Lastoursville. "All over our world," I pointed out to the Patchwork Project women in my living room, twirling the plastic planet, "women do patchwork. In Europe and America and Australia and even in Africa. I recently learned that women are doing patchwork now in Cameroon and Togo and Senegal, as well as Kenya and South Africa. But to my knowledge, you are the first to learn patchwork in Mali.

"We are all sisters in patchwork," I said, embracing the room with my thin, white arms. The African women, each holding her teacher-training booklet in her lap, smiled broadly and nodded. They appeared to understand me.

- - - - - - - - - - - - -

Unlike the first semester lessons, which I'd offered twice a week for sixteen weeks, this time the women divided into three groups which would meet three times per week — Tuesday, Thursday, and Saturday mornings — for fourteen weeks. If a woman could not attend a lesson on her regularly scheduled day, she was free to join the same lesson given on another day that week. If a woman wanted to use my library to find inspiration or ideas from my quilting books and magazines, she could do so any weekday morning. This flexibility allowed the women to better balance their patchwork training with their many family obligations.

Each lesson began in my guest room-turned classroom, where I outlined the week's agenda in simple French on the front blackboard under four headings: *"REVISION"* — questions meant to review and reinforce what they'd learned the previous week; *"EXPLICATION"* — that week's lecture, explaining the next step in the ten-step patchwork process; *"DEMONSTRATION"* — the hands-on how-to I would show them that day, which they would then replicate individually on work-tables we pulled out onto my terrace; and *"DEVOIR"* — their home-work assignment for the next week.

In the clean and brightly lit classroom, each group of women sat attentively and took notes from the blackboard in their notebooks. They arrived on time, all earning stars in my attendance book for punctuality. None of them brought their babies. No one fidgeted, whispered with her neighbor, or fell asleep, as had sometimes happened during the first semester's classes at Benkady. These handpicked students took it all very seriously. They were literate and intelligent. They appeared extremely anxious to learn.

- - - - - - - - - - - -

"Yesterday's class — Lesson 3, Group 2," I noted in my journal, "went very well. Six students, plus their assigned *stagiaires* arrived. All had done their homework correctly: They'd made two identical Nine-Patch designs, and the points met perfectly. We all applauded each one in turn, and I gave all of them stars in my attendance book for doing their homework so well."

Cutting the borders for their tote bags — with *exactitude* — was a challenging process for them, however. I'd set up three tables on my terrace, given them the necessary measuring, marking, and cutting equipment and an hour and a half to cut the borders for both sides of their bags: side borders of 8 cm width; and top/bottom borders of 6 cm width. They approached this challenge timidly, seemingly fearful of making a mistake.

Pilippine, the tiny nun from Madagascar, finished first, so I was able to use her pieces to demonstrate how to sew the borders. Ultimately, everybody finished and left understanding their homework assignment: "Make a tote bag of your own design to use to put all your patchwork papers and supplies in for next week," I instructed. "Be creative," I said. "Surprise me!"

- - - - - - - - - - - - -

And how the women surprised me. When they arrived the following week with their completed tote bags hanging from their shoulders, already put to work as receptacles for their course papers and supplies, I was thrilled to see their creativity. Every bag was as colorful and individual as its creator. In our classroom, each woman in turn stood and exhibited her handiwork, to everyone's applause. All received gold stars beside their names.

I found that using the felt board in the front of the classroom became an effective learning tool. To illustrate how many different patchwork designs can be made from triangles, I had each student use some pre-sewn triangles to create on the felt board the designs shown on their Underground Railroad code list. It became like a game for them, and they loved it.

When we learned of a crafts fair sponsored by the Peace Corps to be held in Bamako on November 7, we set to work making large, square pillowcases in a patchwork Log Cabin design to be sold at the fair. This time we strove to make the pillowcases identical, from two-inch-wide strips of *bazin* dyed in shades of pink, purple and blue I'd cut in advance of their Log-Cabin-design class.

Eighteen of the women completed this pillowcase assignment as their homework in time for a friend to take them to the crafts fair. Ten of the eighteen sold for 7,500 CFA (about $10) each at the fair, and the earnings went directly to each maker. The women were overjoyed. This, more than anything I had said so far, more than all the gold stars they'd earned next to their names, spurred them to achieve even greater success. This was proof for them that *"les choses en patchwork sont très* recherchés"— that *toubobs* really do appreciate beautiful things made of patchwork and are willing to pay good money for them.

- - - - - - - - - - - - -

Nevertheless, I felt the need to reinforce the economic aspects of our project at every opportunity. One week, as an illustration, I pulled out the poorly made patchwork *pagne* (wrap skirt) I'd bought at the *marché* earlier in the year and which my Benkady students had told me I'd paid too much for.

"What if," I said to each of the three morning groups, holding up the amateurish patchwork effort, "we could locate the person who made this *pagne* and invite her to come join our classes and learn how to do patchwork properly so she could raise the quality of her workmanship and increase her income?

"And what if," I continued with this fiction, "she comes once, but she decides that doing patchwork well is just too much work. She makes excuses. She claims she is too old to learn, our classroom is too far for her to travel, she prefers her own tried-and-true, hodge-podge methods. She tells us, 'I've been doing it this way all my life, as has my mother, and her mother before her. I can't change.'

"But before she turns to leave, she puts out her hand and begs for money. '*Donnez-moi l'argent*' (give me money), she says. '*Je suis pauvre*' (I am poor).

"Should we give her money?" I ask the class, and they all shake their heads. The moral of this story, I don't have to tell them (but I do anyway) is, "*Il n'y a pas le develloppement sans un changement.*" No change, no gain. "It's easy to say, '*Donnez-moi l'argent,*' isn't it? It's hard to learn something new." The women nod in unison.

- - - - - - - - - - - - -

But in the quietness of my study in the evening, when I was all alone with my thoughts, I worried. Had I said the wrong thing? I knew it was one of the five firm tenets of Islam to give to the poor, no questions asked. Was I undermining their belief system by suggesting we should turn this poor woman away?

At times, the chasm between the culture I'd been steeped in and theirs felt unbridgeable to me. We in the "developed" world were so anxious and driven *(toward what?* I wondered. *Fame? Fortune? Acquisitions? A sense of purpose?)*. Africans, on the other hand, from my observations, were more serenely accepting of their given realities.

I mused on the stark cultural contrasts regarding materialism: Africans live in another world from us, and it's not a material world. They prefer, it seemed to me, to travel more lightly through life than we do, unencumbered by weighty baggage. When we in the West first encounter Africans, living as they do in their little roughly made huts in compounds filled with scantily dressed children, cooking outdoors over wood or charcoal fires, riding bikes or driving donkey carts to get around, we tend to whip out our own materialistic measuring tape and pityingly pronounce, "Oh, these people are SO POOR! They don't have anything!"

The sad truth that I was learning was that we in the "developed" world have been thoroughly brainwashed into believing that the measure of a person's or a people's wealth was the number — and brand names — of their *things*. We'd become so conditioned to thinking along these lines we couldn't seem to embrace the notion that for the most part Africans are not interested in things; their measures of wealth lie elsewhere — notably and especially in family ties and human relations.

Africans, I'd observed, *choose not* to knock themselves out trying to get and hang onto high-paying jobs so they can shop for and impress others with their things. No, on their scale of values, it appeared to me, *time* is more important to them: Time to relax, time to spend with friends and family, time to listen to music, time to do as they please.

We might label this harshly as "lazy," but in fact, I'm sure most harried people in the West would envy the Africans' leisure. It seems one cannot have it both ways. "It's all about tradeoffs," my friend Ron in L.A. is fond of saying. We in the West have traded Time-to-relax-and-enjoy-life for Material Things. I would guess that if Africans could slap a harsh label on us, corresponding to our "lazy" for them, it would be "empty."

Most people in Mali, I observed, *choose* to live in simple, small houses because they spend most of their time — day and night — outdoors. It's TOO HOT to be inside. Kids run around scantily dressed because it's HOT. Women cook outdoors because indoors it would be TOO HOT. The "rich," "developed" world is cold; people have to move more quickly and take shelter indoors. Africa is HOT, for goodness' sake. People have had to adapt in order to survive.

To me, the Africans I worked with and came to know in Ségou were far from the "poor-African" stereotypes most Westerners cling to; they were strong survivors, incalculably rich in their own non-material ways.

- - - - - - - - - - - -

Our combined class project, my nephew Tyler's king-size quilt, loomed. *How could we possibly finish this monstrous task by our last class on December 21st?* I fretted. I began to doubt my sanity.

"Are you sure your son needs this quilt?" I wrote to Heather. But I knew the answer. We needed to meet this challenge. This quilt would become the prototype for all the bed quilts that might follow. It could become the apex — the apotheosis! — of our nascent Patchwork Project. If we could do this quilt, we could do anything. I was driven, as well as anxious.

We started, of course, with Step 1: We made a plan on paper.

Tyler had seen and liked a photo I'd sent to his mom of a baby quilt Delphine, one of my Benkady students, had made during our first semester. Delphine's baby quilt was filled with colorful pinwheels and framed by a sawtooth border. "That's the type of quilt he'd like," Heather wrote to me. "Simple, bright pinwheels on a blue background. Lots of crayon colors."

We drew the design on graph paper and colored it in with crayons. For a finished face size of 260 cm (about 102 inches) square, we'd need 49 blocks 30 cm (about 12 inches) square — 24 of which would be solid light blue *bazin* and 25 would be pinwheels made with colorful African-print fabric. We would then frame this face with four successively wider borders, alternating solid blue *bazin* strips with wild, blue-printed designs, ending with multicolored triangles forming a sawtooth border.

Each student agreed to make at least one pinwheel block at home, following Steps 2, 3, and 4 (wash/iron, cut, and sew) in their teacher-training manual. A few of the outstanding students arrived with several pinwheel blocks, so we had more than 25 to choose from when it came time to sew the rows of blocks together. Using the brightest, wildest African prints we'd collected in our scrap baskets, everyone made at least a half dozen triangles to make the final sawtooth strip

When it came time to make the "sandwich" — spread this patchwork face over the polyester batting my sister had sent, which was resting like a low-lying cloud on the solid blue *bazin* backing — and baste the three layers together, we all held our breath. This quilt-to-be was huge. "It's a football field," I wrote to Heather.

We laid it all on the freshly washed-and-dried tiles of my living room floor, where it looked like wall-to-wall carpeting. It filled the room the way my second-semester students had for our first class. On our hands and knees, with our bottoms pointing to the ceiling, we basted this sandwich in large running stitches to hold it all together.

We were now ready for Steps 8 and 9 — marking our quilting designs on the face and proceeding with the quilting. *Quilting?! How*, I wondered, *would we ever manage to quilt this thing?*

The women trusted me to come up with an answer.

- - - - - - - - - - - - -

A South Carolina Plantation, December 1860

It was a long while before Jeneba washed Moses' markings off her floor. When her grandchildren came in and asked what those black marks were, Jeneba made up a story to satisfy their curiosity. She told them a missionary had come to see her and in trying to convert her to her God and save her heathen soul she'd told Bible stories — assuming Jeneba had never heard them before — and illustrated them by drawing pictures on the floor.

"This one," Jeneba pointed out to the children at the time, "is Jacob's ladder, the stairway to heaven. And this eight-pointed star is the Star of Bethlehem that led the three wise men to baby Jesus asleep in a manger. But you already know these stories." The children nodded.

Jeneba told the children not to walk on the designs or smudge them in any way — "Tiptoe around them," she said — because she was still considering the missionary's message. In truth, she needed time to study Harriet's designs so she could apply them to her quilting. As a new agent on the Underground Railroad, she wanted to be sure to adhere correctly to the code.

In all the years she had been making quilts, Jeneba had created her own designs, choosing odd shapes and bright colors of scrap fabrics as she wished — or as the ancestors led her — and sewing them together to tell her stories. If she were able to write, like her son Beau had learned how to do, she would have sewn words together on paper with a quill pen and black ink. She would know how to make the threadlike marks in ink, with their knots and curls and straight lines, mean something to readers. But Jeneba could only write with a needle and cotton thread and scraps of colorful fabric and hope that her message came through to those with the insight to read her designs.

Oh, she was proud of her quilts! She knew that if she was a sinner, her sin was pride. Jeneba's quilts said things. They shouted. They sang. Some even danced. Sometimes she would hang a new one out on her clothesline as though it had just been washed, but in fact it had never touched soap and water. She just wanted to show it off. She'd sit back and watch proudly from her porch as people in the quarters admired it slow-dancing in the morning breeze as they passed by.

"Nice quilt, Jeneba!" a passerby would say to her, nodding toward her clothesline. "When're you go'n t'make me one? I could use somethin' fiery-hot like that t'keep me warm on these col' nights."

"Soon," Jeneba would say as if she meant it. "I'll make you one just like it, real soon."

When she began to incorporate Harriet's designs into the quilts she made, Jeneba became more generous. Making coded quilts became her passion, her mission, and she gave these quilts as gifts at every opportunity. Mostly, she gave them to newlyweds, with a strict admonition to the new bride that she keep the quilt clean and alive by gently hand-washing it frequently and hanging it outside in the sunshine to dry. "Quilts need to breathe fresh air," Jeneba would say.

So at any given time in the almost ten years since Moses's first and only visit to the Wilson plantation, there had always been at least one coded quilt dancing in the open air for all to see, the way those Confederate flags flapped from the government buildings there in Charleston. Jeneba didn't know how many passengers on the Underground Railroad had seen her quilts airing, but she had faith in her God that many brave travelers had followed her eight-pointed North Star like a beacon to freedom far north, in a place called Canada.

Jeneba never told the true meaning of Moses' designs to those good Christian newlyweds she gave her quilts to. She told them the same stories she told her grandchildren, Bible stories that they could more comfortably live with. Perhaps one or two of the remaining elders, who, like Jeneba, remembered the hand-painted secret messages in the mud cloth of Mali, suspected the deeper meanings in her gift quilts. But those few left who were born in Africa knew better how to keep secrets.

One thing that couldn't be kept secret anymore, Jeneba knew, was that freedom was coming. She could feel it in her feet the way you can feel the earth tremble before you can even see an arriving train. Just last month a man named Abraham Lincoln was elected President of the United States. Would he set all of the slaves in this whole country free? Will that include us in South Carolina, Jeneba wondered? There were whispers that South Carolina was planning to leave the Union.

The slaves on Wilson's plantation lived in hope and fear and anxiety and anticipation. It was a whirling, swirling of feelings they could hardly give names to. Jeneba found herself holding her chest with both hands sometimes, just to keep herself from bursting.

Some of the people in the quarters talked among themselves in low tones, scratching their heads: What will this man named Abraham Lincoln really do when he becomes President next year? What will become of us? If we are set free, where will we go? What work will we do if we don't work with cotton? What will freedom feel like? Where will we live? Who will take us in? Where do we belong? Will there be big ships waiting to take us back to our motherlands in Africa? Will the ancestors welcome us home? ...

No one had any answers.

Well, Jeneba said to herself, I hope to live to see the day this new President fulfills his promise, because my work as a secret agent on the Underground Railroad has had to come to an end. He'll have to do it all now, without my help. I can no longer see well enough to quilt or sew. My eyes have grown cloudy, and my hands are too stiff and thick to handle a needle and thread. My legs, too, hurt so much I can barely walk. I don't go anywhere anymore — not that I went far before.

- - - - - - - - - - - - -

Although she could no longer see well enough to sew, in some ways Jeneba could see better than ever. When she looked back on her life, she could see some things more clearly than when they occurred.

For example, when she was in her twenties and her owner owned her nights as well as her days, no other man on the plantation ever came near enough to touch her. They were, she could see now, afraid. She was the owner's woman — everyone except his wife and daughters knew this. Jeneba was Wilson's property in bed as well as in the cotton fields; and no one dared trespass on his property for fear of his merciless whip.

Then, when she was in her thirties, after baby Carolina had just learned to walk unsteadily, and Wilson had found another slave woman's body to claim while his innocent wife lay sleeping in their marriage bed, a handsome African man named Jonah came to call. He and Jeneba would sit on her porch on Sunday afternoons and talk in hesitant Bambara. He too was from southern Mali and remembered the griots' stories and songs from his childhood. Jonah once spoke shyly to Jeneba of marriage and children. He said if they had a son, they could name him Sundiata, after Mali's

Lion King. The boy's nickname could be Sunny. The warmth of Jonah's wide smile melted Jeneba's heart. She saw love in his kind eyes.

People saw them together and talked. One day Beau approached Jonah and shouted, "What are you doing with my mother? You don't belong here!" Jonah and Jeneba looked at each other in silence; they could feel the ancestors tremble. Soon after, when word of Jonah's interest in Jeneba reached Wilson, he sold Jonah to a plantation across the state line in Georgia, where the owner was known for his brutality. No other man ever came to call.

During those years, when Jeneba's body ached for love it had never known, the quilts she made and slept beneath were filled with fire. The yellow, red, and orange fabric fragments she sewed together resembled wild flames. Each quilt was the picture of a house on fire.

It was a good thing, Jeneba could see clearly now, that Moses came along when she did, to give Jeneba's quilts new meaning, to help her redirect her passion when the flames inside her were so high she could have burned her cabin — and maybe the entire slaves' quarters — down.

- - - - - - - - - - - - -

For Jeneba's daughter Carolina, who was now in her thirties, her passion is her church. Her owner, whom she doesn't know is her father, has succeeded in converting most of his slaves, especially the younger generation born on his plantation, to his Christianity. Carolina grew up to be a passionate follower, a true believer.

She married the young butler, Roland, who came with Wilson's new wife when he remarried the year after his first wife died. This woman was a rich widow from his church, and Roland, a devout Christian, was her most loyal and obedient slave. She sold all of the others; Wilson already had plenty of slaves.

Sometimes Carolina tells Jeneba what her husband Roland overhears over dinner parties at the big, stone house — that Lincoln will surely fail in his efforts to free the slaves because "cotton is too important to the country's economy." Jefferson Davis, Roland also overhears and therefore believes, is a good man who knows what's best for the South. For those like Roland, and

Carolina too, who know no other world, loyalty and subservience to powerful white Southern men are among the highest virtues.

Jeneba shakes her head but says nothing. She knows there is no use disputing with her daughter. Jeneba knows the freedom train is coming. She cannot prove it, but she can feel it. She can feel it in her feet.

To her great sorrow, Jeneba knows that she and her daughter Carolina live in different worlds and believe in different Gods. Carolina's Christian God, she threatens her mother every chance she has, is going to damn Jeneba to hell. She tells Jeneba repeatedly that she fears for her soul. "If you don't become a Christian," she shouts at her mother, "if you remain a heathen from darkest Africa, your soul will burn in hell for eternity after you die!"

Carolina continues reproachfully: "I," she says, "am giving my children a good Christian upbringing! They have a mother and a father. Marriage was ordained by God, and I am a faithful, married woman. I don't sleep with any man who happens to be passing through — and bear children out of wedlock in all shades of brown!"

Jeneba doesn't reply. She doesn't argue with her daughter, fearing the truth would hurt Carolina more than her false accusations hurt her. Carolina calls Wilson — the father who has never taken any notice of her — "Master," and she tries her best to please him by being the fastest and most productive worker in his fields. She leads the row; she sets the pace. She believes this man, this rich, distinguished-looking, white-haired old man, is a good Christian because this is what she's been taught in his church.

"We are fortunate to be here on his plantation," she tells Jeneba emphatically. "Master takes good care of us — like a shepherd does his flock. We have shelter and clothing and food. Tell me," she says, shaking her finger at Jeneba like a whip, "have you ever been hungry? Have you ever been whipped? Have you ever slept outside in the cold? Master Wilson provides for all our needs."

Jeneba does not answer her. She knows her daughter's beliefs are absolute. They are the wide, wooden planks that make up the high platform on which Carolina stands straight and tall looking down on her African mother. Jeneba knows if she tried to pull the planks away, Carolina would fall and break. She is my child, Jeneba repeats to herself, I cannot hurt her.

"Everything is God's will," Carolina preaches to her mother. "It is God's will that Master Wilson is our Master. We must be grateful, hard working, and obedient in this life. If we are, we will be abundantly rewarded in Heaven."

"Maybe so," Jeneba says, and then turns from her daughter heavily. Jeneba knows it won't be long before she will know first-hand whether there's a Christian Heaven or Hell. But here and now she suspects there is neither — just a spirit realm where the ancestors gather, as if for a celebratory feast. Jeneba is sure her mother and father and brothers are there by now. She longs to join them soon at that feast.

- - - - - - - - - - - - -

"The patchwork is a project for the development of the women. … For me, I love patchwork very much."

— Bassam Sacko, Patchwork Project graduate
(translated from the French)

Griots

I RODE MY BIKE INTO TOWN WITH A HEAVY HEART, choking back tears. The U.S. 2000 Presidential election results had finally been decided, by none other than the United States Supreme Court, and the sorrow I felt was profound. Although it was a beautiful, mild, December morning in Ségou, I was oblivious to the beauty around me as I rode. My thoughts were half a world away.

I had not been able to vote in this election, despite having tried. Several times over the past months, I'd requested an absentee ballot, but none ever arrived in the mail. *How many other Americans living overseas*, I wondered, *have been similarly disenfranchised?*

Every night for the previous five weeks, ever since Election Day, I'd been following the news of the disputed election, my hopes rising and falling with each twist and turn. I'd sat in my study intently listening to the Voice of America and Radio France International on my short-wave radio as I worked at my sewing machine. At first, they reported the election "too close to call." Then, on Wednesday, November 8th, one day after the election, Radio France announced, *"Bush a gagné le presidence!"* (Bush won the Presidency). *"Quelle suspense!"*

Despite Al Gore's "superior competence," the radio announcer said, "the people have chosen Bush due to his superior charm and charisma." Then, just the next day, the Voice of America broadcast news of possible fraud. A recount was demanded. Radio France announced on Friday that the election decision was to be postponed until November 17, allowing time to hand-count Florida's votes and add in absentee ballots.

"What a dramatic time we're all living through," I wrote to my sister on November 10. "Everyone — even here in Ségou, where a nuclear bomb dropped somewhere else on the planet wouldn't concern most of the locals — is glued to his or her shortwave radio to get the latest on the U.S. Presidential elections. They're rooting for Gore, of course, because having been Bill Clinton's VP, they believe he will follow in Bill's footsteps. They all LOVED Bill. ..."

By Thanksgiving the 2000 election still hadn't been decided. Each night, as I listened to my shortwave, the news was the same: "the suspense continues" as to the winner; "this is the closest race" in U.S.

history. Finally, the matter went to the Supreme Court.

Early Wednesday morning, December 13, I tuned into Radio France to learn the Supreme Court's decision. The day before they'd decided 5 to 4 for Bush. The Court, ignoring the popular vote in Al Gore's favor, gave the Presidency of the United States to George W. Bush. One radio commentator called this final decision "a miscarriage of justice." The election "was not stolen," another said. "It was expropriated."

What good are elections if the electorate's votes no longer matter? I wondered. *Where is our democracy heading? What kind of example are we setting for the world?*

I decided to ride my bike into town and visit my friend Mohammed who owned a small stationery store, where overpriced paperbacks and faded, outdated magazines lined the store's shelves and collected dust. Mohammed and I had talked frequently about the election over the past months. He was sure Al Gore would win because Gore was the better man — smart, able, and honorable. Mohammed believed that if Africans, living so far away, could see this, surely the majority of Americans would also.

When I got to town, I chained my bike to a post and walked heavily into Mohammed's dark and cluttered store. I approached the front counter feeling like a lost child, or a woman without a country.

"C'est decidé. Bush a gagné le presidence," I said.

"Oui. Je sais" (I know), he said. He'd heard the news too.

Pent-up thoughts and fears tumbled out of my mouth.

"This isn't good news for Africa," I said. "Well, I mean countries in Africa that don't have oil, such as Mali."

And then, as if I could see into the future, as if I knew with certainty what this new Administration would bring, I said, "There's going to be a war, Mohammed. Bush will start a war. You'll see."

- - - - - - - - - - - - -

MUSIC WAS AS INTEGRAL to the life of my Club Crochet girls as it is to Malians of all ages. The thirty-or-so neighborhood eight-to-twelve-year-olds who gathered on my front terrace every Wednesday afternoon enjoyed crocheting to music.

Sometimes the girls would sing among themselves traditional songs in Bambara, bobbing their heads and keeping time with their bare feet as their little hands worked skillfully with the silky strands of plastic. Sometimes, if the electricity had not been cut that day, I'd pull my small boom box onto the terrace as far as its electric cord allowed and turn to the local radio station that played nonstop Malian music. Or I would play for the girls some of the well-worn cassette tapes I had at hand: Tracy Chapman ("Talkin' 'bout a Revolution"), Elton John ("Candle in the Wind"), Willie Nelson ("Georgia on My Mind"), or Luciano Pavarotti ("Nessum Dorma"). Their favorite tape by far, though, was by their own homegrown and world-renowned singer-composer-musician Salif Keita.

The girls knew that I, following the practice of American Peace Corps volunteers in Mali, had informally adopted a Malian name to signal my membership in the large, predominantly racially tolerant, and generally embracing Malian family. The name I'd picked for myself was "Bani Keita" — Bani being the name of the sister river to the Niger (pronounced, conveniently, exactly like my actual first name), and Keita being a regal Malinke name held by descendants of Sundiata Keita, the Lion King, founder of the Mali Empire. I told the girls, jokingly, every time I put in his cassette, *"Salif Keita est mon frère"* (Salif Keita is my brother), to which they nodded earnestly, as if this fib could well be true. After all, Salif Keita, an albino, had white skin too.

Born in 1949 in the small rural village of Djoliba southwest of Bamako in the Koulikoro region of Mali, Salif Keita was outcast by his family and ostracized by his community because at the time albinos were thought to bring bad luck. He further earned his royal clan's scorn by becoming a musician, a line of work traditionally held by a lower caste, the griots, itinerant entertainers and oral historians who sang their stories in a haunting, plaintive wail.

Salif Keita's wide-ranging and timelessly soulful singing voice — borne, no doubt, of his early personal hardships and pain — brought him international stardom after he moved to Paris in the mid-1980s. Interviewed by Quincy Troupe for the *New York Times Magazine* in 1995, Keita said, "I'm trying to mix the past with the future. ... We [his band] are always gaining experience by working in the present for the future. The mix of the traditional and modern is the future. Not just in Africa, but everywhere." Soon after the New Millennium, Salif Keita returned to Mali from Europe to live and record in Bamako.

Because it was their favorite, I played Salif Keita's tape repeatedly for my Club Crochet girls, until I knew by heart every note of every primal sound he made. My mind could anticipate where his voice would go next, when it would dip sharply or rise in a prolonged, warbly wail. I didn't know the words he sang in his own tongue; but all of the girls did, and they sang along.

- - - - - - - - - - - - -

One day the girls surprised me.

"Viens" (come), Bintou, their spokesperson and main translator, said to me one afternoon soon after the girls' arrival. *"Nous avons une petite surprise!"* She took one of my hands, Aminata took the other, and the rest of the group followed us away from my house, down a narrow side street, and onto the wide, main unpaved road in Pelengana that led to Mariko's nursery.

Some of the older girls had been acting strangely lately, I'd noticed — suddenly asking to withdraw money from the bank I held for them but without giving any reason. "For school books?" I asked, and they hesitated in answering, obviously not wanting to lie. Now I learned why: They had pooled their own money to pay for professional musicians to play for us. They had organized a surprise street party in my honor.

As we approached, I saw three grown men, serious musicians, sitting on stools by the side of the dusty road. They then began to play their percussion instruments — large and small drums and a melodious *balafon* (West African-style xylophone) — while the designated griot began to sing. I heard my Malian name sung as if in praise — "Oh, Bani Keita...!" — and only a few bars later the name of Sundiata Keita. *Were we being linked in some familial way,* I wondered? *Was the griot saying I, too, was descended from the Lion King?*

The girls, clearly thrilled by their successful coup, found a stool for me to sit on and formed a circle around me and the musicians. They clapped and moved in time with the music and sang along with the refrain. Our group took up half of the road, so that the occasional clomping donkey cart or whizzing car kicking up dust had to go around us, but no one seemed to mind. Those who passed us waved benignly, as if a street party consisting of one middle-aged *toubob* and almost three dozen African girls in party dresses held on a hot Wednesday afternoon in the middle of the main, dusty road in *quartier* Pelengana was a normal, everyday occurrence.

One by one, the girls pulled me up to dance with them in the center of the circle. At first I felt embarrassed and unsure. The heat, the dust, the musicians' muscular drumming, the griot's plaintive singing, and the excited little girls clamoring around me made my head spin. But then I gave in to the music. I let the music dance through me. To my surprise, and for the duration of my surprise party, Bani Keita was an African woman who could really dance.

- - - - - - - - - - - - -

Baltimore, Maryland, December 1936

Rose Jeffers MacNeal
Slave Narrative
Interviewed at Baltimore, Maryland
Interviewer not identified
Age when interviewed: 88

I was born on the mornin' of January 4, 1849, in Beaufort County, South Carolina. That would make me near to 88 now. I belonged to an old, white-haired gentleman named James Beaufort Wilson. His family since way back owned a whole lot of slaves and a whole lot of land, too, in those parts. They was really rich due to their fields of cotton. My granny used to say Wilson was like a king who made his subjects turn cotton into gold.

My granny came over from somewhere in Africa on one of the las' slaver ships when she was only a chil'. Wilson bid the highest for her at the slave market in Charleston and brought her back to his plantation in Beaufort. People used to say she was real pretty when she was young. They said she walked tall and straight with her head held high, as though she was wearin' a big crown.

My granny became a special seamstress for the big house. She made clothes for Wilson and his family when they was all young. She made quilts, too, but none of them survived the big fire. I sure would like to have one of them quilts now to keep me warm.

My granny had three light-skinned chil'en. Some say they were the overseers', but she would never say who they daddy was. Granny didn't talk much. She kep' mostly to herself when I knew her, all the time stayin' in her cabin and sewin'. But sometimes she would tell us chil'en stories about Africa.

My mamma, born Carolina Wilson, was granny's younges' child. I never knew her two older ones because they was gone from the plantation before I was born. My mamma married the butler at the big house, name Roland Jeffers, and they had four chil'en — me, Junior, Sarah, and Hugh. I'se the oldest, but I'se lived the longest.

Before the war, our plantation was a nice place to be. When I was a chil' Master Wilson was already old, so he didn't have the strength left to whip his slaves no more. And his new wife, a fine Christian lady, wouldn't allow him to have anyone else whip us neither. So we wasn't afraid. We worked and played and went to church meetin's. That was my life growin' up there. There was no readin' or writin', though. Master didn' 'llow slaves to get such education.

Then the war came. I'se sorry my granny didn't live to see how those Yankees swooped down from the North like hungry grasshoppers and ate up all there was to eat and then set fire to the whole place — the big house and cotton fields and cabins and all. My granny would have nodded her head in approval and clapped her big black hands. She didn't like Wilson no-how. The Yankee soldiers didn't kill ol' Master and his wife, though. They just left them out there on the front lawn under the smoky sky, huggin' each other and wailin' like babies.

After the war we all had a hard time gettin' used to bein' free. My parents took us from place to place, sharecroppin' here and sharecroppin' there, always on the run from the Ku Kluxers. My daddy was no good at farm work because he had always worked in the big house takin' orders from the Master's wife. He didn't know how to work with land or with his hands. He didn't have the gift.

So we chil'en were often hungry and scared, and my mamma would scold my daddy harsh, sayin', "We were better off with Master Wilson! We had enough food and we had protection! Now what do we have? You can't take care of us! God has deserted us!" She seemed to prefer slavery over freedom. Like I said, those were real tough times.

In 1869 I married a good-lookin' ginger-cake man named Ben Mac-Neal, and we moved up here to Baltimore, where he got work as a caulker. Yes, he was mighty proud to work at the first black-owned shipyard in the whole nation — the Chesapeake Railway and Dry Dock Company, run by Isaac Myers. Why, I can still remember the names!

Ben was a good man, a good worker, and he made good money. We raised three chil'en. They'se all dead now — "gone to the ancestors," as my granny would say. My gran'chil'en scattered to the four winds. I can't keep track of how many they is now and where they's all at. Oh, one is in Philadelphia, if I recall. Her name is Sally Jones. She sometimes keeps in touch.

- - - - - - - - - - - -

*"The Patchwork Project is a project of development.
We women must unite to create an association for working together.
And then we can teach other women in other women's centers.
I will never forget the Patchwork Project,
because it has developed an esprit of women working together."*

— Rокоатои Ван, Patchwork Project graduate
(translated from the French)

The Quilt

ONE OF THE THINGS I WAS DETERMINED TO DO before I left Ségou was to see that Aminata attended school. My first step was to enlist my friend Mariko's help in this campaign. I knew that he, as a retired elementary school principal, would take up my cause. I knew, too, that as my friend and neighbor, he would do anything to help me.

So Mariko and I arranged for him to stop by my house one Wednesday afternoon while Aminata and her fellow Club Crochet members were gathered on my front porch, busily crocheting with plastic bags and singing along with Salif Keita. After greeting the girls in Bambara and getting a warm response, Mariko asked Aminata to invite Camara to join him in my courtyard. She ran to fetch her uncle, and he arrived right away.

I sat with the girls, crocheting too, as the two men stood together in the walkway of my front yard and talked. Both of them were tall, well-built men in their mid-fifties, dressed in traditional Malian robelike clothes — Mariko in a clean, pressed, flowing white *boubou* and Camara in a crumpled, ragged, dusty brown one. Facing each other, the two men were alike in their characteristic Malian dignified and respectful stance; but I knew that on the subject of schooling they faced in opposite directions: one toward the future and the other toward the past.

Mariko was an educated man, a career educator, whereas Camara had never been to school. Camara knew how to hammer scrap metal into usable, saleable objects, how to be a faithful husband who supported his disabled wife and adopted child, how to attend mosque services every Friday and pray five times a day; but he had never learned how to read or write or question. He believed in tradition. He feared education.

As Malians' conversations customarily do, theirs began with elaborate greetings back and forth and inquiries into each other's and their respective family's health and well being — time-honored social lubricants that smooth the way for more serious discussion. Although I couldn't understand their words, I could tell from their body language how the negotiations were going: Mariko was making a case for Aminata's schooling, gesturing in her direction — a bright and diligent little girl among the more than two dozen little girls on my porch, most of whom, as Mariko knew, already attended school. Then Camara gave his reasons against the idea, ticking each off on his long, work-worn fingers. The two men listened respectfully to one another, as Malians excel at doing. Neither raised his voice in anger.

The Club Crochet girls and I kept our heads low, pretending not to be paying attention. We'd hushed Salif Keita's singing to a whisper. To a person, we were silently rooting for Mariko. All of us were aching for Aminata to be allowed to go to school.

"How did it go?" I asked Mariko in French after Camara returned to his home next door and Mariko joined the girls and me in the shade of my front terrace.

"At first he said no — Aminata must stay home and help her aunt with the housework —"

I shook my head. "This is a crime —"

"But then I convinced him to reconsider. He agreed to think about it," Mariko said, conceding that this was a big step forward for such an intransigent man.

Within a few days, I learned through an interpreter that Camara and Sarah had agreed to let Aminata attend the local Franco-Arab school — if, that is, I agreed to pay for it. The cost, I learned, was only about 1,000 CFA per month, or the equivalent of roughly $2. Of course, I agreed.

The next time we met, the Club Crochet girls were jubilant at the news. Aminata would be going to school! She would no longer spend her entire days as her aunt Sarah's slave.

This "Franco-Arab" school, however, turned out to be the Koranic school in *quartier* Pelangana, housed in a small, tent-like hut near the dusty local *marché*, where raggedy poor children sat on rows of long, rough, wooden benches and did nothing but recite the Koran in Arabic for hours.

"Alphabet?" I asked Aminata, the next time she came by. I drew the ABC's on a pad and tried to appear quizzical.

She shook her head.

"Numbers?" I wrote 1, 2, 3…

She shook her head again.

I felt angry that I'd been duped into paying for a school where she would learn nothing useful, in my opinion. But when one of my Ben-kady women friends inquired of Aminata in Bambara on my behalf, she learned that Aminata liked the school. It gave her a chance to spend time with other children and make more friends. It took her away from her mean-spirited aunt and the drudgery of days filled with house-work. Aminata was happy and proud to be a schoolgirl at last.

I resolved to redouble my efforts to be her private tutor — if not in math (always my own weakest subject), then at least in the ABC's.

- - - - - - - - - - - - -

Whenever she could — whenever she saw me leave my house and she could break away from her unrelenting chores — Aminata would call to me, then rush to the cement wall divide between our houses to show me her progress. In the past, this progress had been measured only in crocheted plastic items; now it also included schoolwork. To me, the Arabic words she'd obviously copied sloppily from her school's black-board were beyond indecipherable. But I praised her efforts nonetheless.

"Bravo! … *Très bien!* … *Bon travail!*" I sang, patting her leathery little hands. Her quarter-moon smile widened almost to the breaking point; her bright eyes danced.

Aminata took special care in dressing for school, I noticed, wearing some of the things I'd brought back for her from my granddaughter Lauren on my last trip to the States. In her short-cropped hair, she wore a big, pink plastic clip shaped like a butterfly. Lauren's outgrown summer sandals — white leather, decorated with daisies — were still too big for Aminata's narrow little feet; but she wore them to school any-way. And Lauren's pink-and-white Cinderella T-shirt, although still too large for Aminata's small frame, seemed particularly fitting.

I often thought about Aminata's future and what it might hold. The likelihood of a storybook ending for this pretty little brown Cinderella was negligible. Without a useful education or trade that might offer her some hope of independence, she would be forced to marry in a few years — certainly not a handsome prince; more likely an older man not of her own choosing — and begin a whole new chapter of servitude and subjugation that would last her lifetime.

Was I wrong to try to guide her toward a different path than that? Was I fighting the tide of Malian traditionalism? Was I mistaken in making her education my business? Mariko didn't think so. He applauded my efforts. He fanned the flames.

As far as I could judge, I had made some progress. Since that first incident soon after I moved to Pelengana, I had not seen Camara abuse Aminata again. She became increasingly freer to visit my home, her refuge, after her household chores were done, to sit quietly with me and crochet or to practice her alphabet in French. She was now allowed to attend school, albeit a Koranic school. Camara and Sarah seemed to appreciate whatever I was able to do for them or share with them, such as the occasional gift of meat for their family's meals, Lauren's second-hand clothes for Aminata, and the monthly tuition I paid for her school. In fact, in time, Aminata's aunt and uncle grew to trust me — but never as fully as Aminata had done from the moment she and I first met.

- - - - - - - - - - - -

My longtime friend Wendy wasn't a handsome prince, but her gift held the promise of a happier ending to Aminata's life story.

Wendy, who had been born and raised in Kenya to a British father and a white South African mother but now lived in Florida, made a trip to Mali with a friend, and they visited me in Ségou. By the time they arrived at my house, they had toured Mali's major attractions; they had seen the sights and bought significant souvenirs. I admired the necklace that Wendy's traveling companion Maria was wearing — a full, fat strand of perfectly sculpted, pale-caramel-colored, genuine amber beads — which she'd purchased on this trip.

She ran her manicured fingers along the necklace. "It cost a fortune," she said. "But fortunately, I can afford it."

Wendy and Maria were there for our Wednesday afternoon Club Crochet gathering. They bought ten of the crocheted plastic change purses the girls had ready for sale. They admired the little girls at work. They met Aminata, who smiled shyly at the two imposing middle-aged American women and shook their hands.

It didn't take long for Wendy to devise a plan: She became determined to share her good fortune with my little next-door neighbor.

The next day, when Wendy and Maria met the women of my Patchwork Project, I explained to Ramata, the president of Centre Benkady, that Wendy wanted to pay in full, in advance, for the Centre's one-year *coupe-couture* course for Aminata. All that remained was to convince Camara to allow her attend.

This time, Camara was confronted on his own territory. Ramata, in a colorful, flowing *boubou* and matching head wrap, strode regally into his compound and interrupted him at his work. Again, from a distance, I could see his resistance; but Ramata, a charmingly forceful woman, would not back down.

"How did it go?" I ventured when she returned to my house.

"At first, he refused," she said. "But I managed to change his mind. I told him that as a seamstress who could earn a good income, Aminata would be able to help support him and his wife in their old age. I told him he cannot pound metal forever."

"How soon will Aminata be able to begin?" I asked.

"He consented to letting her attend our sewing school starting with the next school year. In the meantime, you must pay for her Koranic school until June."

I happily agreed.

- - - - - - - - - - - - -

APART FROM PICTURES of finely made wooden kits advertised in the back of quilting magazines, I'd never seen a quilting frame. In the entire fifty-five years of my life, I'd never touched one, sat at one, quilted at one, nor watched anyone else do so. I didn't come from a quilting tradition. There were no stories in my family of old-time quilting bees held at an Aunt Clara's cabin in the country, where her handyman husband, Uncle Jake, had rigged up a quilting frame that descended from the bedroom ceiling on ropes and pulleys. In my life, such stories were strictly fiction.

So when the time approached for the Patchwork Project to hand-quilt the wedding gift my sister had commissioned us to make for her son Tyler, I was faced with a challenge at least as enormous as Tyler's king-size quilt-in-progress: What would we use for a quilting frame? Where would I find one? How could I make one, having never even seen one?

There were certainly no quilting frames for sale in Mali, since quilting was, up to that point, essentially unheard of in that country. It was not practical, nor even possible, for me to buy a quilting frame through a quilting magazine ad and have it shipped all the way to Ségou. For one thing, the frames I saw for sale cost hundreds of dollars, well beyond my budget. Plus, even if I could afford to buy and ship one, I couldn't count on its ever arriving in Mali intact — if at all. No, I knew I had to be resourceful and creative — as resourceful and creative as most Malians needed to be to make do without many manufactured products and without money.

During sleepless nights, when my faithful Muslim neighbors woke to the call to prayer sung from the minaret of the local mosque, I prayed for a workable solution to my quilting-frame dilemma. In the pre-dawn darkness, beneath the mosquito netting covering my rooftop bed, with eyes still closed, I drew various quilting frame designs in my mind. Then one morning over tea in my study, I sketched my winning design on graph paper.

It was simple, really: Three, nine-foot, sturdy bamboo poles resting on two sawhorses. The sawhorses would be one meter (39-1/2 inches) long and slightly taller than tabletop height (80 cm, or 31-1/2 inches) — to allow quilters to sit at the frame comfortably, with one hand under, and the other hand over, the quilt. Two of the bamboo poles would act as scrolls, onto which the "sandwiched," basted, and ready-to-be-quilted quilt would be attached and rolled, then tied with plastic cord to each end of both sawhorses. The third pole would support the center length of the quilt. On paper, this frame made perfect sense. But would it work in practice?

I had a local carpenter, the same young man who had made our classroom worktables, make the wooden sawhorses to my design. I bought the poles in town, from a bamboo merchant on the banks of the Niger, attached them to my bike, and pedaled precariously home — thankful it was a straight route because with the bamboo tied on both sides to my handlebars and rear basket, I couldn't make turns. Once home, I wrapped the poles tightly with clean muslin cloth, sewing the cloth securely in place, to both protect the quilt from the bamboo's rough joints and to give the quilt something to be temporarily sewn on to. I set up this makeshift quilting frame in the middle of my living room and hoped for the best.

When Group 3 basted Tyler's quilt to the bamboo poles and we rolled the poles onto the sawhorses, I was ecstatic. *It worked, it all worked!* I thought. What I'd envisioned and hoped for was gradually coming to pass. I thought of Emily Dickinson's line, "You never know how tall you are til you are asked to rise…" My Malian women students were tall indeed.

I suspected that they would especially enjoy hand quilting at the quilt frame because of the sociability of it. They could sit side by side around the frame, talk, laugh, sing, listen to music; maybe make a party of it. They were always up for a celebration.

Then I did the math: There were 49, 11-1/2-inch squares in the quilt; a maximum of 18 women currently in the project; four working lessons left in which they could do the hand quilting. Allowing for absences, if 15 women were able to complete one square per two-hour lesson, that meant 15 x 4 = 60 squares (which translated to 49 squares, plus borders). *So it* is *possible we can complete this project in this century,* I told myself.

Four women could sit on cushioned chairs along both sides of the frame within arms' reach of each other and work on the squares directly in front of them. The women worked bare-footed, having left their shoes on my front porch before entering my house. My living room, with all of its windows and doors open to the occasional breeze, was relatively cool, well lighted, and clean. The atmosphere was more pleasant and social than strenuous. The women seemed happy to be there and to learn this new skill.

We used masking tape as a guide for our quilting designs: On the solid, blue *bazin* blocks, we quilted squares within squares; on the pinwheel blocks, we outlined the triangles that formed the pinwheels.

As I'd suspected, my Malian students enjoyed hand quilting, and they had an abundance of patience for it. The repetitive, up-and-down motion of the short quilting needle seemed to mirror Malian music, so much a part of their culture. In fact, we often listened to Malian music as we worked.

Our lessons became quilting bees, and word of these bees drew interest beyond those directly involved in our project. Women in high places — the mayor's wife, the governor's wife and her entourage — stopped by my house to see what this quilting gathering was all about. Young female Peace Corps volunteers came by on their bikes, pulled up a chair, and pitched in with the quilting. Other European women friends and acquaintances came for a visit and found themselves learning how to hand-quilt. This makeshift quilting frame filling up my living room became like a long, narrow harvest table where an international group of women of all ages regularly shared a happy feast.

It was here at the quilting frame that I got to sit with the women side by side, instead of standing in front of them as their instructor. It was here that we could all talk and laugh and sing, while our hands did the monotonous (only to me) work of hand quilting. It was here that I got to know the women better as individuals, and I learned some of their life stories for the first time.

I was also able to take photographs of the women at work at the quilting frame for an album I planned to give to my nephew Tyler, along with his finished quilt.

Here are some of that album's photos and stories, frozen in time:

The white woman with the graying dark hair is my new friend Mieke Bastianssen, 53, from Holland. She and her husband Yoss, an irrigation engineer, arrived in Ségou recently on a two-year contract. Mieke has just become a grandmother. She wants to learn quilting so she can make a baby quilt for her new grandson, Bram, to bring to him for Christmas in Holland.

Fily Diallo, 33, the young Malian woman with a shy smile, to Mieke's right, is one of the Benkady *stagiaires*. She also cleans my house two mornings a week now, allowing me the freedom to do other things. To help her arrive for work on time, I gave her the watch she's wearing — only to learn afterward that she has never learned how to tell time. She can't read or write either because she never went to school. As the only girl in her family (one of her many older brothers is now a judge in Bamako), Fily had to stay at home to help her mother with the cooking and housework.

Fily was married briefly, but her husband, who beat her regularly, with his fists as well as with lengths of rebar, divorced her because she failed to get pregnant in three years. (His subsequent wife has failed to get pregnant as well.) Fily now lives with her aunt Ramata, the president of Centre Benkady. Despite her misfortunes, Fily maintains a sunny nature and is quick to smile, however shyly.

Across from Fily, in the green-and-beige-patterned dress and matching turban, is Rokiatou Bah, 30. Rokiatou has never been married and has no children, which is quite unusual among African women her age. Instead, she has her own tailor shop, Express Couture, in *centreville* Ségou, with three employees. She is an extremely capable seamstress and now a conscientious quilter.

Next to her is Fatimata Traore, 38, who is on her way to becoming an excellent quilter. She is the mother of one child — a teenage girl — and at the time of this photo was a week away from divorcing a husband she called "insupportable." I'm hopeful that when the women form an association to carry on the Patchwork Project, she'll be one of its leaders because she has the time and talent, as well as the newfound love of quilting that would make her outstanding.

The two young white women on the far right are new Peace Corps volunteers in Ségou. Erin, 26, is a small business volunteer from Nashville; and Christine, 24, with the honey-color hair, is an agricultural volunteer from Boston posted in a nearby village and working on a chicken-raising project.

Rokia Dembele, the very pretty 22-year-old woman in the brown and white puffed-sleeved dress with matching turban, is the youngest of my students but very able and conscientious. She is a newlywed and, in this photo, three months pregnant with their first child, whom she says she'll name Bonnie if it's a girl. She is typical of many young Malian women — quiet, shy, willowy, elegant, and somewhat mysterious. Malian women tend to become more interesting, outspoken, and textured with age.

Bassam Sacko, in pink, is 38 years old and the mother of six children. Of all my students, Bassam was the most enthusiastic about learning patchwork quilting. Whereas the others sometimes missed classes due to family obligations and celebrations — baptisms, weddings, funerals — which always took precedence over everything else, Bassam never missed a class. *"Le patchwork est le plus important pour moi"* (patchwork is the most important for me), she told me one day, adding, "marriages and funerals can wait." I was delighted to learn that she's been chosen by her classmates to be the president of their soon-to-be-formed patchwork association.

Marie-Augustine Diarra, 43, is the mother of seven surviving children (three others died), a devout Catholic, and a complete character. Among many other things, she is a member of a theater troupe, in which her role is usually the clown — banging a drum, dancing, and jumping around like a kid. She seems to try her hand at everything: Here it's quilting, which she does badly because she can't see without her glasses — if in fact she owns a pair of glasses; she never seems to have them with her.

Guylaine Fortin, 31, the white woman with a pixie haircut standing at the far end of the quilt frame, is from Quebec. She came to Mali this year as a volunteer with a Canadian development organization called PACCEM, and promptly fell in love with her boss, another Canadian, named Gino. When her volunteer service ends, she plans to stay in Ségou to be with him.

Korotimi (Koro) Traore, 36, is the mother of six children and is one of the liveliest of the group. She is always singing (her name, Korotimi, means "little bird" in Bambara), putting new words to well-known African tunes. One of the ditties she sings for the group in French while quilting is, "If you want to succeed at Patchwork, you must do a good job…"

Philippine Razafin, the light-brown-skinned woman in a yellow short-sleeve shirt with a silver cross on a long chain (standing), is a seemingly ageless Catholic nun from Madagascar and the most conscientious of my Patchwork Project students. She travels to remote villages to teach sewing and other practical skills to village women. She hopes now to share her newfound love for patchwork quilting with the women she teaches.

Other photos show individual students at work, such as Ami Sylla wearing a bright red *boubou* and matching turban, looking up over her big eyeglasses at my camera. Ami has just recovered from a grave illness, in which she suffered severe headaches and partial paralysis of her arms and legs. When I visited her at home, she seemed quite shaken by this experience. Like me, she is terrified of physical incapacitation. We're all happy to have her back at the quilting frame.

And this photo is of Delphine Dembele, head close to her stitching, struggling to see because she doesn't own glasses. If you look closely, you can see the bent finger that her husband broke in one of his drunken rages.

In this one, Fatou Diallo, in pale blue, is intent on threading a needle with the white quilting thread my sister had sent us. Fatou, who works at the nongovernmental organization ALPHALOG, helped me round up the students for this semester. She is also intent on mobilizing the women into forming a patchwork association to prove to me the project will go on.

And here is a photo of two young Peace Corps volunteers from Gabon who showed up at my house for a visit after completing their two-year service there and embarking on a six-month-long grand adventure traveling around Africa, India, and Australia. These two smart and funny American adventurers, Cara and Chula, both in their mid-twenties, became close friends while serving as agricultural volunteers in Gabon.

I not only gave them my guest room for several days but also a crash course in quilting. Cara, from Michigan, told me she'd never sewn anything in her life before, so she sat at the quilt frame with shaky hands. Chula, from Steamboat Springs, Colorado, on the other hand, said she'd been sewing since early childhood, so she took to the quilting right away.

When my guests were gone, however, and my students returned to their homes and families, and I was left with my thoughts, quilting alone at the quilting frame, I couldn't help but worry. Would the Patchwork Project continue after my departure? Would it succeed in being an income-earner for these newly trained women? Despite the women's talk of a planned association, despite their reassurances to me, I had serious doubts.

The fact was, I was left doing most of the hand quilting. My optimistic mathematical projections weren't working out as I'd calculated. The women, despite their best intentions, could not complete one square per person in a two-hour lesson, as I'd hoped. They were too slow, sometimes too careless, and too inexperienced with deadlines and standards of quality to apply themselves completely to this painstaking work while sitting at the quilting frame enjoying our sisterly quilting bee. They were also preoccupied with other familial and religious priorities in their lives, such as their current observance of Ramadan.

The women, I knew, were doing their best under the circumstances — circumstances they were reluctant to change because they were comfortable, familiar, and familial — but these very circumstances handicapped them, preventing them from doing the job well enough to compete in the world market. It seemed to me to be a vicious cycle.

My job, I kept having to remind myself, *is only to teach them patchwork. The rest is in God's hands.*

Yes, but I wasn't content to leave things at that. I held weekly meetings at my dining room table in the evenings among interested, influential women who might help the project survive. The mayor's wife, Ulla, an Oxford-educated German woman in her forties, generously gave of her time. She brought along her sister-in-law, Aissata, from Guinea Conakry, who owned a successful gift shop in *centreville* Ségou that catered to tourists, plus a young volunteer from Germany named Suzanne, who was under a two-year contract to work with women artisans. I invited Erin, the new Small Business Peace Corps volunteer, as well as my Dutch friend Mieke, who'd been a teacher in Holland for nearly thirty years.

At these meetings we women talked — in English — for hours. I learned that FNAM, the German nongovernmental organization in Bamako that had given me my contract, now had "no money." Suzanne reported she had "no time." Ulla suggested I stay in Ségou and continue the Patchwork Project on my own. I explained that without a phone, a computer, a car, or financial (or any other kind of) support, that would be impossible for me. I'd taken the project as far as I could on my own, I told the group; now it would be best to turn it over to someone with the business, computer, and international marketing skills that I lacked.

Together, we did the math: rent, electricity, salaries (for two people — a manager and a secretary) would come to about 250,000 CFA per month; the sale of one big quilt would bring in 225,000 CFA (maximum — depending on its quality). Sadly, it appeared unlikely that the current group of women could produce even one large quilt per month.

It came down to this: the project needed a home (after mine would no longer be available), which would have to be clean and central and have electricity; and it also needed a person (after I'd gone) to love it, supervise the quality, keep it alive. And, of course, it needed more trained and dedicated workers.

Everyone agreed these were great ideas, and there was definitely a market out there for our Malian "ancestor quilts." The missing link was right here: *Can the women organize, mobilize, rise to the challenge?* Erin said, "This is an American business we're starting up here, and not a small one. We need someone with American business experience, as well as quilting experience."

The fact that we were speaking English allowed me to speak plainly, direct from the heart: "Call me stubborn," I said, "but I remain determined. I believe this project was and is inspired, and I must continue to push for a positive, creative solution to these seemingly insurmountable problems."

The women at my dining room table nodded, then went on their way to their respective homes.

Meanwhile, in the afternoons, women of all colors, nationalities, and backgrounds continued to gather at the quilting frame in the living room of my rented house in *quartier* Pelengana, Ségou, to hand quilt the first king-size bed quilt ever made in Mali, a quilt destined to help keep a young married couple in Denver, Colorado, warm on many cold winter Rocky Mountain nights.

These women worked with love, if not First World efficiency. Their uneven quilting stitches were flecked with laughter, song, and personal stories that united us all.

On the first page of the quilt's accompanying album, which I put together for my nephew Tyler, I quoted *The Prophet* on "Work": "…What is it to work with love? … It is to charge all things you fashion with a breath of your own spirit…" *This quilt*, I thought, as I admired its painfully slow progress on the frame each passing day, *has so much spirit it will one day fly.*

AFTER I LET PIERRE GO in mid-September 2000, I had no choice but to find another night guardian. My Malian women friends would not allow me to live in my house alone, insisting, as they had before they'd found Pierre for me, "Women do *not* live alone here! It is not safe. You *must* have a guardian." This time, though, I chose to find the new guardian myself. *If this one doesn't work out,* I decided, *I'll only have myself to blame.*

The man I chose, who lived somewhere in *quartier* Pelengana and worked most days as a shoe repairman near the Hotel Independence, a few blocks away from my home, had been neighborly and helpful to Youssef and me when we first moved in. He'd helped us dig and plant our vegetable garden, after which he sometimes stopped by to visit with Youssef and admire our garden's growth.

I approached David as he worked beneath a small, open, ramshackle shed near the main road, hammering on the sole of a threadbare leather shoe. Leather shoes were rare sights in Ségou, I'd noticed; most people simply wore plastic flip-flops. So business for David must have been slow. After the usual greetings, I asked whether he might be interested in becoming my new night guardian. *"Oui,"* he said, nodding and smiling broadly, displaying bad teeth. Yes, he was available, and, yes, he could start right away. *"Pas de problème!"* he assured me.

From a distance, Pierre, my first night guardian, and David, whom I was lining up to be my second, could not have been more different. Whereas Pierre was a short, erect, devout Christian man in his early forties, David was a tall, stoop-shouldered, irreligious man in his late fifties. David's body, beneath his tattered long-sleeved shirt and oversized trousers belted in gathers at the waist, was skeletally thin. He walked slowly, with his arms dangling lifelessly, like an old, old man.

Unlike Pierre, who had been, it seemed to me, mentally deficient and childlike in his irresponsibility, David appeared at first to be intelligent and trustworthy. He told me, in educated French, that he had been a night guardian once before and had held the job for several years. He said he wasn't married, had no children, and was neither Muslim nor Christian. *"Je ne crois pas de Dieu"* (I don't believe in God), he told me proudly, flashing his rotten front teeth, as if not having to answer to anyone, including God, would make him a more devoted employee. He seemed proud, too, to tell me he was a member of Mali's Bozo tribe. "Traditionally, Bozos are fishermen," David said to me, "but I don't like water."

In this respect, David and Pierre were similar; neither liked water well enough, it appeared, to bathe. But I had to keep reminding myself that cleaner, nicer-smelling Malian men had girlfriends or wives and children and better things to do with their nights than to sleep alone in a narrow bed in the guardian's quarters (*case*) beside the front gate of a *toubob* woman's house.

To firm our agreement, David extended his boney right hand to me, the same hand he'd been using to work on the filthy old shoe. It was like shaking the hand of a skeleton. I wondered what I'd just done.

- - - - - - - - - - - -

Youssef had often told me about Mali's many proud and diverse ethnic groups and the Malian citizenry's unique ability to good-humoredly embrace such diversity throughout their country. It was common, Youssef said, to make a joke when meeting someone from another ethnic group for the first time. This was the standard one: "Oh, you belong to the [such-and-such] tribe — the people who eat a lot of beans and pass a lot of gas!" Instead of being offended, the accused just laughs, and tensions are defused. For the most part, Youssef said, Mali's major tribes, despite their great differences, managed to coexist peacefully.

Youssef himself, like the fabled Lion King Sundiata Keita, was a proud Malinke from the westernmost region of Mali. The Tuaregs — often called "the blue people of the desert," because the indigo dye from their clothing rubs off on their light-brown skin — inhabit the almost uninhabitable northern regions of the country in the Sahara Desert.

The Fulani, or Peul, nomadic cattle herders, are spread over a more than 100-mile radius from the east-central city of Mopti. The Dogon tribe, mainly farmers and modern-day cliff dwellers, live in ancient villages tucked into a stretch of embankment off the Bandiagara Cliffs near Timbuktu. The Bambara, Mali's largest ethnic group, whose language most Malians speak, are at the heart of the country both in geographical and governmental terms, centered in and around the capital, Bamako, as well as in the Ségou region.

David's tribe, the Bozo, from the southern flood plains between the Niger and the Bani Rivers, are known as fine fishermen and boatmen. Bozos, Youssef told me, would not likely be found so far inland, hammering shoes. "David is like a fish out of water," Youssef had joked to me. "He claims he was cursed by a *marabout* when he was a child," Youssef said, "and I believe it. He looks cursed."

- - - - - - - - - - - -

When David arrived for work that night at nine, he tried to wrap his filthy arms around me in greeting. I wanted to scream. Instead, I pulled away and showed him the *case* I had prepared for him, with clean bedding, clean towels, and a new, clean kerosene lamp.

He soon fell into his new routine, arriving at nine and sleeping soundly with his door closed, until seven in the morning, when he reluctantly drizzled water on my thirsty plants and trees before moseying off to spend his day pounding shoes. In this respect, my garden and I missed Pierre's overzealous watering—even in the rain. David couldn't seem to finish his watering chores fast enough. He appeared to have a true aversion to water. Or perhaps it was to work.

- - - - - - - - - - - -

Sometimes a woman in the neighborhood would sing all night. Her singing—wailing, really—and the drumming that accompanied it, all highly miked, were part of a mysterious ceremony that kept me awake and on edge. Ear plugs didn't help. The woman's voice was piercing, painful, incessant.

Who was she wailing for, I wondered? A large group who stayed up all night to watch and listen to her? Why? Was it a marriage celebration? Some other kind of ritual? Was I the only other non-attendant who was kept up all night by the noise? Maybe so. Africans, I'd observed, had the enviable ability to sleep anywhere, any time, under any conditions.

One morning, as I was letting David out of the front gate I asked him what the noise was all about. Neither a marriage, nor a *fête*, he said; it's a woman who drives out demons. *"C'est diabolique,"* he said. While the wailing and drumming are going on, David explained, people get up and dance one at a time in a frenzy, until they drop and are then carried away.

"Aha," I said, never questioning David's explanation. I figured he was something of an authority on such things.

It wasn't that David was exactly diabolical, but I did find him spooky. His face was cadaverous and his smoker's cough cavernous. He walked listlessly, like an apparition. He seemed to me to inhabit some gray middle ground between life and death. Too often, when he arrived for work well after sunset, he reached out to touch my arms or shoulders with his claw-like hands, as though reaching for a lifeline in the darkness. I pulled away from him, repulsed.

Just as Pierre had done, David profoundly shook my beliefs in my own capacity for tolerance. He, too, made me question everything. Was he in fact ill? Should I show more compassion? Was he friendless and looking for a human connection? Were Bozos just more demonstrative than other ethnic groups? Or did he think that I as a woman living alone was lonely and would welcome affection? Should I fire him too and begin a brand-new quest for another night guardian?

The truth was, I didn't want a guardian. Any guardian. I didn't want a strange man within the confines of my home at any time, but especially at night. Having to employ a guardian, a virtual gatekeeper, made me feel caged, invaded. It became increasingly clear to me that if it wasn't safe for me to be alone in my own home, if I couldn't find refuge there and restore my soul in peaceful solitude, then I couldn't stay in Mali. Youssef was right after all; I couldn't live in Mali on my own, without him. I would have to leave.

As much as I'd tried to surmount cultural barriers and differences during my more than two years in Mali, there was one more I knew I couldn't overcome: my need for aloneness. As a born introvert, I've always needed large daily doses of solitude, as much as, if not more than I need food. In stark contrast, the majority of Malians I knew were naturally social people, thriving on togetherness. "No one here, it seems," I lamented in my journal, "understands my need for quiet time, private time, solitude. Africans live such communal lives — always together, amid large families and friends streaming in and out all the time. I'm sure the concept of solitude is unimaginable to them."

Sundays were the days I tried to call my own, when I ached to do the soul-restorative activities I loved best — reading, writing, gardening, cooking, sewing, napping, listening to the radio, thinking. But especially on this treasured day of rest, visitors arrived at my front gate and hammered on its metal door incessantly. I knew their visits were meant to be flattering — an expression of respect and honor in their culture — but their effects on me were only unnerving. I felt trapped, with nowhere to turn for tranquility. I considered making a "Do Not Disturb" sign in French for my front gate, but on second thought realized how useless that would be. Most of the people who came and thoughtlessly knocked non-stop — women, little children, neighbors in the *quartier* — couldn't read.

I grew overly tired and consequently irritable. I found I couldn't get enough sleep or solitude to refill my physical, emotional, and spiritual tanks. I felt old and raggedy. At last I came to realize that the life I needed to live — independent, self-sufficient, quiet and safe — was not possible in Ségou, Mali. The life I'd been trying to live there — neither African nor European — without the aid and comforts of modern living, such as a car, a telephone, a washing machine, or air conditioning, was impossible to sustain. Africans, on the other hand, had each other to rely on: many hands to help with the household chores, many little feet to run errands and relay telephone-like messages here and there. I didn't have any of these things.

"Africa is for Africans!" they say. As much as I loved Africa and yearned to belong, I knew I could never be African. I knew it was time for me to leave.

"Soyez bienvenues tout le monde!" (Welcome everyone!), I greeted the women as cheerily as I could, in an effort to ease the anxiety in the air. Unlike our first class on September 21 — when the whole group seemed as buoyant as brightly colored helium balloons — on this Thursday morning, December 21, the final day of our Patchwork Project classes, the assembled women appeared weighed down with worry. They were about to take their final exam.

"Félicitations on your achievement!" I added in my introductions, applauding them excitedly. "You have come this far! You have done so well!"

But as we all knew, there was still far to go. In order to receive a certificate of successful completion on graduation day, which we'd set for January 25, 2001, they each had to pass this final exam, plus submit their individual projects, a baby quilt of their own design, to me by January 18. In addition, no one could ignore the elephant in the center of the room: The Patchwork Project's final, group project, my nephew Tyler's king-size quilt, still rolled like a scroll on the bamboo quilt frame stretching the length of my living room, was not yet fully quilted.

I stood at one end of the quilt frame and scanned the faces of the fifteen women (three students were absent; we'd ended with as many students as we'd begun) looking up at me earnestly. They sat in chairs surrounding the frame, on the living room sofa, at the dining room table, at the sideboard in my dining area. For most of them, I suspected, this would be the first such exam of their lives. Their anxiety, so uncharacteristic on their normally smooth, serene, sunny faces, was painful for me to see. Was the price of development always stress? *Must* it be "no gain without pain"?

"Ne vous inquiétez pas!" (Don't be worried), I tried to reassure them. "I know you'll do fine."

I distributed the three-page, typewritten exam I'd written and had photocopied on large, white sheets of paper. Then the women set to work, with Bic ballpoints in hand and brows furrowed, answering the multiple-choice questions, drawing the required patchwork designs, and answering a short essay question.

Here is the English translation of the exam they took in French:

A. Choose the sole correct response for the following questions:
  1) The first step in patchwork is:
     a) to wash your hands
     b) to cut the fabric
     c) to make a plan
  2) The plan is made on:
     a) the fabric
     b) a piece of paper
     c) the table
  3) The seam allowance for patchwork is always:
     a) 1 cm
     b) ½ cm
     c) 2 cm
  4) The best fabric for patchwork is:
     a) nylon
     b) silk
     c) cotton

5) The difference between sashing and borders is:
   a) the sashing is larger
   b) the borders are always dark
   c) the sashing is between the blocks
6) After you make the "sandwich," you:
   a) eat it
   b) baste it
   c) iron it
7) The most practical reason for doing the quilting is:
   a) to stitch the "sandwich" together
   b) to pass the time
   c) to make a design
8) Patchwork bed quilts are very valuable in countries that are:
   a) hot
   b) south
   c) cold
9) The three primary colors are:
   a) orange, green, violet
   b) blue, yellow, red
   c) white, black, red
10) How many principle methods of quilting are there?
   a) two
   b) five
   c) three
11) When you quilt by hand, the knots are always:
   a) on the surface
   b) under the back
   c) buried in the batting

12) When the batting is too thick for quilting by machine, you do it:
   a) by hand
   b) with knots, using cotton thread
   c) you cannot do it

13) You make a baby quilt for:
   a) a wedding gift
   b) an old person
   c) a newborn

14) The Patchwork Project is a project for:
   a) economic development
   b) distraction
   c) pastime

15) During the period of slavery in the U.S., the slaves are said to have used patchwork quilts as a:
   a) game
   b) map to freedom
   c) carpet

16) The eight-pointed star design is a symbol of:
   a) protection against evil forces
   b) happiness in life
   c) God in heaven

B. In the spaces provided, design the following blocks:
1) Nine-patch
2) Pinwheel
3) Hourglass
4) Sailboat
5) Wild geese
6) Eight-pointed star

C. On the other side of this paper, tell me what you think of the Patchwork Project and how you will use what you have learned.

- - - - - - - - - - - - -

As each woman finished and handed me her exam with a big sigh of relief, she pulled a chair up to the quilt frame and quietly quilted while the others continued writing. When all were done, I broke the news to them:

"I have decided to leave Mali at the end of February."

The women gasped in unison.

"I must return to my country and my family," I continued, framing my reasoning in a way they would surely understand. "I have been away from my daughter and my two grandchildren for too long."

These women, most of whom were mothers and many already grandmothers, then nodded knowingly.

"If you give me proof that you will continue the Patchwork Project, I will leave you everything we have here to keep the project going — the tables, chairs, blackboard, quilting frame, all of our supplies, such as the rotary cutters and mats, scissors, needles, pins, even my nice sewing machine — *tout* (all)! If you are *not* interested in continuing, that's okay. But if you *are*, how will you go about doing so?"

At this point, Fatou of ALPHALOG got up and took my place at the head of the quilting frame. With hands folded resolutely in front of her as if in fervent prayer, she addressed the group in French:

"This project must not depend on Bonnie! It is necessary that we organize to work together to apply the lessons we have learned. One person alone cannot make a big patchwork quilt. But together — *ensemble!* — we can do it and we all can profit! We must form an official association to keep the Patchwork Project going. We must meet at my office next week to draw up the papers and to elect officers. *D'accord?*"

The women, whose faces were starting to look sunny once again, wholeheartedly agreed with Fatou's entreaty.

- - - - - - - - - - - - -

As soon as I was alone again, I graded their final exams. Two students, Bassam and Philippine, got 100%, A-plus's. Six students — Koro, Rokia, Fatoumata, Nathalie, Mariam Coulibaly, and Rokiatou Bah — earned

A's. Mariam Dolo, Fatou, and Assitan earned A-minus's. Marie-Augustine got a B-plus. Everyone else, including Fily who was illiterate and had to take her exam separately, orally, received a grade of C. Not one of these students from our second semester failed her final exam.

With tears welling in my eyes, I read their essay responses, trying my best to decipher the creative French spelling and grammar written in the European-style script they had learned in elementary school. Here are some roughly translated snippets from those responses:

"The patchwork is a project for the development of the women. For me, we are going to make an association for continuing the patchwork. For me, I love patchwork very much." — Bassam Sacko

"The Patchwork Project is a very interesting work that helps in development. It is also very demanding and very meticulous. One must have courage to complete all the steps. With what I have learned, I will make things for my family [religious community]. I will teach the women in the villages where we work. We have already talked with the village women, and they are interested." — Philippine Razafin, nun

"I like the patchwork project a lot because I learned a lot of things, and I ask the Good Lord that the project continue and that we have the courage to continue it after the departure of Bani." — Nathalie Berthe

"The Patchwork Project is a project that I have loved a lot because I think it is a good thing for us. I will never throw scraps [of fabric] away in the future; instead, I will make good things [from them]." — Mariam Dolo

"The Patchwork Project is a good project of development. It is a project that can succeed here because Malian textiles are very rich. It will also permit women to have money, which will make them economically independent." — Fatou Sogoba

"Patchwork is the beginning of a new life for me... Truly, I love patchwork with all my heart. I adore it. [This] Patchwork Project creates a liaison between our country and other, cold countries, where patchwork is appreciated. What I have learned in patchwork I will use to perfection ... if it pleases the Good Lord." — Assitan Togora

"The Patchwork Project is a project of development. We women must unite to create an association for working together. And then we can teach other women in other women's centers. I will never forget the Patchwork Project, because it has developed an *esprit* of women working together." — Rokiatou Bah.

"The patchwork project is a source of development in Ségou, or rather in Mali, to help us to fight poverty. I believe that if we create an association, we will be well organized to continue this art, to teach new people, and to work in a timely manner on the orders [that come in]. Thank you." — Koro Traore

I gave the women their grades and returned to them the first pages of their exams, but I asked if I might keep the essay answers. Their handwritten, heartfelt words, carved in blue ballpoint ink on this white paper, were like gifts of pure gold to me. I knew I would cherish them forever.

"ANYONE CAN *BUY* THINGS," my mother used to say to my sisters and me when we were little and my father couldn't keep a job due to his drinking. "But not everyone can *create* things!" My then young and buoyant mother cleverly upended our have-not status and turned it into a plus. Instead of buying the latest-fashion dolls at a toy store, for example, she would *make* one-of-a-kind sock dolls for us.

"So *adorable!*" she'd say, praising her own creative efforts and admiring each doll's pudgy legs, poufy dress, fluffy yarn hair and expressive hand-embroidered face. "No other girl *in the world* has a dolly like yours," she said, proudly giving each of us one of her adorable creations. I, for one, felt sorry for those girls whose parents could only give them assembly-line-manufactured, store-bought dolls.

In the Peace Corps in Gabon I'd taught the women in my crafts classes how to make sock dolls. Their little girls, who had never owned a toy or doll of their own, lovingly carried these sock dolls strapped to their backs the way their mothers did their babies.

Remembering the power of these simple, homespun dolls, I made one to help me give my closing remarks at the Patchwork Project's graduation ceremony on January 25, 2001. I named this baby-doll sock doll — made of chocolate-brown socks, with short, black yarn hair, and dressed in nothing but a thick, white diaper — Benjamin; and I pulled him out, like a rabbit from a hat, at an appropriately dramatic moment.

"*Le projet a ce moment est un nouveau-né, comme mon bébé*, Benjamin" (The project at this moment is a newborn, like my baby...), I said, scooping Benjamin up in my arms. "And like a fragile baby, it could die of negligence or indifference, or it could grow up to be famous. It all depends on you..."

The women watched and listened, riveted. They understood the love and care that newborns required. They knew motherhood backward and forward. They got the analogy. They nodded, knowingly.

Then I unfolded Tyler's quilt, asking the women closest to me to hold it up for all to see: "*Voilà, notre grand projet!*" I said. "*Voilà le preuve que c'est possible à faire ici!*" This giant-size quilt, completed at last, was proof that they could do it, that they had indeed succeeded. The audience gasped at the sight of it, clearly an original work of art like nothing they'd seen before.

This time my living room could not accommodate the crowd. In addition to all of my Patchwork Project students and *stagiaires*, there were the three Peace Corps volunteers posted in Ségou who'd helped with the quilting, people from the German ONG that had supported me, officials from the governor's office, some of my students' husbands, and Ulla, the wife of Ségou's mayor. As my students filled the rows of white plastic chairs at the foot of my front terrace, the rest of the audience stood, dotting my mango-tree-shaded courtyard and applauding as I used my terrace "stage" to present prizes (for best baby quilt and most gold stars earned), payment from my sister who had commissioned Tyler's quilt, and certificates to the graduates.

Thirteen women received certificates that day for their successful completion of the course — for passing the final exam, creating a baby quilt of their own design, and participating in the *grand projet*. I'd had these certificates printed in town on fine paper of lasting value, and I signed my name boldly above *"Créatrice."* What a beautiful French word, I thought: *créatrice*. My mother would have liked the word too.

- - - - - - - - - - - - -

Certificat d'Achèvement

---

a reussi à faire

la Formation des Formatrices

de 14 leçons

du 21 september au 21 decembre 2000

avec succès

Bonnie Lee Black

Créatrice et Chef Formatrice

WORD OF MY IMMINENT DEPARTURE spread quickly in Ségou. More unexpected visitors than ever arrived at my house at all hours to see me and wish me well. What they couldn't know was how exhausting their visits were to me. I tried to be gracious and appreciative of their kindness, but underneath it all, I was getting grouchy. Deprived of my requisite, restorative afternoon naps, my nerves became frayed, and my thoughts ricocheted:

What I won't miss about Mali: a so-called "guardian," who silently creeps up on me in the pitch-blackness when the electricity's been cut, as I'm fumbling with my key ring to find the one for the front door so I can grope my way to the kitchen for matches and candles.

"David?" I call to the stalking sounds.

"Oui," he says.

"Do you have a flashlight?"

"Oui," he says. The sounds get closer.

"Where is it?" By this time, I'm becoming agitated. Everything is blackness, and I can't find the keyhole.

"It's in the *case,"* he says.

"Then GET IT." I'm practically screaming now.

"It doesn't have a battery," he says.

"Oh, great. Do you have matches?"

"Oui."

"WHERE ARE THEY?!"

"Right here in my hand."

"THEN LIGHT ONE!"

No, I will not miss: the ignorance, negligence, and indifference that are the hallmarks of Africa's retardation. I won't miss the dust and dirt, the fact that everything is always dirty — everything one touches, every place one sits. I won't miss the toxic fumes from my neighbors occasionally burning plastic bags in their cookfires. I won't miss the fact that I have NO privacy, the fact that I am constantly being swarmed by people — especially kids — calling my name, "Bani! Bani! Bani!" incessantly, wanting to come into my courtyard and visit — as if I, like them, had nothing better to do than sit in my courtyard and visit.

I won't miss: the ever-present mosquitoes at night, threatening malaria with every high-pitched whine, nor the need to sleep under a protective net that smells of dirt and dust only days after being washed. I won't miss the fact that it's so hard to make a decent meal; that the meat, if not pressure-cooked to death, is impossible to chew; that the water, even after being boiled, is probably the cause of whatever is giving me such intestinal grief.

I won't miss: the danger of a potentially crippling accident that I risk every time I bike to and from town several times a week, because no one is looking where he's walking, riding his *moto,* or driving his car or truck.

I certainly won't miss: the hot season, which causes my over-heated, thin white skin to erupt in ugly, itchy boils.

What I WILL miss, though, is my work with the women and the deep feeling of satisfaction and accomplishment that work gives me. I will miss the recognition I enjoy among a large number of people here now, and the respect they give me, even though — or *because* — I am an older woman. I will miss my Club Crochet girls; I will miss the chance to watch them grow into women.

It will be difficult to go somewhere new and be a no one again. But I must do it.

Funny, isn't it, I mused, *how the heart changes its course. In the beginning, when my heart was filled with hope — and when Youssef and I were still together — I thought I could live out my life in Ségou. I fantasized about living happily-ever-after by the banks of the teal-blue Niger. Now I know without question I must go.*

HELLOS AND GOODBYES, greetings and farewells, are inordinately important in Malian culture. I'd observed the traditional greeting-exchanges countless times in my thirty months in Ségou — the ritualistic back-and-forth of queries as to the other's (and that other person's family's) health and welfare. Early on, I'd remarked to Youssef how time-consuming these exchanges appeared to me to be. His response was, "Most Malians don't own watches."

In time, though, I came to see the beauty in these exquisite, almost balletic greetings and the implied messages of respect and caring that they convey. Between the lines of questioning, they say: "You are more important than time to me."

How many of us in the West could say that sincerely to our friends and acquaintances, I wondered.

As my departure date from Ségou drew closer, I began to learn firsthand about Malian goodbyes. On February 17, I visited the Tounkara family in town for a farewell celebration. I spent most of the day there — playing with the children, helping Fatimata and Nene with the lunch preparation, having lunch (rice and sauce, eaten *à la main*) with the women, while the kids (including my little favorite, Mohammed) sat and ate their lunch in a circle nearby. Then I stayed until tea was prepared, after having taken a family photo. Their warmth, hospitality, and generosity touched me deeply. I appreciated this gesture enormously, and they appreciated the gifts I brought for them — French textbooks, drawing paper and crayons for the children and my prettiest Malian *boubous* for the women. Youssef was not there, and no one spoke of him or his whereabouts.

On February 20, my Patchwork "sisters" surprised me with a farewell *fête*. At lunchtime, when they would have otherwise been at home, serving their families' main meal in their respective courtyards, and I would have been reading *Newsweek* while eating alone at my dining room table, more than a dozen women arrived at my house bearing large, round platters of cut-up roasted meat and bags of bottled cool drinks.

As it happened, I'd just made a big bowl of macaroni salad to last my remaining days in Ségou, so I added this contribution to the platters of meat. We sat in round clusters on woven mats spread out on my terrace, eating the meat chunks and still-warm macaroni salad with our right hands and sipping sodas straight from the bottles, as Salif Keita's ubiquitous voice serenaded us from the radio.

After we'd eaten and cleared the terrace of mats and platters, we turned up the radio's main Malian music channel, and the party began. As I noted in my journal the next morning, "Some of these women can really whoop it up, especially Bassam, the newly elected president of their new Patchwork Project association!" Marie-Augustine changed into her clown outfit and behaved like the court jester she always was at every *fête*. Fily danced and sang a song about me and my admonitions to them — "*Il faut faire soineusement!*" (You must do careful work!). And at one point, as though drunk on wine, though I'd only had one Fanta orange soda, I danced the Highland fling for them, to the beat of an improvised African drum — an inverted plastic bucket.

Rokiatou Ouattara's husband, who worked for ALPHALOG, arrived by car toward the end of our *fête* to give his wife and some of her friends a ride back into town. Before they left, he translated for the women their heartfelt sentiments from Bambara to French for me, because, he said, they feared they didn't know the French words that would adequately express what their hearts needed to say. He said the women didn't know how to thank me enough for what I've given them, but they did know God would bless me for my efforts. He said the women promised to continue doing patchwork so that the project would succeed. He said the women said (and this meant the most to me), "Patchwork is now our Life."

His words made me feel richer than the richest woman alive.

Later in the afternoon, little Club Crochet visitors brought me love notes in envelopes addressed to my Malian name, Bani Keita. Their letters, written in large, looping schoolgirl script read, *"Je t'aime Bani jusqu'à ma mort"* (I will love you until I die). They also gave me small bags of roasted peanuts, which must have been a traditional Malian farewell gift. I tried to tell them, with ten-year-old Bintou acting as my translator: "Study hard … use your heads … I love you all … you will always be in my heart…" As I spoke, then waited for Bintou's translation, my heart clenched and my eyes filled with tears. All the while, Aminata sat beside me on the terrace steps, with her head down, quietly crocheting with plastic bags.

In the evening, Abdoulaye Djiabate came by to pick up my kitchen stove, which he'd bought from me for his wife so that she would have a "modern" kitchen in their newly built house. I didn't tell him how unbearably hot her modern, indoor kitchen would be. As a farewell gift, he surprised me with two beautiful *bogolan tableaux*. I wanted so much to wrap my arms around this sweet, shy man to thank him. But I didn't. I stood over an arm's length away and said, *"Merci mille fois, mon ami."*

- - - - - - - - - - - -

The day before my departure from Mali in late February, 2001, Fatou and Rokia arrived at my house with a *charette*, which we loaded precariously high with all of the things I'd promised to bequeath to the ongoing Patchwork Project — the tables and chairs and blackboard and sewing machine and disassembled quilting frame, plus all of the smaller items — such as mats and cutters and baskets of fabric scraps — packed in boxes.

Soon after, Mariko arrived with his *charette* and several sons to take the potted plants I was giving to our new neighbor, Abdoulaye Djiabate, plus a garden hose for himself and the tall, pottery water jar from my front porch. While his sons waited outside the front gate, I took Mariko's hand and walked with him slowly around my courtyard so he could admire my gardens.

"*C'est paradis,*" he said with obvious pride at having played a god-like role in its creation. Indeed, it looked like paradise compared to the bare, baked earth it had been when I moved into this house over two years before. When the owner of the house, a wealthy Malian businessman in Bamako, had stopped by to visit for the first time a few days prior to this and I gave him a tour, he'd said the same, "*c'est paradis,*" adding sweetly, "This is more *your* house than mine now. But now you're leaving. *C'est dommage*" (that's too bad).

I took Mariko inside the house, now empty. In the large living room, where the Patchwork Project's bamboo quilting frame had been, where the women had worked and laughed and sung songs about their newfound love of quilting, he held out his arms to me and I walked into them. His large frame beneath his long-sleeved rugby shirt was bone-thin. His faded jeans hung on him loosely. He smelled of earth.

"Will I ever see you again?" he said.

"Yes," I answered, "in the next life."

He rested his large hands on my bottom and gave a slight squeeze as if to prove we were both still alive.

"When I was young," he said softly into my hair, "I was *aflame.*"

"I know," I said. "And you still are."

- - - - - - - - - - - - -

February 23, 2001 — 5:35 am:

> The sky is turning gray-blue. Soon the soft early morning light will wake people, more effectively than the call to prayer. Soon the roosters will crow, the sheep and goats will begin to bray, and maybe, if I'm lucky, a wild parrot will swoop into my courtyard and dazzle me. Soon women will begin their heartbeat-like pounding of millet in wooden mortars for their families' breakfast porridge, the way women here have pounded millet for millennia. Soon this light, these sounds and sights, this thudding heartbeat, will be history for me, a pleasant history. I'm glad you, my faithful journal-friend, have helped me to preserve it.

- - - - - - - - - - - -

"It's so difficult to say goodbye to those you'll likely never see again," I wrote as I waited at the airport in Bamako for my flight back to the States. Tyler's finished quilt — colorful, joyful, and somewhat magical — was checked in with my baggage. It would indeed fly.

"My farewells in Ségou were tearful," I told my journal: Ramata had tears streaming down her face. Fily was nearly sobbing. My little Club Crochet girls looked crestfallen, almost in shock; Aminata was wooden. Suzanne and her two girls came to say goodbye. Abdoulaye Djiabate spent almost the whole morning with me, talking, as we'd always done, on the front terrace steps. Mieke came and took pictures of the tearful, fond farewells.

The driver I'd arranged to take me and my baggage to Bamako arrived right on time, at noon. After he'd packed my things into the SUV, and after more tearful hugs outside of my front gate, I left *quartier* Pelengana, stopping briefly in *centreville* Ségou to say goodbye to some of the Patchwork women who were manning booths at a crafts fair there, selling some of their smaller patchwork items.

I cried for nearly an hour as the driver, Ali, and I sped away on the N-6 main road to Bamako. I thought about asking him to stop here and there so I could take photos of the landscape — the teal-colored Niger, the monstrous baobabs, the vast fields of lush mango trees… But then I thought better of it: *No, I can take and keep such pictures in my mind.* Ali and I continued the three-hour drive to Mali's capital in silence.

Epilogue

It's been more than twelve years since I left Mali to return to the U.S., and I haven't been back since. I've told myself, *If I had the time and money and stamina for such a long and emotionally grueling trip, I would go in a heartbeat,* because it would be such a grand reunion; in so many ways my heart is still there. But circumstances haven't allowed me to return in person. Instead, I've kept Mali in my thoughts daily, like a home movie I replay for myself alone. And now, with a heavy heart, I read news reports of political upheaval, military conflict, and humanitarian crises in that once-exemplary and peaceful African country.

I sometimes wonder: If I *could* return to Mali, what would I find? That Mariko has died of complications from his diabetes? That Aminata is married to a much older man she didn't choose? That a few of the brightest Club Crochet girls are now at university in Paris? That the Patchwork Project is limping along — not yet connected to the World Wide Web, but not yet dead either?

I know that Youssef's extended family in Ségou is well because I've been corresponding with his cousin Makan all these years. I regularly send Makan some money for his son Mohammed's schooling; and Makan writes me gracious, grateful letters in return. He never mentions Youssef, and I do not ask.

From time to time I get letters from the Patchwork women, enclosing a photo or two of their latest completed quilt and asking me to see what I might do to find a buyer for it. Several of my willing friends have bought their quilts in the past. Others have shown some interest but have not been able to follow through. The Patchwork Project still needs a leader with all the international-business and computer skills that I lack. It has been my fervent prayer than this book will take on a life of its own and find that person somewhere in the world.

Sometimes, when I think of Mali, I let my imagination wander. I imagine my original dream coming true: I see the Patchwork Project's quilts somehow coming full circle, warming and comforting African American women whose ancestors may well have come from Mali. I even imagine my fictional slave-quilter Jeneba's great-granddaughter, Sally, or a real person just like her, visiting Ségou as a tourist one day and stopping to buy a quilt and connect.

I imagine:

The tour company's air-conditioned SUV is speeding toward Mopti, the driver and guide intent on getting there before sunset. One of the four tourists inside the car, an African-American woman in her mid-thirties, is having an animated conversation with the person beside her. Suddenly, she sees something that looks like a quilt on a clothesline by a sign for a women's center, and she interrupts herself—.

"STOP!" she calls to the driver. "Please stop the car! Please pull over!"

The young tour guide, Hadi, a multilingual Malian, turns and says to her in English, "Is something wrong, Miss? Are you not well?"

"I'm fine," she says. "But I saw something... Oh, please, we must stop and go back."

Hadi instructs the driver in Bambara to turn around. The driver, Ali, knowing how many kilometers lie ahead and how fast the sun is sinking, shakes his head in silent protest but does what he's been told.

The new-looking sign by the side of the road says,

CENTRE DE FORMATION FEMININ
BENKADY PELENGANA
COUPE COUTURE

and the stars-and-stripes-patterned flag-like quilt nearby, obviously faded from age and wind and the intense sun, looks as though it were once a bright red, white, and blue.

The tourist apologizes to the others in her group. "Forgive me," she says to them, hastily unbuckling her seatbelt. "But I have to investigate this. I'll be as quick as I can."

The afternoon heat envelops her like a thick quilt as she emerges from the air-conditioned car. In a rush, she walks the dusty distance to what looks like a small shop near the women's center. Its door, she's relieved to see, is open. As her eyes adjust to the dimness inside, she sees a tall, commanding African woman dressed in a billowing boubou, who appears to be in her mid-fifties. This African woman, more than anyone she's noticed since arriving on this her first trip to Mali, reminds her of someone from her distant past. Yes, she resembles her Grandma Rose, whom she visited a few times in Baltimore when she was a little girl.

"Bonjour," the American tourist says, using the French she studied in advance of this trip, and extending a nervous right hand — as if to a phantom, a memory, an ancestor long gone. "My name is Sally Jones. I'm a nurse in Philadelphia. I wrote a letter to this women's center many years ago. Do you remember me? I must buy one of your quilts."

- - - - - - - - - - - - -

Acknowledgments

Without the support and encouragement of those who believed in my dreams, neither the Patchwork Project of Ségou, Mali, nor this book about that life-changing experience would have ever come to be.

My heartfelt thanks go first to my Malian "Patchwork Project sisters," whom readers have met and, I hope, have come to know in this narrative. I will be forever grateful to them for embracing me and teaching me so much. Their hunger to learn new things, their forbearance with my lessons, and their blind faith that elsewhere in the world people need quilts to keep themselves warm at night made this project possible.

Friends and family helped from afar while I lived in Mali. They are: my sister Heather Black Wood, my cousin Jean Wotowicz, and my dear longtime friends in the States, Wendy Tyson, Ronald Goldhammer, Paul Matteo, Martha Cooper and Belmont Freeman. Friends in Europe provided support and encouragement as well: Marie-Laure Besançon, Isabelle Deleze, and Janine Slukova. And Amparo Llanos in Australia was my link to Clean Up the World.

While I lived in Mali, many new friends, including young Peace Corps volunteers posted near Ségou or passing through in their travels, took part in the Patchwork Project, sitting at the quilting frame and enjoying the lively, cross-cultural quilting bees. Among those friends whom I must thank are: Paulette Valliere, Vivica Williams, Sonia Kassambara, Kathleen Fox, Mary-Denise Tabor, Kristin Weinhauer, Chula Walker-Griffith, Cara Trautman, Guylaine Fortin, and Mieke Bastiaansen.

In writing and revising the many drafts of this book in recent years, I've benefited from a number of early readers' suggestions. My special thanks go to: Dawn Marano, Harvey Frauenglass, Judith Kendall, Teresa Dovalpage, Allison Price, Wendy Tyson, Jeannie Admire, Eileen Sherry, Paulette Valliere, and Marge Reading.

Finally, without the enormous talents of Barbara L. Scott and Rebecca Lenzini of Nighthawk Press, this beautiful book would still be just one of my dreams. I cannot thank them enough.

Notes

Centre Benkady

1 Dorothy Frager, *The Quilting Primer, 2nd ed.* (Radnor, PA: Chilton Book Company, 1979).

4 Photo of author's room in Tounkara family compound, Ségou, October 1998.

11 Photo of Mohammed Tounkara, age four.

14 Photo of Youssef Tounkara in *centreville* Ségou, October 1998.

17 Photo of Aminata at the wall between her home and author's in *quartier* Pelangana, Ségou.

22 Photo of author by her front gate in Pelangana, headed for the *marché*.

27 Photo of author's rented home in Pelangana, soon after moving in; the window to her study is on the right.

31 Gabon flashback from: Bonnie Lee Black, *How to Cook a Crocodile* (Peace Corps Writers, 2010).

34 Youssouf Tata Cissé, *Seydou Keita* (NY: Scalo Publishers, 1997).

37 N.J. Dawood (translator), *The Koran* (Middlesex, England: Penguin Books, 1956).

45 Photo of author on her front porch, weaving a doormat from fabric scraps on a frame loom.

49 Eli Whitney: www.eliwhitney.org/cotton.

49 David Brion Davis, *Inhuman Bondage: The Rise and Fall of Slavery in the New World* (NY: Oxford University Press, 2006).

50 From "L'Or Blanc" exhibit at the National Museum of Mali, Bamako, 2000.

50 "Follow the Thread," Alan Beattie, *Financial Times*, July 22, 2006.

51 "Those Illegal Farm Subsidies," Editorial, *New York Times*, April 28, 2004.

A South Carolina Plantation, late 1822

52-57 This and all other italicized slave-narrative sections are fictional; they are works of the author's imagination.

Puppets and Primers

60 Photo of life-size puppet, Jelimuso Jeneba (Jenny the Storyteller), made by author for storytelling.

61 Gabon flashback from: Bonnie Lee Black, *How to Cook a Crocodile* (Peace Corps Writers, 2010).

63 Werewere-Liking, *Marionnettes du Mali: Statuettes Peintes D'Afrique de L'Ouest* (Paris: ARHIS), p. 11.

64 Elisabeth den Otter: www.euronet.nl/users/edotter.

66 Werewere-Liking, *Marionnettes du Mali: Statuettes Peintes D'Afrique de L'Ouest* (Paris: ARHIS).

68 Photo of Club Crochet girls on author's front porch, displaying their handiwork; Aminata is second from right, bottom row.

69 "Flower of Africa: A Curse That's Blowing in the Wind," Marc Lacey, *New York Times*, April 7, 2005.

71 Photo of some of the Club Crochet girls concentrating on their creations.

72 Dorothy Frager, *The Quilting Primer, 2nd ed.* (Radnor, PA: Chilton Book Company, 1979), p. 1.

74 See photo of Chinese sewing machine on p. 238.

75 Photo of Ami Sylla (left) and Sali Traore at Centre Benkady.

77 Photo of Ségou wall quilt.

A South Carolina Plantation, 1833

79-82 This and all other italicized slave-narrative sections are fictional; they are works of the author's imagination.

The Way God Works

87 Clean Up the World literature: www.cleanuptheworld.org.

88 The prize-winning child's drawing used on Mali's Clean Up the World T-shirts.

100,104 Gabon flashbacks from: Bonnie Lee Black, *How to Cook a Crocodile* (Peace Corps Writers, 2010).

110 Photo of author (center) with Club Crochet girls at Centre Benkady, celebrating International Women's Day; Aminata and Bintou are directly in front of author.

112 N.J. Dawood (translator), *The Koran* (Middlesex, England: Penguin Books, 1956), p. 213.

113 N.J. Dawood (translator), *The Koran* (Middlesex, England: Penguin Books, 1956), p. 434.

113   Photo of the front of author's house with newly installed iron ladder to her rooftop "hideaway."

116   Katherine Ashenburg, *The Dirt on Clean: An Unsanitized History* (NY: North Point Press, 2007), p. 19, 285.

117   ibid, p. 2.

120   Photo of Irwin in his cage in the front mango tree.

121   Gabon flashback from: Bonnie Lee Black, *How to Cook a Crocodile* (Peace Corps Writers, 2010).

123   Senegal Parrots: "European Ban Hurts African Export Industry," Associated Press, Hans Nichols, January 6, 2006; and www.senegal-parrots.com.

129   Jacqueline L. Tobin and Raymond G. Dobard, *Hidden in Plain View: A Secret Story of Quilts and the Underground Railroad* (NY: Random House, 1999), p. 3.

A South Carolina Plantation, early 1850s

131-4   This and all other italicized slave-narrative sections are fictional; they are works of the author's imagination.

Pioneers

146   N.J. Dawood (translator), *The Koran* (Middlesex, England: Penguin Books, 1956), p. 348.

147   Photo of author lecturing in her living room on the first day of the Patchwork Project.

150   Linda Parker, *Montana Star Quilts* (Helena, Montana: Montana Quilts, Inc., 1997).

161   Photo of Sali Traore at Centre Benkady working on the "Stars and Stripes Forever" wall quilt intended for the American Embassy.

171   Photo of author teaching in the Patchwork Project classroom at her home; note completed "Stars and Stripes Forever" quilt on the wall.

175   N.J. Dawood (translator), *The Koran* (Middlesex, England: Penguin Books, 1956).

176   Maryse Condé, *Segu* (NY: Penguin Books, 1996).

176   Roland L. Freeman, *The Communion of the Spirits: African-American Quilters, Preservers, and Their Stories* (Nashville: Rutledge Hill Press, 1996).

188   Photo of author with Tyler's quilt-to-be on her living room floor.

A South Carolina Plantation, December 1860

191-6 This and all other italicized slave-narrative sections are fictional; they are works of the author's imagination.

Griots

203 "Beat King: Salif Keita," Quincy Troupe, *New York Times Magazine*, 1995.

Baltimore, Maryland, December 1936

207-8 This fictionalized slave-narrative was inspired by Norman R. Yetman's *When I Was A Slave: Memoirs from the Slave Narrative Collection* [of the WPA] (NY: Dover, 2002).

The Quilt

218 Photo of the bamboo quilt frame set up in author's living room.

220 Photo of some of the Patchwork Project women at the quilting frame.

226 Photo of Mariam Dolo, one of the Patchwork Project teacher-trainees, quilting at the frame.

232 Photo of Patchwork Project women about to take their final exam on December 21, 2000.

238 Photo of author's hand-cranked Chinese sewing machine at her dining room table.

244 Photo of Tounkara family (Youssef's cousins and their families) in their compound in *centreville,* Ségou.

Book Club Questions
and Topics for Discussion

1. Why did your book club choose to read this particular book?

_____

_____

_____

2. How does this book compare with other books your group has read in the past?

_____

_____

_____

3. What is the metaphorical significance of the main title of this work?

_____

_____

_____

4. Did the true stories in this book alter your preconceptions of Africa in any way? If so, how?

_____

_____

_____

5. What effect did the fictional account of Jeneba and her descendants have on you as a reader?

_____

_____

_____

6. If you — or someone you know — is a quilter, what would you say makes this particular craft so appealing and even "addicting"? Why do you think it appealed to these Malian women?

_____

_____

_____

7. Which real-life characters in these stories stood out for you and why?

_____

_____

_____

8. Mali has been in the news lately. Has this book helped you to understand the place and its people better and given you more empathy for their current situation? If so, how?

_____

_____

_____

9. Belonging to women's organizations and celebrating International Women's Day every year were important to the women in this book. How does this compare with the women in your own community?

_____

_____

_____

10. What other issues did this narratrive raise for you?

_____

_____

_____

About the Author

Bonnie Lee Black is the author of the memoir *Somewhere Child* (Viking Press, 1981), which was instrumental in the creation of the National Center for Missing and Exploited Children. Her second memoir, about her Peace Corps service in Gabon, *How to Cook a Crocodile* (Peace Corps Writers, 2010), won a "Best in the World" award from Gourmand International in March 2012. The manuscript for this Mali book won first place in the memoir-book category in the SouthWest Writers Annual Writing Contest, 2011.

Black earned a bachelor of arts degree from Columbia University in New York in 1979 and an MFA in Creative Writing from Antioch University-Los Angeles in 2007. She was a professional writer and editor in New York City for twenty years and has been an educator in the U.S. and overseas for nearly twenty years.

Her essays have appeared in a number of published anthologies and literary journals. She now lives in Taos, New Mexico, and teaches at UNM-Taos. In 2012 she was chosen one of the Remarkable Women of Taos. Visit her website at www.bonnieleeblack.com.

Photo: Lenny Foster

Made in the USA
Charleston, SC
09 August 2013